W9-CZU-696

Paths to Homelessness

Paths to Homelessness

Extreme Poverty and the Urban Housing Crisis

Doug A. Timmer, D. Stanley Eitzen, and Kathryn D. Talley

Westview Press
Boulder · San Francisco · Oxford

Copyright © 1994 by Westview Press, Inc.

Published in 1994 in the United States of America by Westview Press, Inc., 5500 Central Avenue, Boulder, Colorado 80301–2877, and in the United Kingdom by Westview Press, 36 Lonsdale Road, Summertown, Oxford OX2 7EW

Library of Congress Cataloging-in-Publication Data
Timmer, Doug A.
   Paths to homelessness : extreme poverty and the urban housing
crisis / Doug A. Timmer, D. Stanley Eitzen, and Kathryn D. Talley.
      p.   cm.
   Includes bibliographical references and index.
   ISBN 0-8133-0782-1 — ISBN 0-8133-0783-X (pbk.)
   1. Homelessness—United States—Case studies.   2. Poverty—United
States—Case studies.   3. Urban poor—Housing—United States—Case
studies.   4. Unemployed—United States—Case studies.   I. Eitzen,
D. Stanley.   II. Talley, Kathryn D.   III. Title.
HV4505.T56   1994
362.5′0973—dc20   94-15668
                                                                                CIP

Printed and bound in the United States of America

The paper used in this publication meets the requirements
of the American National Standard for Permanence of Paper
for Printed Library Materials Z39.48-1984.

10   9   8   7   6   5   4   3   2   1

For Mary

Contents

Acknowledgments   xi

PART 1   OVERVIEW

1   **Understanding Homelessness:**
     Industrial and Urban Decline   3

2   **The Root Causes of Homelessness in American Cities**   10
     Major Issues Concerning the Homeless, 11
     The Sources of Rising Urban Homelessness, 17
     Conclusion, 30

PART 2   PATHS TO HOMELESSNESS

3   **The "Old" Homeless: Sam Sheldon and Henry Walsh**   33
     Labor Market, 36
     Welfare State, 42
     Shadow Work, 47
     Extreme Poverty, 48
     Alcohol Myths, 49
     The Demise of the SRO, 52
     Sam, Henry, Housing, and Homelessness, 53

4   **Work Versus Welfare—A False Choice: Sue Jackson**   55
     Villains of the 1990s: Welfare Moms, 55
     The Facts on AFDC, 56
     Occupational Segregation of Women in the
        Low-Wage Economy, 58
     Child Care for Working Mothers, 60
     Insufficient Subsidized Housing, 62

Work Versus Welfare: No Choice, 66
The Role of Mental Illness, 66

5   **The Economic Marginality of Young Families:
    Sara, Dave, Elizabeth, and Joshua**   69
    The Near Homeless and a "Precipitating Event," 70
    The Declining Economic Status of Young, Non–College
        Educated Parents and Their Families, 73
    Shelterization Is Not the Solution, 79

6   **Left Behind in a De-industrialized, Low-Wage Economy:
    Bob and Nancy Shagford and Their Children**   81
    What Has Happened to Jobs? 83
    Why Is the Economy Changing? 85
    Conclusion, 89

7   **Eviction: Debbie Jones and Her Children**   91
    Housing Demand for the Poor Is Greater
        Than Supply, 92
    The Poor Pay More for Housing and Other Services
        and Commodities, 94
    The Relative Powerlessness of Low-Income Renters, 96

8   **Social Service Bureaucracy and Homelessness:
    Diane Moore**   99
    Unsuspected Sources of Homelessness:
        Social Service and Welfare Programs, 99
    Bureaucracy Meets the Urban Housing Crisis, 103
    Homeless Shelters, 104
    "Class" Divisions Among the Homeless, 107
    One Woman's Experience in the Shelter, 109
    The Myth of Family as the Solution to
        Homelessness, 111
    No Culture of Poverty, No Welfare Dependency, 115
    Notes, 116

9   **Runaway and Throwaway Teens: Jeffrey Giancarlo**   117
    Youth Homelessness, 117
    The Myth of Dysfunctional Families as the Cause
        of Homelessness, 120
    Antifamily Social Policy, 121
    The Failure of Child Welfare Agencies, 123
    Marginalization of Teens, 124
    Teens Who Don't and Won't Conform, 125

Declining Household Size, 126
Bad Trends and Policies, Not Bad Kids and Families, 126

**10   A Black Teenage Single Mother and Her Son:
      Michelle and Andre**   128
      Black Teenage Single Mothers, 130
      The Children of Teenage Single Mothers, 135
      Values Versus Structure, 137

11   Battered Women and Homelessness: Barbara Evans   140
      An Epidemic of Violence Against Women, 140
      Battered Women and Housing, 147
      High Aspirations Meet Discrimination and the
         Low-Wage Economy, 150

PART 3   CONCLUSION

12   The Complex and Simple Reality of Homelessness   155
      A Note on the Complexity of Homelessness, 155
      The Concrete Reality of Homelessness, 156
      A Final Note on the Simplicity of Homelessness, 173

13   Making Homelessness Go Away: Politics and Policy   175
      Industrial Decline, 175
      Urban Decline, 178
      Meager Welfare State, 180
      Urban Housing Crisis, 181
      The Shelterization Response, 183
      Clinton and the New Democrats, 189
      Policy, Not People, 190
      Notes, 190

References   191
About the Book and Authors   201
Index   203

Acknowledgments

This research was assisted in part by a Dana Foundation Faculty Development Fellowship Grant from the University of Tampa and a Lilly Foundation Development Grant from North Central College, Illinois.

We want to thank the people who shared their lives with us. We have learned much from them and want to give something back. Therefore, the royalties received from this book will be given to not-for-profit community groups in the struggle for low-income and affordable housing in Tampa and Chicago.

Doug A. Timmer
D. Stanley Eitzen
Kathryn D. Talley

I am eating outside of a ribs joint early on a Sunday evening in late July, at the corner of 53rd and Dorchester on the South Side of Chicago. A young black man—maybe in his mid-to-late twenties—comes up to my table.

"It's a tiresome world, isn't it? I've been livin' in my van for the last two months. Got my last check [unemployment] and there still ain't no work. I'm goin' to get out of here to Boulder or Wisconsin. My buddy wants to go to Colorado but I just want to go up to Wisconsin. You can find the same things there as you can in Colorado. We're gonna try to find a cave. I'm tired of this big-city, big-city prices. You get a cave and you ain't got to pay no rent. Ain't nobody can take it from you."

Before I can say much, he's on his way, leaving as quietly and quickly as he appeared.

"Take care, man," he says.

PART ONE

Overview

1

Understanding Homelessness:
Industrial and Urban Decline

The homeless are the most visible of America's social problems. Homeless people are found everywhere: in cities, small towns, suburbs, and rural areas. They are on the evening news, especially when it is very cold and during the winter holidays. We see them huddled in frigid temperatures on steam grates. We encounter them as they beg for handouts along the sidewalks in front of the trendiest stores as well as in the alleys of the most run-down neighborhoods. We cannot escape them as they seek refuge in church doorways, subway terminals, libraries, parks, and stores. They are everywhere and their numbers are increasing.

The homeless are the poorest of the poor. Like other poor people, the homeless receive inadequate or no medical care, tend to be malnourished, experience discrimination, and are the objects of scorn and condescension by those more advantaged. But the poverty of the homeless is extreme. They are homeless because their economic resources are exhausted. They have no personal safety net and they have escaped the one supposedly supplied by society. Finding food and shelter are troubles every day. And, most notably, the homeless are much more visible than other poor people. Whether they sleep in the streets or in shelters, they are quickly and easily identified as social pariahs.

Homelessness is not just a matter of social class. Race is also a crucial determinant, since people of color are disproportionately among the very poor. For example, in 1991, 11.3 percent of whites were below the poverty line compared to 28.7 percent of Latinos and 32.7 percent of African Americans. If we look at those at half the poverty rate or lower, 3.9 percent of whites were in this extreme category of poverty compared to 9.9 percent of Latinos and 15.8 percent of African Americans (U.S. Bureau of the Census 1992:17–19). Within these impersonal statistics are institutional racism, which disadvantages racial minorities through residential segregation patterns, job discrimination, and inferior education, and the personal tragedies and indignities resulting from discrimination that disadvantages people of color.

Although homelessness is found throughout American society, it is particularly an urban phenomenon. Homelessness is especially urban because the cities are the endpoint of industrial and urban decline. The government's data for 1991 show that 43 percent of the nation's poor were found inside central cities (U.S. Bureau of the Census 1992:1). Homelessness in the United States is predominantly a problem of the inner cities because the poor there are especially vulnerable to the structural forces that lead to unemployment, layoffs, and plant closings. The poor in the inner cities are also relatively defenseless against the problems endemic to poverty because the cities are generally financially unable to provide a sufficient safety net to meet their needs. Finally, the poor in the cities find special difficulty in finding affordable housing because of high costs and ever fewer available units. This lack of housing supply for the poor is the primary reason, as we will document throughout this book, for the rapid rise in the homeless population in U.S. cities since the middle 1970s.

How are we to understand the phenomenon of homelessness? The most commonly used explanation focuses on the faults of those individuals who are homeless. This type of explanation is based on the ideology that opportunities for economic advancement are readily available for those willing to try. In this view, individuals are personally responsible for their successes or failures. Thus, homeless persons are to blame for their deprivation because of their drinking habits, their immorality, their mental instability, their illiteracy, or their lack of purpose and initiative. In other words, the homeless are homeless because they are drunk, unstable, or lazy. The problem with this approach is that it blames the victim and ignores the powerful structural forces that push many people into difficult situations beyond their control.

If the individualistic approach is correct, then the proportion of homeless should be about the same in all large cities of the world. Personal irresponsibility certainly occurs everywhere. If that is the reason for homelessness then there should be about the same proportion of homeless in Tampa as in Toronto or in Chicago as compared to Copenhagen. Since this is not the case, socioeconomic factors must account for the differences. Elliot Liebow argues (and we agree) that "the only things that separate people who have a home from those who do not are money and social support: Homeless people are homeless because they cannot afford a home, and their friends and family can't, or won't, help them out. I don't want to overlook the differences among us but I don't think they're as important as the samenesses in us" (quoted in Coughlin 1993:A8).

The structural approach focuses on factors such as the shortage of low-income housing, the impact of changing technology on work, the globalization of the economy, and the dual labor market that dooms certain kinds of workers to economic marginality. The only problem with the structural approach to homelessness is that whereas it has great explanatory power, by itself it does not capture the human suffering involved.

A third type of explanatory scheme, the "politics of compassion," prevails among contemporary social scientists (for a critique of this approach, see Hoch and Slayton 1989). In this view, the "old" homeless (i.e., the homeless prior to the middle 1970s) are characterized as people whose flawed personal characteristics doomed them to homelessness. The "new" homeless, in sharp contrast, are portrayed as victims—victims of economic dislocation, bad marriages, the deinstitutionalization of the mentally ill, physical handicaps, and the like. As victims, the new homeless are seen as deserving of society's help. There are two fundamental problems with this approach, as Hoch and Slayton (1989) have argued. First, it overlooks the common economic and class origins of the old and new homeless. Second, the "politics of compassion" view leads to interventions by various professional interests, both public and private, to provide specialized care for the different "types" of homeless persons (e.g., single mothers with children, battered women, and the mentally ill). Although such interventions are surely needed in some cases, this approach has the negative consequence of leading toward permanent dependence on professional care and shelter for all of the homeless. In Hoch and Slayton's words:

> Appropriate professional skills and organizational services are matched with the need of a segment of the homeless. This need becomes the social problem which these specialized caretakers can satisfy. And as the needs of various groups of homeless increasingly justify specialized treatment, those treating the homeless soon perceive this need as the reason for homelessness itself. ... Public service providers and professional caretakers have ... promoted a politics of compassion in their efforts to secure the development and expansion of specialized shelters and services for the homeless. ... These efforts are not only rapidly expanding the number of ... dormitories for the poor but are legitimizing their institutional value as a solution to the problem of homelessness. (Hoch and Slayton 1989:5)

In this way, the "politics of compassion" fails to address the structural sources of homelessness in extreme poverty and in industrial and urban decline. The strategy for understanding the homeless employed in this book provides antidotes to the problems inherent in each of these approaches. Five themes guide our inquiry:

1. Homelessness in the United States is especially an urban phenomenon. It is not a special social problem but rather the result of industrial and urban decline. The homeless are not a "special" group of people with "special" problems. Homelessness is simply the endpoint, the "logical" outcome for part of the population—the extremely poor—under conditions of industrial and urban decay. Solutions to homelessness, then, must address this urban and industrial decline.

2. The homeless are extremely poor, the poorest of the poor. The number of people living in extreme poverty, defined as two-thirds or less of the official poverty line, has doubled since 1970. The homeless come from this group, those with the least income and the fewest basic necessities (see Rossi 1989).

3. People of color are overrepresented among the poorest of the poor and race is an important factor in the genesis of urban homelessness. Probably the single best estimate of the racial composition of the homeless population in the United States found it to be about 45 percent white, 40 percent African American, 10 percent Latino, 2 percent Native American, and 1 percent Asian American. This compares to a national population that is approximately 12 percent African American, 7 percent Latino, 0.5 percent Native American, and 3 percent Asian American. Most studies done before the mid-1970s found the homeless to be predominantly white. This suggests an important change during the 1980s. The current overrepresentation of people of color among both the homeless and the larger poverty populations indicates persistent racial discrimination in the job and housing markets as factors contributing to homelessness (Wright 1989).

4. Homeless people are not, for the most part, people disabled by drugs, mental disease, or physical affliction but rather are people negatively affected by socioeconomic trends and forces. The homeless are not deficient and defective; they are resilient and resourceful.

5. The approach will be explicitly structural, not cultural. Just as there is no "culture of poverty" that makes and keeps people poor, there is no "culture of homelessness" that makes and keeps people homeless. Just as there is no urban underclass with different and distinct values and behavior that traps them in inner-city poverty, homeless persons do not hold values or behave in ways different from the housed population that are responsible for their situation (see Reed 1992; Inniss and Feagin 1989). Rather, whatever "different" values, behaviors, and routines the homeless may develop are a response to their homeless circumstances (see Snow and Anderson 1993).

Our approach to studying homelessness begins with ethnography. This, unfortunately (from our point of view), makes our research unique. A recent review of the explosion of literature on homelessness during the 1980s found that little of it actually involved observing and talking with homeless persons on the streets and in shelters. If there was contact with homeless people, it was usually only to complete a quick survey or questionnaire. Little ongoing field observation or in-depth interviewing has been done. Instead, sociologists David Snow and Leon Anderson (1993) found, nearly all of the existent research used survey research techniques in which homeless caretakers and service providers, rather than the homeless themselves, were asked for information about the demographics or disabilities of homeless people. We believe that this is fraught with the danger of producing what ethnographer Clifford Geertz (1983) has called "experience-distant" representations and understandings of homelessness. The ethnographic approach, in contrast, provides more "experience-near" representations and understandings. In this regard, we see our study as having more in common with the few notable exceptions to the main homelessness research thrust over the past decade, exceptions such as Kozol's *Rachel and Her Children* (1988), Glasser's *More Than Bread* (1988), Snow and Anderson's *Down on Their Luck* (1993), and Liebow's *Tell Them Who I Am* (1993).

In spring 1986, we began in-depth interviewing of homeless persons and collected their life stories, including their accounts of the circumstances that led to their homelessness. This interviewing was done in Tampa, Denver, and Chicago. It took place in parks, on downtown streets, in abandoned houses, in neighborhood restaurants, and waiting in soup lines. Altogether about twenty single men were interviewed; about half were black and half were white, and they lived on the streets without shelter.

Later, we moved on to homeless shelters. Between the summers of 1986 and 1988, we interviewed another twenty people, who lived in two different shelters. The interviewing took place in a shelter for homeless women and their children on the South Side of Chicago and in a shelter for families near downtown Tampa. In the Chicago shelter nearly all of the residents were black; in Tampa most were white but there were some blacks and a few Latinos.

The interviews are best characterized as semi-structured and open-ended. Most were tape recorded with the remainder written as close as possible to verbatim after the interview. The interviews ranged in length from two to five hours; some were done in two or three separate sittings. All of the interviews were done in the context of longer-term participant observation and were not undertaken until we had established a significant degree of familiarity and rapport with those who were interviewed, both on the street and in the shelters. We believe this provided a more than adequate "check" on the truthfulness of those who told us their stories.

Thus, to counter the impersonality of the structural approach, we examined intensely, through in-depth interviews, the lives of homeless persons and families. These personal accounts reveal the isolation these persons feel as social outcasts. After all, these persons are, in the words of Patricia Cayo Sexton: "cast off, degraded, uprooted, excluded from rewarding work—by other classes, by economic policies, and by a value system that cherishes individual achievement, despises individual failure, and is profoundly suspicious of misfits" (Sexton 1983:79). We learn from the words of the homeless how they cope on a day-to-day basis with deprivation, degradation, and denial. They inform us of the extent to which cooperation and victimization prevail among and between the homeless. These glimpses into the lives of the homeless reveal that the homeless are not, for the most part, disabled by habitual drunkenness or by mental instability. To the contrary, these people are especially resilient and resourceful. Conversations with homeless persons also help us understand the degree of effectiveness of private charitable efforts and public agencies in meeting their needs. We see that the homeless are not a "special" group that requires a special solution. Rather, we see that the answer lies in policies that address urban and industrial decline in the United States.

The tendency to blame the homeless for their plight is overcome in two ways. Chapter 2 provides the context for the personal accounts of homelessness by addressing the structural sources of the problem. Some examples of these sources are (1) public and private policies that have caused a shortage of low- and moderate-income housing in American cities, (2) economic transformations such as deindustrialization, and (3) various governmental efforts to dismantle the American welfare state.

The second strategy to overcome the inclination to blame the victim is the judicious selection of homeless persons included in this book. Each homeless individual or family described here was included to illustrate a particular path to homelessness. Their personal accounts will show how individuals are affected, sometimes dramatically, by impersonal social and economic forces. In effect, we employ C. Wright Mills's "sociological imagination" (1959) to understand the private troubles of the homeless as public issues. This approach emphasizes how homeless persons are trapped in a socioeconomic contradiction at a particular time in history. Thus, the personal accounts by homeless persons will go beyond the facts of the urban housing crisis, evictions, economic decline, plant closings, and the like to capture their human reality. We want to understand homelessness in human terms. This requires that we understand how individuals and families act and react to the powerful structural forces in which they find themselves. To accomplish this goal each chapter will examine a particular path to homelessness. There will be a general discussion of the particular population at risk (e.g., those unemployed because of deindustrialization) with interview data from an individual case to give the problem its human face. The second part of each chapter will focus on how individuals caught in this structural bind face an urban housing crisis leading to homelessness.

Our approach is what sociologist Michael Burawoy (1991) has described as "ethnography unbound"—ethnography freed from simple description and done, rather, in a Millsean way. We intend to find the links between biography and history, the personal and the political, based on the case at hand. Using the "extended case method," the concrete experience of homeless persons is connected to the historical and socioeconomic forces that condition and influence it.

Although the homeless deserve our compassion, we must overcome the tendency to view them as incapable of independent action. We must seek solutions to homelessness that recognize the structural roots of the problem and that meet the needs of those affected *without* making them dependent on shelters and professional caregivers. The final chapter summarizes what we have learned from the accounts of homeless people. The focus in that chapter is on the social policies that these different paths to homelessness indicate would do the most to diminish significantly the homelessness experienced by growing numbers of Americans. In short, we end with the social policy question of what to do about this vexing social problem. Understanding the socioeconomic sources of homelessness, along with the appreciation of how homeless persons are affected by these structural forces, leads us toward appropriate social policies and solutions.

2

The Root Causes of Homelessness
in American Cities

The facts concerning poverty in the United States are grim. Data from 1991 reveal that 14.2 percent of the population (about 35.7 million Americans) were below the official poverty line (the data in this section are taken from U.S. Bureau of the Census 1992:vii–xviii). Over one-fifth of all children (21.8 percent) were poor. About one-third of all African Americans (32.7 percent) and almost three out of ten Hispanics (28.7 percent) were poor.

As bleak as these data are, they severely understate the actual magnitude of poverty. John Schwarz and Thomas Volgy, in their book *The Forgotten Americans* (1992), argue that the 1991 official poverty line would have been $21,600 for a family of four (instead of the $13,359 used by the government) if it had been determined as it was originally in the early 1960s. The first poverty line was calculated by determining the lowest cost for feeding a family of a given size at an acceptable nutrition level. Because it was assumed that one-third of an average family budget went for food, the food cost was multiplied by three to determine the official poverty line. Since then the official poverty line has been adjusted each year by the consumer price index (CPI) to account for inflation. The problem with this procedure is that the cost of basic necessities such as food and housing has risen much faster over the past thirty years than the overall CPI. If a more realistic poverty line were used, *at least 25 percent of Americans—more than 60 million people, would be classified as poor (The People* 1993a:3).

This chapter is a much revised version of Doug A. Timmer and D. Stanley Eitzen, "The Root Causes of Urban Homelessness in the United States," *Humanity and Society* 16 (2) (May 1992):159–175.

The poor face a number of obstacles. They are rejected and despised by others. They are looked down upon as lazy, shiftless, dirty, and immoral. They often receive inferior educations because they live in economically depressed school districts. They often are exposed to toxic chemicals. Many of the poor are malnourished and have health problems. In 1991 some 35.4 million Americans had no health insurance and many were refused medical care for financial reasons. The result is that on average low-income families pay one-fifth of their incomes toward health care—twice as much as the one-tenth paid by high-income families (Economic Policy Institute, reported in Associated Press [1993]).

Whereas misery, ill health, malnutrition, and discrimination are endemic among all the poor, the most disadvantaged among them also live in substandard housing without adequate plumbing, heat, or other facilities. The poorest of the poor are often just an illness, accident, divorce, or other personal disaster away from homelessness. During the 1980s and the early 1990s the proportion of poor people who became homeless increased dramatically. An ever-increasing number of homeless were visible on the streets as the demand on shelters far outstripped the supply. Much more than at other times in U.S. history, the homeless are experiencing a severe housing shortage, which is forcing many of them to sleep in temporary shelters or even in doorways, on heating grates, in dumpsters, in cardboard boxes, and in abandoned buildings.

The goals of this chapter are to examine the important issues, dispel commonly held myths, and outline the root causes of homelessness. Over the past decade a flood of information on homelessness has appeared. This "information explosion" is overwhelming in terms of its sheer quantity. Also, it is becoming more and more difficult to draw political and policy conclusions from it. The intent of this chapter is to integrate and make sense out of what is known about homelessness and its structural sources. This overview of the socioeconomic forces impinging of human lives will provide a framework for understanding how people become homeless. This understanding of the causes of homelessness will also help to provide solutions to the problem, which is our task in the final chapter.

Major Issues Concerning the Homeless

Three questions are raised and answered in this section: (1) What is the extent of homelessness in America? (2) Is homelessness caused by personal disabilities? and (3) Are the "new" homeless different from the "old" homeless?

The Homeless: How Many?

The homeless are typically defined as those who have no permanent home and who must resort to streets, shelters, or other makeshift quarters. The number of homeless is impossible to determine accurately since they may be living with relatives or friends or hidden beneath bridges, in alleys, in abandoned buildings, in shelters and are therefore difficult to find and count. The low estimate, by the U.S. Department of Housing and Urban Development (HUD) during the Reagan administration, was that between 250,000 and 350,000 Americans were homeless. Political conservatives find appeal in this low figure because it means that the problem is relatively insignificant and not in need of additional public programs and resources to ameliorate it. Estimates at the high end come from advocacy groups like the National Coalition for the Homeless, which put the figure at between 3 and 4 million. Reformers, convinced of the magnitude and seriousness of the problem, are prone to accept these higher figures (for discussions of the methodological and political reasons for the wide discrepancies in the estimates of the homeless, see Kozol 1988c:9–11; Wright 1989:19–27; Rossi 1989:45–81; Wiegard 1985; and *Population Today* 1986).

Whatever the actual numbers of the homeless, three points must be underscored. First, the proportion of Americans who are homeless is the highest since the Great Depression, with a rapid rise in the past fifteen years or so and still climbing. Second, the numbers actually minimize the seriousness of the problem because so many of the urban poor are on the brink of homelessness and many who lack housing are hidden by doubling or tripling up with relatives or friends. Jonathan Kozol estimates that there are over 300,000 hidden homeless in New York City alone and that nationwide more than 3 million families are living doubled up. When these households are added to those poor people paying more than half of their monthly income for rent, more than 10 million families are living near the edge of homelessness in the United States (Kozol 1988b:1, 14). Another estimate, this time by the American Affordable Housing Institute of Rutgers University, states that between 4 million and 14 million families live on the edge of homelessness (quoted in Mercer 1990). And third, we should not become unduly focused on the numbers because they deflect us from the problem itself and the homeless themselves. In Kozol's words:

> We would be wise ... to avoid the numbers game. Any search for the "right number" carries the assumption that we may at last arrive at an acceptable number. There is no acceptable number. Whether the number is 1 million or 4 million or the administration's estimate of less than a million, there are too many homeless people in America. (Kozol 1988b:3; see also Daley 1987)

Homelessness and Personal Disabilities

A recurrent belief among politicians, journalists, social scientists, and the public is that homelessness is a consequence of personal disabilities. That is, homeless persons tend to suffer from chronic alcoholism or from chronic physical or mental disorders and these disabilities explain their homelessness. This is a myth with damaging consequences. Although some homeless persons suffer from alcoholism, most do not. Some suffer severe mental or emotional disturbances, but most do not.

Typically, the recent rise in homelessness is seen as a consequence of the deinstitutionalization of mental patients that began in the 1950s. The data appear to support this notion, since the average daily census of psychiatric institutions dropped from 677,000 in 1955 to 151,000 in 1984 (Kozol 1988a:18). The numbers of former mental patients swelled as a result of deinstitutionalization, but this does not necessarily explain the increased numbers of the homeless in the 1980s. Almost all of the reduction in mental patients had occurred by 1978, yet the homeless did not begin overflowing the streets and shelters until 1983.

Several other cautions must be raised concerning the emphasis on the homeless as mentally ill. First, although it is undeniable that some homeless people are mentally disturbed and incapable of sustaining personal relationships and steady work, most of the homeless are *not* mentally ill; most are quite capable of functioning in society. There is solid research evidence to indicate that no more than 10 to 15 percent of persons living on the street are mentally impaired in some way. Researcher James Wright, using data from the national Health Care for the Homeless (HCH) program, has concluded that as many as one-third of the homeless probably are mentally ill (Wright 1988a). But more recent research has confirmed the 10 to 15 percent estimate. Piliavin, Westerfelt, and Elliot (1989) have found Wright's higher figures to be biased by his sample, which was limited to homeless persons who used health clinic services. These researchers have found the homeless who use these services to have significantly higher rates of mental illness than those homeless persons who do not use them. Yet the myth is perpetuated in the media that the majority of the homeless have a history of chronic mental illness (see, for example, Morganthau 1986).

A second caution concerns context. Elliot Liebow, in his description and analysis of homeless women, argues that judgments about the homeless often involve descriptions of them as deviant—mentally ill, alcoholic, drug addicted—descriptions that would receive more positive judgments if they were in another setting.

Like you, I know people who drink, people who do drugs, and bosses who have tantrums and treat their subordinates like dirt. They all have good jobs. Were they to become homeless, some of them would surely also become "alcoholics," "addicts, or "mentally ill." Similarly, if some of the homeless women who are now so labelled were to be magically transported to a more usual and acceptable setting, some of them—not all, of course—would shed their labels and take their places with the rest of us somewhere on the spectrum of normality. (Liebow 1993:xiii)

In short, there is a class bias involved here. When homeless people do have mental difficulties or problems with alcohol, these situations are identified as the cause of their homelessness. But when well-housed middle-class and upper-middle-class people are mentally ill or alcoholic it is identified as an unfortunate situation requiring attention and treatment. Clearly, then, the source of homelessness is not behavior—mental illness or alcoholism—but the different social or class context for the behavior.

A third caution has to do with cause and effect. Does mental illness cause homelessness or do the stresses induced by extreme poverty and homelessness cause mental illness? Although some argue that mental illness is a cause of homelessness, there are no data to support this claim. The much stronger argument is that mental illness is a probable consequence of homelessness. This is based on the assumption that a stable life leads to mental stability and an unstable one to mental instability. In Jonathan Kozol's words:

Many pregnant women without homes are denied prenatal care because they constantly travel from one shelter to another. Many are anemic. Many are denied essential dietary supplements by recent federal cuts. As a consequence, some of their children do not live to see their second year of life. Do these mothers sometimes show signs of stress? Do they appear disorganized, depressed, disordered? Frequently. They are immobilized by pain, traumatized by fear. So it is no surprise that when researchers enter the scene to ask them how they "feel," the resulting reports tell us that the homeless are emotionally unwell. The reports do not tell us we have made these people ill. (Kozol 1988a:155–156)

A fourth caution is that the emphasis on the personal sources of homelessness blames the victims for their problem and deflects attention away from its structural sources. To do so leads to faulty generalizations and public policies doomed to fail. In the words of David Snow and his colleagues, leading researchers on the presumed connection between mental illness and homelessness:

It is demeaning and unfair to the majority of the homeless to focus so much attention on the presumed relationship between mental illness, deinstitutionalization, and homelessness. To do so not only wrongfully identifies the major problems confronting the bulk of the homeless, it also deflects attention from the more pervasive structural causes of homelessness, such as unemployment, inadequate income for unskilled and semi-skilled workers, and the decline in the availability of low-cost housing. (Snow et al. 1986:422)

In this regard, sociologist Michael Sosin's (1992) recent study of homeless persons in Chicago is instructive. Comparing a sample of homeless persons to a sample of "vulnerable" persons—not homeless but impoverished and precariously close to losing their shelter—Sosin found the lack of access to various social and institutional supports and resources to be a much better predictor of homelessness than any personal disabilities or "deficits."

We must stress that various disabilities such as alcoholism and mental and physical illnesses are not the causes of homelessness. As James D. Wright has summarized:

Some of the homeless *are* broken down alcoholics, but most of them are not. Some *are* mentally impaired, but most of them are not. ... In a hypothetical world where there were no alcoholics, no drug addicts, no mentally ill, no deinstitutionalization movement, no personal or social pathologies at all, there would *still* be a formidable homelessness problem. (Wright 1989:18, 50)

This last point is a major theme of this book—people are homeless not because of their individual flaws but because of structural arrangements and trends that result in extreme impoverishment and a shortage of affordable housing in U.S. cities. We believe that Wright's analysis is correct. The extent to which the homeless population is made up of the mentally ill, the physically handicapped and disabled, alcoholics, and drug abusers and addicts results from their being more vulnerable to the kind of impoverishment that excludes them from the urban housing market. Their vulnerabilities mean that they may be the first to lose permanent shelter. But the absolute shortage of low-income, affordable housing in the United States ensures that even if no one were plagued with these personal disabilities, the size of the homeless population would be roughly the same. Only then we would not be able to identify the homeless population as drunk or crazy and therefore identify the causes of homelessness as these personal defects. The homeless would be like everyone else (as they, in reality, are now) except that they would not have a home.

In short, the homeless are not deficient and defective. We found them to be much the opposite. The homeless people we came to know are much like those that Snow and Anderson encountered in their study of homeless street people—resilient and resourceful.

> What has impressed us most about the homeless we came to know and whose stories we have endeavored to tell is their resourcefulness and resilience. Confronted with minimal resources, often stigmatized by the broader society, frequently harassed by community members and by law enforcement officials, and repeatedly frustrated in their attempts to claim the most modest part of the American dream, they nonetheless continue to struggle to survive materially, to develop friendships, however tenuous, with their street peers, and to carve out a sense of meaning and personal identity. To emphasize this is not to romanticize the homeless and their lives but simply to recognize the many ways they confront their often brutalizing circumstances. (Snow and Anderson 1993:316)

The False Distinction Between the Old and the New Homeless

Many recent observers of homelessness have concentrated on the differences between the "old" homeless and the "new" homeless (those homeless since about 1975) (see, as examples, Rossi 1989; Wright 1989). They find, for example, that the new homeless, when contrasted with the old homeless, are more visible, younger, and composed of a larger proportion of African Americans, Latinos, women with children, and families with both spouses present.

Although these differences between the old and the new homeless are correct empirically, they are subject to two common misinterpretations that lead to wrong conclusions and subsequently ineffective social policy. First, they imply that the new homeless are unique and, therefore, constitute a new social problem. Actually, the old and the new homeless are alike in that both are extremely poor and their differences only reflect the changing demography of U.S. cities. As Hoch and Slayton have argued:

> The "new" homeless endure the same economic difficulties as the "old" homeless and have the same class origins. Both come mainly from the ranks of the urban poor. The differences in demographic characteristics and vulnerabilities between the two reflect differences mainly in the compositions and afflictions of the urban poor. For instance, the "new" homeless are more likely to be younger and single mothers with children because the contemporary urban poor are disproportionately composed of younger, single mothers with children. (Hoch and Slayton 1989:6)

The essential point is that whatever differences are found between the old and the new homeless, they are differences in the demographic composition of the urban poor in different historical periods, not differences in their origins in the economic marginality endemic to market economies and class societies such as the United States.

The second misconception of many who distinguish between the old homeless and the new is that because there are now so many more women, children, and families among the homeless, and because the homeless now are poorer, and more mentally ill, and because they are more likely to be victims of events like plant closings, the new homeless are much more deserving of our compassion than were the old homeless, who were mainly disaffiliated single men who had, allegedly, rejected the work ethic. Hoch and Slayton have called this approach the "politics of compassion." This approach emphasizes how the poor are "overcome by a combination of their own vulnerabilities and changing circumstances" (Hoch and Slayton 1989:4). Two problems result. First, the moral outrage evoked by the plight of the new homeless tends to focus "public attention on *individual* vulnerabilities rather than on the *institutional* roots of homelessness" (Hoch and Slayton 1989:5). Second, the emphasis on individual vulnerabilities directs solutions aimed at meeting those particular needs. This results in both public and private interventions by social workers and other professionals aimed at each "type" of homelessness, which when combined with sheltering leads to an increasingly dependent homeless population.

Homeless people are seen and treated as a "problem population," like other "problem populations" such as delinquents, criminals, and the mentally ill; they are perceived as "clients" in need of services and control provided by professional caregivers and social service bureaucracies. All of this ignores, once again, the structural causes of homelessness for both the new and the old homeless. In sum, it ignores how extreme poverty and homelessness derived from the structure of a market society in both the 1930s and in contemporary urban America.

The Sources of Rising Urban Homelessness

Although the extent of differences among the old and the new homeless is disputed among social scientists, there is no doubt that the number of homeless in American cities has increased dramatically in the past decade and a half. The question is why. What are the factors that explain this spreading social problem now?

The current and expanding crisis of urban homelessness results from the convergence of two contradictory and proximate forces: the rapidly dwindling supply of low-income housing and the increased economic marginality among the poor and the near poor, caused by the changing economy, changes in family structure, and shifts in government policies.

These proximate causes of urban homelessness, it must be remembered, are in turn embedded in and derived from the structure of a historically changing corporate capitalist economy and society.

The Low-Income Housing Shortage

Our analysis of housing does not focus exclusively on the homeless. To do so risks adding to the deviant identity homeless persons have thrust upon them. Singling out homeless people exacerbates their supposedly "special" character. To do so encourages a view that they are considerably different from those who are housed. In truth, the homeless are not distinct persons, nor do they have a completely distinct problem. They happen to be at the extreme end of a shelter continuum—ranging from those who are sufficiently housed, through those who are ill-housed, to those who have no housing at all. Thus, the urban homeless problem is fundamentally a housing problem.

There is not enough low-cost housing available for the economically marginal in U.S. cities. The low-income housing supply has shrunk dramatically in recent years. The inflation of the 1980s is one source of this shrinkage: The cost of housing at all levels rose rapidly. The median price of a single-family dwelling sold in 1970, for example, was $23,000; in 1980 it was $62,200; in 1989 it was $92,900; and by 1993 it was $104,000. This varied by locality, of course, with the cost of a median house in Honolulu, San Francisco, and Anaheim well over double the median and Los Angeles, San Diego, Newark, Boston, and New York City just below double the national median (*USA Today* 1993:10B).

Some might argue that the low interest rates of the 1990s (in July 1993 the interest rate costs for housing were at a twenty-one-year low) will alleviate the housing crisis for the poor. This is not the case, however, because the required down payment (typically 5 to 10 percent) is prohibitive for the economically marginal. Some lenders offer first-time buyers a mortgage with no money down. The catch for those on the economic margin is that these plans typically require a parent or close relative to guarantee 30 percent of the sales price by investing in certificates of deposit held by the bank. Clearly such a plan is not directed at solving the housing needs of the urban poor. Most significant, lowered interest rates also have not meant a decline in rents. Moreover, there is a general tendency for rent increases to outpace the rate of inflation (see, for example, Ringheim 1993).

The cost of renting followed the inflationary trend of the 1970s and 1980s; in fact, it rose faster than renters' incomes. This was partly a function of the high cost of home purchases, which floods the rental market, putting upward pressure on rents. Between 1970 and 1990, for example, rents tripled while renters' incomes only doubled (Gilderbloom 1991:30). This inflation in the housing market at all levels has placed increased pressures on the poor, who simply cannot afford the increased rents or must sacrifice essentials such as food to pay the higher rents. The federal standard for affordable housing is less than 30 percent of household income for rent. A survey of forty-four cities by the Center on Budget and Policy Priorities found that 75 percent of low-income households (those earning less than $10,000 annually) paid more than 30 percent of their incomes in rent. In thirty-nine of the forty-four cities surveyed, housing costs alone normally exceeded the entire grant for a family of three receiving assistance from the Aid to Families with Dependent Children (AFDC) program (reported in Gugliotta 1992:A6). Data from 1989 indicated that nearly one-half (47 percent) of those households below the poverty line *spent more than 70 percent of their incomes for housing* (DeParle 1991:1). Paying such a high proportion of their low income for rent places these households on the brink of homelessness, one medical crisis, one layoff, or one pay cut away from losing their shelter.

One factor explaining the increasing lack of affordable rental housing is the "rent squeeze" caused by concentrated ownership of rental housing in U.S. cities. In both New York City and Houston, for example, 5 percent of all landlords control more than one-half of the rental housing stock. In Boston, only twenty individuals own 40 percent of the city's rental units (Gilderbloom 1991:31). When rental housing is controlled by a few, rents rise. The poor and the working class have been especially affected negatively by the reduced competition among the owners of rental housing (Gilderbloom and Appelbaum 1988).

Although the rising cost of low-income housing is an important reason for the increased rates of homelessness, other factors are also important. Foremost, there has been an absolute loss in low-income units. From 1970 to 1989 the number of rental units for the poor declined 14 percent to 5.5 million while the number of poor renters—those who made less than $10,000 in 1989 dollars—increased from 7.3 million to 9.6 million (Gugliotta 1992:A6). This shortfall of 4.1 million rental units for the poor is a major reason for the dramatic rise in homelessness (see Figure 2.1). And it is estimated that by the year 2003, the gap between those needing low-income housing and the number of available units will be 7.8 million (Shapiro 1989:20).

Conspicuous among the reasons for the decline of low-income housing has been the loss of single-room occupancy (SRO) hotels, often the housing of last resort for the economically marginal in cities. About a million SRO units have been torn down nationwide since the 1970s (Levitas 1990:84). In New York City, for example, the stock of SROs shrunk from 127,000 units in 1975 to 14,000 in 1985 (Siegel and Levy 1985).

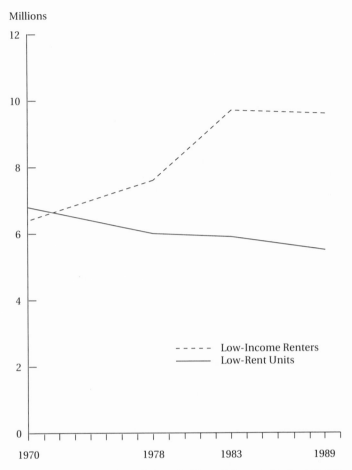

FIGURE 2.1 The Number of Households with Income Under $10,000 a Year and the Number of Houses and Apartments Renting for Less Than $250 a Month (all in 1989 dollars)

SOURCES: Center for Budget and Policy Priorities; National Low Income Housing Information Service.

SROs and other low-cost rental housing have disappeared because of two related trends. One is gentrification—the process of converting low-income housing to condominiums or upscale apartments for the middle and upper-middle classes (Kasinitz 1984). Condominium conversion involves taking rental units and turning them into apartments for sale. This practice often replaces those who cannot afford a down payment or qualify for a home mortgage with those more affluent persons who can. Gentrification typically includes buying up older and sometimes run-down property in poor and working-class neighborhoods and rehabilitating it into middle-class condominiums, townhouses, single-family dwellings, and upscale lofts and apartments. Often, the original residents of the area are displaced because they cannot afford the increased rents, purchases prices, and insurance and property taxes associated with the neighborhood's rising property values. The poor, who once had housing, are left out. Especially harmed by this process are nonwhites. Research by Phillip Clay (1979) studied fifty-seven gentrifying neighborhoods in thirty cities and found that before gentrification about half the neighborhoods were predominantly black. After gentrification, 80 percent were dominated by whites and only 2 percent were predominantly nonwhite.

Slumlords have also contributed to the inner-city housing shortage. Slumlording occurs when investors buy rental properties in poor neighborhoods and purposefully fail to maintain them. Typically, the slumlords are middle class and white, the tenants poor and black. Over time serious housing code violations develop as roofs leak, stairways deteriorate, plumbing fails, and electrical wiring becomes dangerous. Slumlords simply squeeze whatever rents they can for as long as they can. The end point of this process is when the city condemns the buildings, evicts the residents, and takes over the property for delinquent taxes and unpaid utility bills.

Another market mechanism that leads to the urban housing crisis is "warehousing." Here, real estate speculators buy property on the edges of gentrifying areas and gradually empty them of their occupants by not maintaining them or by not renting them when renters leave. The goal is selling these properties to other developers for a profit. Developers are especially attracted to "warehoused" properties since they spare them the difficulties of removing poor and working-class leaseholders who will not be able to afford the newly gentrified property.

These actions by urban developers and real estate interests to increase their profits result in removing affordable rental housing from the market, driving up rents in the remaining apartments, and displacing tenants from their homes and communities.

These sources of shrinkage in the urban housing market have been met with, and at times encouraged by, failed federal housing policies. From the 1960s on, for example, federally financed urban renewal projects have focused on the demolition of blighted properties in poor and working-class neighborhoods. In theory, urban renewal funds were supposed to follow the bulldozers with rehabilitation and redevelopment. In practice, something quite different occurred.

In the first phase of urban renewal, cities applied for designated federal funds and when they were received they used their legal power of eminent domain to declare an area blighted. Once so designated, all structures were demolished. The razing of huge expanses of buildings often facilitated the development of public projects such as airports, colleges, medical centers, sports arenas, and even private commercial projects on the now vacant land (see Hirsch 1983). The second phase of federal urban renewal was to include replacement housing for those who lost their homes to the bulldozers. For the most part, however, funds were never appropriated for this phase, leaving many poor people permanently displaced from shelter. Urban renewal projects continued to reduce the supply of low-income housing throughout the 1970s. Much of the housing stock that was lost was indeed blighted, but for many occupants it was at least an affordable place to live.

Urban renewal by government combined with the actions by developers to make housing precarious for nonwhites. Micaela di Leonardo states:

> The housing destroyed by urban renewal was never replaced, and two-thirds of those displaced were black or Hispanic. The real estate speculation spiral of the 1970s and '80s was the poison cherry on the arsenic cake for poor minorities' housing aspirations, pricing them out of the private housing market just as the federal government abandoned its commitment to providing low-cost housing. We white middle-class Americans know what housing price inflation has meant in our lives—higher and higher shares of income siphoned off, being unable to buy a house or apartment, or being so ridiculously house-poor that you can't afford a meal out. Just imagine, then, what it has meant for those not only poor or working-class but also minority, since it's well-documented that high percentages of banks, landlords, and realtors still discriminate by race. (di Leonardo 1992b:33)

A comparison of all blacks with all whites in U.S. society showed that blacks spend more on rent than whites do. This is because African Americans are concentrated in urban areas where rents tend to be higher and because their housing options are limited by discrimination (Burns 1993:45).

Rollbacks in public housing have further reduced the supply of low-income housing in U.S. cities. Federal low-income housing programs, including government subsidies for its construction, declined dramatically during the Reagan presidency. Federal support for subsidized housing dropped from $32.2 billion in 1981 to $6 billion in 1989 (Appelbaum 1989:7). The U.S. Department of Housing and Urban Development (HUD) authorized the construction of 183,000 subsidized dwellings in 1980 but only 20,000 in 1989 (Appelbaum 1989:7). Ameliorating the problems of the poor and the homeless was clearly not a priority of the Reagan administration: "When Reagan came to office in 1981, the federal government spent seven dollars on defense for every dollar on housing. When he left office in 1989, the ratio was forty-six to one" (Appelbaum 1989:9).

These recent cutbacks in public housing exacerbate an already meager public housing sector. When compared to the industrial democracies of Europe, for example, U.S. public housing makes up a paltry share of the total housing stock. In Europe, urban public housing often accounts for as much as 40 percent of the total housing stock, compared to only 1.3 percent in the United States. Only 6 percent of U.S. households qualifying for low-income housing assistance receive it from the government (Gilderbloom 1991:31). And only one-fifth of the poor live in government-subsidized housing of any kind, whether public housing run by local housing authorities, privately owned projects subsidized by HUD, or private apartments for which tenants pay rent with government vouchers (Dreier 1992:21). This is the lowest rate of assistance of any industrial nation in the world (Dreier and Atlas 1989).

The Department of Housing and Urban Development currently provides aid to about 4.5 million families, either through public housing or the subsidizing of rents in private apartments. HUD estimates that as many as 13 million more families qualify for housing assistance but cannot be helped because of a shortage of federal funds. Of the 13 million lacking assistance, 5.1 million are considered to have "worst-case needs" because they spend more than 50 percent of their incomes on rent or live in "severely substandard" conditions (DeParle 1993).

The federal government's reliance on the private sector has proven to be an inefficient, ineffective, and a contributing factor in the dwindling supply of low-income housing in U.S. cities. Beginning in the late 1960s, hundreds of thousands of apartments were built with government-subsidized, very low interest loans. For the duration of these loans, usually twenty years, the owners were required to rent a percentage of their units at below-market rates to low- or moderate-income households. When the developers paid off their mortgages, they were free to displace low-income renters and charge prevailing rates, which they did. When this problem became apparent in the 1980s Congress passed a law compensating owners with *new* subsidies in exchange for not raising the rent. The result was that HUD spent hundreds of millions of dollars a year in new payments to landlords, simply to preserve existing units, not to create new low-cost housing.

HUD foreclosures also show the negative effects of subsidizing the private sector. HUD now manages 48,000 apartments that were repossessed when their owners defaulted on their HUD-insured mortgages. HUD wants to sell these units to private investors but it will cost about $2 billion in additional subsidies to make the apartments attractive to new investors (DeParle 1993).

The inherent problems associated with subsidizing the private sector in order to provide low-income housing are exacerbated by the high potential for corruption whenever public moneys are used. This was evidenced throughout the 1980s when already scarce HUD dollars for low-income housing assistance were often diverted to politically connected real estate developers who were given exemptions from the federal law requiring that a percentage of their units be rented to low-income persons. Sometimes these federal dollars earmarked for the poor were even used to develop townhouses and golf courses for the affluent.

Finally, the failed government policies regarding low-cost housing are seen in this bitter irony: While low federal expenditures to house the poor are subjected to the budget ax, housing subsidies for the affluent, in the form of mortgage interest and tax deduction write-offs, continue. In 1990, home owners received approximately $47 billion in tax subsidies whereas HUD spent $9 billion on low-income housing programs (Gilderbloom 1991:31; *Economist* 1992:24). This $47 billion disproportionately benefits home owners with high incomes and second homes; 60 percent of these tax shelters go to families in the top 20 percent income bracket. One-quarter of this subsidy goes to the 2 percent of all taxpayers with annual incomes over $100,000 (Dreier and Atlas 1989:29).

To summarize, the dramatic shrinkage in the supply of low-cost housing is both a problem of affordability and supply. Clearly, market forces, which, according to conservative analysts should work to solve social problems, have *not* worked to furnish an adequate supply of low-cost housing in America's cities (Gilderbloom and Appelbaum 1988). In reality, market forces are the source of, not the solution to, the problem. Nor did the federal government step in to meet this need. The result was a shortage of affordable housing units for the poorest of the poor. And this structural change in urban housing markets was occurring at the very time that the numbers of the very poor were increasing.

The Swelling of the At-Risk Population

Another way in which housing becomes less affordable is through declining wages and income. Poverty in American cities has been intensifying and expanding because the urban poor have fewer dollars for housing. This situation results from a number of fundamental changes in society.

The Changing Economy. The changing economy has made certain segments of the population especially vulnerable to increasing economic marginality and poverty. The structure and changing imperatives of corporate capitalism have transformed the American economy in at least four ways (Eitzen and Baca Zinn 1989a:1–17). Briefly, these are (1) a shift from an economy dominated by producing goods to one based on services (including both "higher-order services" such as finance, insurance, government, medicine, and education and "lower-order services" such as clerical, secretarial, custodial, restaurant, and retail); (2) capital flight (overseas investment by U.S. firms, the relocation of American businesses in other countries and to the suburbs or Sun Belt in the United States, and corporate mergers and leveraged buyouts); (3) the globalization of the economy, which means competition from abroad; and (4) technological breakthroughs in microelectronics, which result, for example, in automated production replacing workers. These trends have combined to transform the American economy in a generation. From 1979 to 1989 some 13.6 million full-time jobs were created. But more than one-half of these jobs were "bad" jobs in the sense that they involved few skills, were poorly paid, had little responsibility attached to them, provided poor job security, and had few if any fringe benefits such as health insurance and pensions. The Census Bureau has determined that 18.9 percent of full-time workers had low-wage jobs in 1979. In 1992 the proportion of low-wage jobs was up to 25.7 percent (O'Reilly 1992a:62). At the same time, many millions of "good" jobs were lost when machines (computers, robots, and the like) replaced workers; factories were relocated in the South, where wages were lower and unions weak or nonexistent; business and industry moved to Third and Fourth World countries; or when businesses failed, decided to sell their assets, shifted to other business endeavors, or became part of a conglomerate. Some of these millions of workers who lost good jobs in the past decade or so were able to find similar work but many had to take low-wage service-sector jobs. Thus those who did not fall below the official poverty line became poorer also. And even when the good jobs were not lost, corporate mobilization campaigns led to wage and benefit concessions and declines in union membership and strength (Sheak 1990).

Another source of low-wage jobs is the proliferation of contingent employment. This employment arrangement refers to employees who work for an employer as "temporaries" or as "independent contractors." Employers like to hire temporary workers because they save money on salaries, unemployment compensation, training, and career advancement. It also means avoiding antidiscrimination laws, health care costs, paid vacations, and pension costs. This "temping" of the work force is a significant trend. In the ten years since 1982, when employment grew by less than 20 percent, temporary employment increased by almost 250 percent. In 1988 about 25 percent of the labor force were contingent workers; in 1993 they were 33 percent of the work force (McWhirter 1992; Castro 1993).

Some of the negative consequences for contingent workers are a lower standard of living, less security, and treatment as a second-class citizen by employers and permanent staff. This trend and its consequences are especially detrimental to women. *Two-thirds of all part-time workers are women.*

The fundamental shift in the economy of the past twenty years is that of deindustrialization. The U.S. economy has evolved from one primarily involved in the production and distribution of goods to the provision of services. Whereas industrial employment characteristically included unionization and resultant higher wages, job protection, and benefits, service-sector employment is less unionized, low paying, less likely to include benefits, and more likely to be part time and temporary. Robert Reich, current secretary of labor, has characterized the service economy as consisting of two escalators—a small one going up, composed of those few jobs in management and high tech that pay well, and a much larger one going down, the fate of the majority of workers who are consigned to retail, information processing, and other low-paying service positions (cited in Dreier and Appelbaum 1991). This bifurcation of the work force has removed the "middle." As a manager of a Toledo branch of the Ohio Bureau of Employment Services remarked: "The whole middle of the job market is gone, the $8-an-hour to $13-an-hour jobs. Those middle, family-supportive jobs we've lost" (quoted in Kilborn 1993). This is evidenced by the decline in real wages. Adjusting the average weekly wage to reflect actual purchasing power, the CPI has declined by 19 percent since 1973 (Jackson 1993).

Recent government data reveal the contours of the "new poor." From 1983 to 1988 nearly 10 million Americans lost jobs to plant closings and manufacturing layoffs. Nearly 4.7 million were longtime workers (workers who had held their previous jobs at least three years). Only 71 percent of them found new jobs. Of those re-employed full time, 44 percent reported making less money (30 percent reported an income loss of at least 20 percent). These workers were downwardly mobile even if they were not living below the government's poverty line. But 1.5 million of these longtime workers are still unemployed and a part of the new poor (*New York Times* 1988). These workers are subject to loss of both income and self-esteem. Their joblessness makes them vulnerable to unanticipated crises such as health problems, a fire, an automobile accident, or divorce. These circumstances, of course, can also result in the loss of their home or apartment.

The structural transformation of the U.S. economy has been especially difficult for racial minorities. African Americans, for example, have been overrepresented in the manufacturing sector, which has undergone a severe contraction. Also, to the extent that blacks have been concentrated in the industrial central cities of the Northeast and Great Lakes regions, they have been living and working in those areas that have experienced the most profound economic decline. De-industrialization has meant that some cities have changed from centers of production and the distribution of goods to centers of "higher-order" services such as administration, finance, insurance, public relations, and government (Kasarda 1985). New York City, Chicago, Boston, Philadelphia, and Atlanta are examples (Noyelle and Stanback 1984). This shift has reduced the overall number of jobs available and changed the requirements for obtaining employment, with education being the critical requirement. In New York City, for example, the number of jobs in industries with lower educational requirements decreased by 492,000 from 1970 to 1984, whereas those with higher education requisites increased by 239,000 (Wilson 1987:40–41). In short, minorities tend to be concentrated in inner cities where unskilled jobs once were much more plentiful than now. There is a mismatch, as blacks have been denied the educational opportunities that would qualify them for the increasing number of higher-order service jobs.

As unskilled and semiskilled jobs are lost in the manufacturing sector, competition for those jobs that do remain in the city is increased, making already marginal working-class blacks more marginal to, or squeezing them completely out of, the labor market. And in many cities the decline of manufacturing employment has been replaced by mostly "lower-order services"—low-wage clerical, retail, custodial, security, and fast food jobs. Cities like Milwaukee, Buffalo, Gary, Flint, and Youngstown have seen little of the higher-order services side of the service economy (Noyelle and Stanback 1984).

Even the relatively few remaining manufacturing jobs have often tended to move from the inner city to the suburbs and nonmetropolitan peripheries. The inner-city poor are disadvantaged by these moves because they do not have access to adequate transportation to these jobs and continued discrimination and high housing costs prevent them from moving nearer to the new job sites. The result is that those with the greatest need for jobs are the farthest from them. An example of this mismatch of jobs and housing is the construction of the new Denver International Airport, which was scheduled to open in 1994. At a cost approaching $4 billion, it is the largest recent public works construction project in the United States. The new airport is located twenty-eight miles from downtown Denver and has no public transportation to it. The airport employment office reported that over 4,000 poor people applied for the relatively high-paying construction jobs but since the job required a car, only 600 were hired (McBean 1992).

These trends—the changing economy and changing cities—have meant that the poor are getting poorer. According to the Census Bureau, in 1978, 31.5 percent of all poor people had incomes that were below half the poverty line. In 1991, this proportion had risen to 39.4 percent or 14.1 million persons (U.S. Bureau of the Census 1992:xvi). Thus, there is an increasing number of disadvantaged individuals and families who have either become homeless in recent years or who are on the edge of homelessness now.

Changes in Family Structure. Families are another at-risk category. For a number of structural reasons, including increasing numbers of women entering the labor force and the changing economy, some dramatic changes in families have increased the probability of poverty and homelessness especially for women and their dependent children. One of these changes has been the rapid rise in divorce. Beginning in the mid-1960s, the divorce rate has moved up sharply, reaching a peak in 1981 with a very slight decline since then. About one-half of marriages now end in divorce. The lower the economic resources of the couple, the greater the likelihood of separation and divorce. In terms of race, black couples have a much greater probability of divorce than either whites or Hispanics. This is related to low income. Research has shown that if black men have the same employment and income as whites, the proportion of stable families between the two races is comparable (Farley and Hermalin 1971). But blacks and whites are not equal in income, with the unemployment rate consistently more than twice as high for blacks as whites and the proportion below the government's poverty line exceeding one in three blacks as compared to about one in ten whites. For those families in economic distress that end in divorce, women and children suffer most. This is especially true for divorced mothers who retain custody of their children, which is the case nine times out of ten. Their former husbands do not have resources for child support and there was little, if any, marital property to divide. Thus, divorced poor women with children are prime candidates for poverty and homelessness.

Even divorced middle-class women with children may find themselves in serious economic difficulty. Many of them do not have the skills for middle-class employment. With divorce they are left with the children and, typically, a low-paying job. They face gender-based inequality, discrimination, and occupational segregation in the labor market. Female workers in American society make, on average, less than $.70 for every dollar a male worker makes. Moreover, many absent fathers, even those who can afford it, do not pay child support.

In sum, the economic situation for most divorced women puts them at risk. The "feminization of poverty" is a reality that reflects the high divorce rate and is a consequence of a patriarchal society in which women earn much less than what men earn. In addition, women almost always end up with the added burden of supporting children (Sheak 1988).

Also contributing to the extreme poverty and homelessness of these kinds of families, according to sociologist William J. Wilson, is male economic marginality, particularly the economic marginality of poor, young, black men living in the inner city. Wilson's research shows that while the birth rate of black teenagers is declining (as it is among teenagers generally), the number and proportion of out-of-wedlock births in the poor black community is increasing. His data from Chicago indicate that when black males have secure employment (something less and less likely in the inner city), marriage and the formation of two-parent households are much more likely to occur. When these males are jobless or they have only temporary or insecure employment, marriage is less frequent and a poor single-parent, female-headed household is likely to result (Wilson 1987).

Wilson's argument is limited, however. Its patriarchal focus on labor-market outcomes for males implies that this, rather than a gender-biased labor market for women, is the primary source of the poverty of women and their children in the United States. His explanation leads to the too facile interpretation that to escape poverty and even homelessness, women must simply marry men with good jobs; his solution does not focus on reforming the patriarchal American labor market (see Reed 1988).

All of these changes in family structure lead to decreasing household size in American cities. The demand for the shrinking supply of low-income housing is not only heightened by intensifying poverty and economic marginalization but also because *more* households or families are being created. Cities are made up disproportionately of both more households in general, even as they are depopulated, and more poor households in particular.

Changing Government Policies. Finally, at the very time in U.S. history when powerful forces were converging to lead more and more people to the brink of poverty, or if they were already poor, to deepen their poverty, government policies shifted dramatically toward more austere social and economic supports and programs (Moore, Sink, and Hoban-Moore 1988; Sheak 1990). In essence, the government "jerked away the safety net," leaving more and more persons vulnerable to the ravages of market forces and poverty. Each of the Reagan budgets cut programs that assisted the truly disadvantaged in American society by tightening eligibility requirements and reducing the moneys allocated. We have already seen how the budgets for low-income housing were cut drastically during these years. In constant 1991 dollars, the national average combined payments for AFDC and food stamps was $10,169 in 1972 compared to $7,471 in 1991, a *decrease* of 27 percent (DeParle 1992). Add to this the cumulative effect of cuts of $12 billion for nutrition assistance, a cut of $1 billion in Medicaid (the federal-state health insurance program for the poor), the elimination of the Work Incentive Program, and severe cuts to family planning programs, and you have a government policy that contributes to extreme poverty and homelessness (Eitzen and Baca Zinn 1989b:96–97).

The problems of the poor who depend on welfare were compounded by the Reagan plan to reduce the scope of the federal government by granting money to the states to be used at their discretion. This "states' rights" or "home rule" strategy, based on the assumption that local governments know what is best for their constituents, has several negative consequences for the poor. First, it allows local patterns of discrimination against women, African Americans, Latinos, Native Americans, and other relatively powerless minorities to flourish unhindered by federal restrictions. Second, the states vary markedly in their ability and willingness to provide welfare for the poor. Data from 1991 show, for example, that the average annual combined payment for AFDC and food stamps for a family of three ranged from a low of $4,764 in Mississippi to $9,906 in California (Rom 1992). And most important, some states still choose not to make AFDC payments to two-parent families.

Conclusion

The dramatic rise in homelessness over the past decade and a half is the result of a severe contradiction unfolding in the United States: As the supply of low-income housing is being reduced, increasing numbers of Americans, especially women, children, and minorities, are becoming more and more economically marginal. Just as too much money chasing too few goods causes inflation, so, too, does too many poor and marginal people chasing too few affordable apartments cause homelessness. Or, to switch the metaphor, think of this as a game of musical chairs, in which the chairs represent apartments affordable to the poor and the players are the poor seeking permanent shelter in those apartments (see Sclar 1990). As the game has been played over the past fifteen years in American cities, the number of chairs has been systematically reduced by failed government policies and private-sector investment decisions. Meanwhile, the transformation of the economy and work, changes in family structure, and cutbacks in public-sector supports for the poor continue to add players to the game. The outcome of this game is that an increasing number of players are losers; they cannot find "chairs" and become homeless.

PART TWO

Paths to Homelessness

3

The "Old" Homeless:
Sam Sheldon and Henry Walsh

Sam Sheldon* is forty-seven years old, black, single, and unemployed. The last job he had was as a temporary painter in Jacksonville, Florida. At the time we interviewed Sam in a downtown park on the banks of the Hillsborough River, he had been in Tampa about three weeks. Sam was living on the streets and "wildcatting"—looking for shelter each night in an abandoned house or under the Crosstown Expressway in a makeshift camp for homeless men or wherever else he could find it. Most of the time, whenever he can afford "a little taste," Sam sips a cheap bottle of wine.

Henry Walsh is sixty-one years old. He is white, single, and sick. His emphysema is in advanced stages and he cannot work. Often, he does not have the money to buy his "breathing medicine." Doctors at Tampa General Hospital will see him and write him a prescription but will not provide it for him. Without it, he is immobilized and can do little but lie on a park bench and wheeze. Several times during the period when we knew Henry, we would have to take his tattered prescription to a sympathetic pharmacist at Walgreen's, who would sell us the drugs to take back to Henry so he could breathe again.

When he can afford it, or get it from a friend like Sam, Henry drinks wine. Lately, he's been drinking rubbing alcohol; it's even cheaper than cheap wine. Seven years ago, a judge in Ocala, Florida, bought Henry a one-way bus ticket to Tampa—to get him out of town. Finally he ended up at "Sallies"—the Salvation Army—and successfully completed their alcohol rehabilitation program. Later, he was put in charge of the front desk at Sallies but was disturbed by having to turn away guys who had

---

*The names of the persons interviewed for this project have been changed to protect their anonymity.

been drinking when they desperately needed a place to stay, so he quit.
Henry left Sallies about three months before we began interviewing him.
At the time of the interview, Henry was living on the street and wildcat-
ting with his new partner, Sam.

Sam sums up their situation:

INTERVIEWER: Where you livin' right now?
SAM: On the streets of Tampa. I'm eatin' on the streets of Tampa. Wher-
    ever I can make a dollar, I'll earn it. And I go to the blood bank to earn
    a buck and me and my partner, we share what we have ... I can go
    seekin' and he'll wait for me. He'll go seekin' and I'll wait for him.
    Somehow we survive. But there's a system that can be improved in this
    town. And I can't speak for everybody in this town. But the way we're
    survivin', we go to the museum and get a cold drink of water. And go
    down in the basement and take a bath—whatever bath it is—and try
    to stay clean. And then we go up there and we seek things out. And it's,
    it works, but it's hard ... I'd rather be in 'Nam right now, alone, than to
    be here. Man, I feel lonely.

Sam and Henry, according to conventional wisdom, are the "old," or
traditional, homeless. They are the older, "unattached," "disaffiliated,"
often alcoholic males who have been around for generations. They are
different than the "new" homeless—the homeless families, women and
children, and youth who have proliferated since the late 1970s. This distinction between old and new is based on two myths: one conservative
and one liberal.

The conservative view is that the causes of homelessness are the same
for both the new and old homeless. Like the Skid Row alcoholics and
derelicts before them, the new homeless are those of weak character and
morality, often choosing the homeless lifestyle. They are the undeserving poor. But this is a conservative myth. As we shall see below, the old
homeless were never particularly alcoholic, derelict, or of weak character and morality. Not then, and not now. So how can we argue that the
new homeless should be characterized this way as well?

The liberal view is that the causes of homelessness are different for the
new and old homeless. The old were and are alcoholic and derelict, personally responsible for their fate. By contrast, the new homeless are victims, of things like de-institutionalization and economic changes. They
are deserving. But this distinction forms the liberal myth because, once
again, it is not the case that the old homeless, earlier or now, stand out as
alcoholic, derelict, weak, immoral, or irresponsible.

The reality is that the new and old homeless come from the same
place. They are structurally similar, produced by the same failing struc-

tures. The labor market and the welfare state have failed the homeless, old and new, then and now. There may be demographic differences between the old and new homeless, but that is where the differences end. Although there are more young single males, women, children, teenagers, families, and people of color homeless now than during the Great Depression, for example, they share a class position with the single white males who were homeless then and with those from that group who are homeless now.

Regarding the extent of social affiliations, even presumed differences between the housed and homeless populations, as well as differences between the old and new homeless, are proving erroneous. In the 1960s and 1970s, social scientists used survey research methods to discover that the homeless often lacked meaningful social ties such as employment and family. Therefore, the process of social disaffiliation and isolation was placed at the center of the causes of homelessness. The homeless in general, and especially the old homeless, the single male, lacked the social relationships found in the domiciled population. But though it is true that many of the homeless often do not have regular employment and have experienced family rejection or abandonment, they are not necessarily socially unattached, disaffiliated, or isolated. Recent ethnographic research among the homeless has found a remarkable effort and ability to create and maintain social relationships, often among peers, which often directly contributes to survival on the streets (see, for example, Snow and Anderson 1993; LaGory, Ritchey, and Fitzpatrick 1991; Lee 1987). Sam and Henry's "partnership," forged under the most difficult of circumstances, illustrates this well. The so-called old homeless may be single, unemployed, and without strong family ties, but their homelessness does not have its source in the inability to make and hold on to social relationships. Their ability to do just that makes them no different than either the new homeless or all of those who are adequately housed.

In fact, other long-term and in-depth observation among the homeless has found that they are not as single and alone as census takers and survey researchers report them to be. Under the precarious and adverse social and economic circumstances that confront homeless persons every day, commitments, relationships, partnerships, couples, and child care arrangements must be flexible and adaptable. Thus on any given day, homeless persons may not be able to act on these interpersonal and familial ties—survival beckons otherwise—and may look and talk as if they are alone when they are not. In addition, homeless parents often do not report either their marriage or their children out of fear of reprisal by welfare officials, who can charge them with neglect and find them or their child's temporary caretakers to be poor parents (see Wagner 1994).

Yet, in spite of all of these similarities, politicians, policymakers, popular opinion, homeless caretakers and service providers, and sometimes even the homeless themselves (see Timmer 1988) continue to refer to "differences" between the old and new that leave single homeless males more personally responsible for their situation. Researchers David Snow and Leon Anderson conclude:

> Even among street people distinctions tend to be drawn. Homeless families and children tend to be treated more sympathetically than homeless street adults. And it is our sense that adult street women are seen as less responsible for their plight than street men, who often tend to be depicted as improvident and lazy individuals who are threats to the property and physical safety of the domiciled. This general perception is reflected in the views of most agencies and individuals who interact with the homeless in a caretaker fashion and who tend to treat homeless men as less worthy or deserving than others. The point, then, is that a community's "span of sympathy" is not as likely to be extended to unattached homeless men as to homeless families, children, and women. (Snow and Anderson 1993:9)

Labor Market

After the Civil War, the industrialization of American society began in earnest. From roughly 1870 through the turn of the century, industrialization produced a huge demand for migrant industrial workers. The large number of transient and unskilled laborers who met this demand gave rise, in many of the growing industrial cities of this era, to a section or district that became home to them. The largest of these districts was located in Chicago, the transportation and industrial hub of America at the time. It came to be known as the "Main Stem," and "stemming" came to refer to the way of life there. The Main Stem was just west of Chicago's Loop (downtown) on West Madison Street, and like other "Main Stems" in other cities, it consisted of lodges, workingman hotels, single-room occupancy hotels, cheap restaurants and taverns, and most other essential services. The men, hoboes and tramps among them, were poor and needed to be mobile in order to respond to the whims of the expanding industrial labor market. But nonetheless, the Main Stem provided the work, inexpensive housing and services, and the measure of privacy, autonomy, and dignity the men needed and desired (Hoch and Slayton 1989).

Demand for migrant industrial labor, however, had begun to decline by 1920. And after World War II, the decline accelerated. Unskilled nonfarm labor as a percentage of all employed workers was 12.5 percent in

1900, 9.4 percent in 1940, and 4.8 percent in 1960 (Hoch and Slayton 1989:89).

This shift in the labor market had important consequences for "Main Stem" communities. The mobile laborers tended to go one of two ways. Postwar prosperity and the efforts of industrial unions meant that some hoboes and tramps became regular industrial workers with improved wages, working conditions, and economic security. Others saw their labor become surplus and were left behind as more stationary—there was no reason to move around anymore since the demand for their labor had dried up—occasional workers. But they were left behind in a smaller and different community.

By 1950, the Main Stem had become Skid Row. Fewer men, hotels, restaurants, and services were found there. It became a deteriorating community, more marginal to the labor market. Nearly every large city in the country had a Skid Row and a stereotype of this part of the city and those who lived there developed across the nation.

The new stereotype was a negative one:

> Gone was the figure of the transient working men—the hobo or the "knight of the road," the tramp—his community memorialized only by phrases like "stemming," referring to the way of life on West Madison Street. Skid Row was now a section of the city where cheap rooming houses, missions, street bums, and alcoholics were concentrated, where only the very dregs of society lived. (Hoch and Slayton 1989:93)

The Skid Row resident was seen as not just poor, but pathological—lazy, immoral, irresponsible, and drunken. It is on this image that the stereotype of the contemporary single homeless male is based. But the stereotype is, of course, a stereotype. It is inaccurate both currently and historically.

The overwhelming majority of Skid Row residents were poor working people and their most common characteristic was their poverty, not their pathology. Skid Row residents worked. The first and most comprehensive study of Skid Row, Donald Bogue's *Skid Row in American Cities* (1963), found 73 percent of the men in the work force. Forty-seven percent had jobs and another 26 percent were looking for one. Sixteen percent were unable to work, because they were either disabled or too old. Among those working, 35 percent had worked more than fifty weeks in the past year and 52 percent had worked forty weeks or more.

However, Bogue also found that only about 40 percent of the men had held only one job in the previous year and 16 percent had worked at jobs of only a day's, or a few days', duration. What all of these data indicate is a Skid Row population quite willing to work, but quite marginal to the labor market—often unable to find any work at all and even more infrequently able to find a regular, permanent job.

Most worked at jobs that were not covered by union contracts and were paid poorly. Bogue found 34 percent working in service industries, most in restaurants, and another 31 percent working as unskilled laborers. The most common jobs were dishwasher, short-order cook, porter, janitor, freight handler, hospital or nursing home aide or orderly, and seasonal work in nearby resorts.

These low-wage jobs and their marginal connection to the labor market kept Skid Row residents poor. Hoch and Slayton summarize Bogue's findings in Chicago and other cities:

> Of all the men, 85 percent made less than $2,500 to $5,000 a year, levels reached by 47 percent of all Chicagoans on the job. Less than 1 percent of Skid Row residents made over $5,000, whereas 13 percent of the workers in the entire city earned this much or more. On the last job worked before the survey, 59 percent earned one dollar an hour or less. An indication that minimal wages were not unique to Chicago's Skid Row came from Bogue's analysis of forty-one cities, which found that whereas 49 percent of the Skid Row residents in these cities earned less than $1,500 a year, only 27 percent of the population of these places earned that little. (Hoch and Slayton 1989:96)

Although Skid Row residents were often unskilled and almost always poor, they were not, contrary to the stereotype, transient and unstable. Bogue found that fewer than 10 percent had been on Skid Row less than a month. Fifty-five percent had lived there a year or more, and 10 percent had been there more than ten years. Seventy-one percent of the men had not moved in the year previous to Bogue's survey, and at roughly the same time the U.S. census found that 68 percent had been in the same apartment for at least two years. Another survey found that only 10 percent had been on Skid Row for less than a year, 81 percent had not moved for at least a year, and 73 percent had lived there for four years or longer (Vander Kooi 1966).

In short, the old homeless on Skid Row did not fit the stereotype—immoral and irresponsible, drifting and too lazy and drunken to work. Instead, most worked and most were stable, kept poor by a changing industrial labor market. And it is the same for the so-called traditional homeless, single males like Sam and Henry, in the 1980s and 1990s.

David Snow and Leon Anderson report in their recent study of homeless street people, the majority of whom were single males, that "research into the employment activities and income sources of the homeless across the country has shown that the vast majority are either working or looking for work, and that some form of employment is often cited [by the homeless themselves] as the most frequent source of income" (1993:144). In their own research, again corroborating many other studies, Snow and Anderson found that the work is typically less than full time and the wages usually minimal. The income homeless men derive from wage labor is irregular, small, and, as we shall see later, seldom sufficient to even support them on the streets.

Of all the studies of homeless people undertaken in the 1980s, one of the largest and most geographically dispersed samples was of clients of the national Health Care for the Homeless (HCH) program. Data for the first year of this program were taken from nearly 30,000 homeless persons seen in health clinics in sixteen large cities all over the country. The data on single adult men in this sample also confirm the view of the old homeless developed above: Just over 50 percent had a job, 3 percent full time, 12 percent regular part time, 35 percent seasonal work, day labor, or odd jobs; another 28 percent were actively looking for work. All together, then, the HCH study found that 78 percent of homeless single males either had a job or wanted and were looking for one. But even those who had one did not earn enough to allow them to secure affordable housing (Wright 1989).

Sam Sheldon's experience reflects this labor market trend—declining demand for unskilled labor.

SAM: I was workin'. I joined the Merchant Marines. I was a Merchant Marine until nineteen seventy-five, then the inflation come in. Shit, I been—fireman, oiler. You know, in the engine room. I worked that. But I worked my way up. I was workin' in the galleys at first: pantry man, second cook, whatever. The oil crisis and all that there. And that fucked me up completely. My grandma died. I didn't have no gig except what I could do, you know, like under a military life. Right? They don't accept that on the streets. So I went to the Longshoreman's Union, ILA, and that failed. Yeah, I been loading and unloading, you know. Doing this and that. Operatin' machinery. I'm still able to do that. Yeah, ILA. But I wasn't a member of the union. I was scabbin'. You want a truthful conversation, I'm givin' it to you. Alright. ILA. At Longshoreman International I was doin' some scab work every chance I get. I was gettin' paid though. So I worked. And I'm workin' now every chance I get. I work every damn where. Landscapin', like this shit. From seventy-five until now. I been up and down the East Coast. I been to Louisiana. I been off rig—offshore. Yeah. Because I have experience in, you know, on a boat. Shit, I can operate a boat. Anybody with common sense can do that. And that's all I have is common sense. I ain't got that much education. What, what but twelve years in school.

INTERVIEWER: How much of that time were you on the street?
SAM: Most of it. And I became an alcoholic.

Sam goes on:

SAM: I need something that I can—I can just guide on. That's me. And
J.C. Because if I had a job, a regular job, an apartment, I can improve.
But sleepin' on the streets, and workin' daily and eatin' where I can:
there ain't nothin' gonna happen good except that I keep strugglin'.
The last time I had an apartment to call my own was about a couple of
months ago. I was, I was workin', Florida Painting Company. I only
worked for them until the job was completed and heck, that only
lasted a month. That was in Jacksonville, Florida. We painted the interior of the Employment Office. We willin' to work for our livin'. I just
felt it—I feel like right now I'm throwed away. But I ain't gonna let it af-
fect me because that's whatever society feels will get me down. All
them millionaires, they go to the Hyatt Hilton and all that there. And
when I was workin', I felt good. That's the way I feel good. You know,
when I'm—when I'm workin'. I can just let myself go and then after the
job is done, I can kick back and say, "Thank you, God. Thank you, Je-
sus." A job well done.

At the time that Sam and Henry were interviewed in 1986, Henry, save
his stay at the Salvation Army, had been living on the streets since 1981.
Even five years earlier, his partner probably would have been closer to
his own age and certainly would have been more likely to have been
white. That his partner is younger and black has to do with important
shifts in the American labor market beginning in the late 1970s.

Race and Labor Market

Since 1980, homeless single males have been younger and much more
likely to be minority, particularly black, than they were on either the
Main Stem or Skid Row. The reasons for this are twofold.

Lack of demand for unskilled labor accounts for the poor employment
and earnings record, and thus the homelessness, of single men. Labor
market factors have worked to lower the average age of single homeless
men over the past three decades. Between 1955 and 1985, there was a dramatic rise in unemployment among young males in American society.
The rise was most pronounced, however, among blacks (Rossi 1989). By
1985, the unemployment rate for black males under twenty-five, for example, had reached a catastrophic 40 percent. Young black males were

more likely to be employed for only short periods and more likely to be fired or laid off than other groups of workers (Freeman and Holzer 1986).

Between 1979 and 1987, the number of "full-time equivalent" white workers with annual incomes below the federal government's official poverty line for a family of four, about $12,000 in 1987 dollars, increased by almost 31 percent. But for blacks, the increase was 44 percent. Over the past decade, the number of black men between twenty-five and thirty-four who found a job but still earned a poverty wage rose by 161 percent. By 1987, black workers were three times more likely than their white counterparts to earn an income below the poverty line. That reversed a trend between 1963 and 1979, when the proportion of low-wage jobs fell for all racial groups and the gap between average black and white wages narrowed (Harrison 1990).

The deteriorating labor market is related to a second reason for the increase in homeless black males. Historically, blacks have cultivated vibrant and active extended kin networks and community life. According to family historian Stephanie Coontz, "Studies of many cities in the nineteenth and twentieth centuries reveal that African-American families maintained tighter and more supportive kin ties than did other urban families, taking care of elders, paupers, and orphans within family networks rather than institutionalizing them as frequently as other groups did" (1992:241). In other words, in spite of all the exploitation and impoverishment that the industrialization of the United States wrought in its black communities, blacks were less likely to be homeless, living on the streets or in missions or shelters, because of the way in which their families, kin, and communities took them in. But these networks of support are now themselves under siege, less able materially to keep their own off the streets and out of the shelters. Since 1978, there has been a nearly 70 percent increase in the number of blacks living below *half* of the official poverty line (Coontz 1992:253). Resources always thin in the black community have grown thinner and thinner. The concentration of extreme poverty begins to break down the strong and supportive black kin networks that once absorbed much homelessness.

Day Labor

The institution that regulated the labor of Skid Row residents was the labor pool, or temporary employment agency. Through this mechanism, men sometimes were given work but always were exploited. Businesses contracted with labor pools to provide cheap unskilled labor on a temporary basis, for "spot" jobs. Therefore, the work was non-union, paid poorly, was often hard and drudgerous, and there were few safeguards in terms of wages, working conditions, and worker health and safety. It was also irregular. The men showed up at an appointed hour early in the morning with no guarantee they would work that day. Some were chosen, others were not needed at that particular time. Most often, deductions from the day laborer's paycheck for taxes, the agency's fees, and transportation to the job site provided by the agency would be as much as one-third to one-half of what the worker earned. On Skid Row, most men ended up working for a dollar an hour or less (Hoch and Slayton 1989).

Again, the similarities between then and now are striking. This same institution is the primary way in which the marginal position of homeless single males is maintained in the American labor market. Sam Sheldon describes his experience in Tampa during the mid-1980s:

SAM: Then if Dave [another friend living on the street] have to go to a blood bank, I'll go. After that I'll shoot over there and try to get a job at the labor pool. ... A typical day tomorrow. Wednesday ... it's an open day. So I'll go over there and I'll try to work. The first thing I try to do is wash up. You know, and look presentable ... I'm presentin' myself. But I know they ain't gonna look at me like, like that [he's eating rice and beans as he talks]. They say, "Well, that dude don't even know how to eat." So I'll go over there and clean up. I'll take another shave. I need that.

  ... Right now they got them some dredges. You got to go down there and clean 'em out. You got to climb down the ladder and shit. I ain't always able to do all that there climbin'. But I'm capable of doin' some work.

INTERVIEWER: You have worked through the labor pool?

SAM: Yes.

INT.: Since you've been here?

SAM: Since I've been here.

INT.: How many days, do you know?

SAM: Three. But I don't go there every day because all they got mostly is, uh, construction. Construction, construction. If you can't handle nothin' real heavy, you won't work. And that's what this town needs right now. Give a person the opportunity to earn some bucks because them labor pools takin' all the money. That's the bottom line. They want you to work and they gonna get theirs off the top, doggone it.

Welfare State

Public assistance did little to alleviate the poverty of men on Skid Row. Fewer than one half, about 47 percent, drew any public funds at all.

Those who did had to qualify for Social Security, military or railroad pensions, Old Age Assistance, or Disability Assistance. Poverty by itself did not qualify anyone for anything. And the public assistance that was available was meager. Bogue found that the state's ceiling for Old Age and Disability Assistance in Chicago, for example, was $80 a month. This was typical of the meager payments in other cities and states. It did not provide the means to reside anywhere other than Skid Row (Hoch and Slayton 1989; Bogue 1963).

And again, the situation is much the same for homeless single males today. Studies from across the country contradict the idea that most of them are on the "welfare dole" (Snow and Anderson 1993). In sociologist Peter Rossi's study of the homeless in Chicago it was discovered that despite their extreme poverty, few were on public assistance. Fewer than one in five were receiving any kind of pension or disability payments, and only about one in four were on AFDC (Aid to Families with Dependent Children) or GA (General Assistance—a program for single adults), with most on the latter (Rossi, Fisher, and Willis 1986).

Compared to most of the industrial democracies of Europe, of course, the American welfare state has always been, and continues to be, much less developed. By comparison, the protections against social and economic insecurity afforded U.S. citizens have been, and are, minimal. The "social safety net" in the United States has always had big holes in it. But the holes for single persons, and particularly single males, have been the largest. This group has been the least covered by public benefit programs. Many states have no benefit programs for single individuals, even if they are disabled. In other states, single persons must be disabled to receive assistance. And some states limit the number of months during a year that a single person can receive benefits (Burt 1992).

The primary public welfare program for poor people in the United States originated in the 1930s. ADC (Aid to Dependent Children) was designed to assist women and their children with welfare payments. A male present in the household meant, and often still means, no aid. Recently, changes have been made: The program is now called AFDC (Aid to Families with Dependent Children), and it allows unemployed males (in many cases a husband or father) to remain in the household that is receiving assistance if they meet certain work history guidelines set by the federal government. But the fact remains that most men, and single women without children, are outside of the federal welfare system. Assistance is for families.

For single, "able-bodied," "employable" adults in the United States, there is no federal assistance at all. Some states, counties, and cities provide aid through General Assistance or "relief," but even this is often only temporary or granted only in "emergencies."

In 1990, there was some form of GA in all but six states. Then, in 1991, Michigan eliminated its program—most of the recipients had been single men in Detroit. Now states throughout the country are moving to eliminate or make reductions in their programs. California, Ohio, and Pennsylvania have already made cuts, and cuts are planned in New York, Connecticut, Rhode Island, and Arizona.

In 1991, Illinois removed 50,000 single men in Chicago from General Assistance. Under the new plan, single adults were categorized as either employable or unemployable. Those considered unemployable received assistance year round, but those determined "employable" lost their benefits (Nicodemus 1993a).

But a study by the Travelers and Immigrant Aid Society's Institute on Urban Poverty found that the 50,000 men were wrongly denied aid. They were not employable. Access to employment was blocked by local job shortages, racial discrimination, a lack of housing that could provide stability, and inadequate public transportation to get to jobs that did exist. The study also found that race figured prominently in General Assistance cuts in Chicago. Eighty-six percent of the 50,000 men forced off GA rolls were black—and all had, according to state records, total assets of less than $500 (see Nicodemus 1993a).

In Tampa, there is no General Assistance.

INTERVIEWER: You got any source of income now?
SAM: No. None.
INT.: None?
SAM: I'm tryin' to improve. I'm tryin' to improve. It's hard because I don't improve. Ain't nobody to help me. And basically what we're talkin' about is street people. I been on the streets, I told you, it's been ten years or more.
INT.: Henry, do you have any income at all on the streets?
HENRY: Not a thing. No. I'll be sixty-two August twenty-second. Him and I just get by.

But we have already seen that even when and where GA exists, few of the homeless are getting it. And even when they do, the amount is so small that General Assistance by itself guarantees extreme poverty and homelessness. The maximum GA check of $154 per month in Chicago is hardly going to gain one entry into a housing market where the average price of a one-bedroom apartment is close to $570 per month.

Tight and bureaucratic eligibility requirements further undermine the meager assistance available to single men. The stinginess of the American welfare state often means that formal rules and regulations enforced by social service bureaucracies override the real needs of extremely poor persons living on the streets. Sam, for example, is going to lose his food stamps because of an error on a new social security card.

SAM: The government made it. Yeah, the government made that mistake and I can't argue about it. It should be two six four dash nine five. Well, they got thirty-five on the card. ... That, that's messin' me up.
INT.: How?
SAM: I can't get food stamps.
INT.: They think you've got the wrong Social Security number?
SAM: They know exactly who I am. ... Now, this one here. That's a nine five. And it don't match ... I tried to correct it. That's my signature ... I even signed it. Look. I'll show you something ... I've got plenty of identification.
INT.: You show this to the food stamp people and they say what?
SAM: They say I gotta get a change.
INT.: Before they can give you the food stamps?
HENRY: They already told him. I was with him.
INT.: So how'd you get those food stamps you got now? Did they give you those?
HENRY: Yeah, they gave him those.
SAM: They gave me one for last month ... twenty-nine dollars.
INT.: For the month?
SAM: Yeah, for this month.
INT.: Then they just said no more?
HENRY: No. I was with him ... Sam isn't gonna get anymore.

Historian and sociologist Theda Skocpol (1992) has recently shown how the origins of social policy in the United States had to do primarily with the protection of soldiers and mothers. The American welfare state has been most "generous" with military veterans and mothers with children. But even here, it has failed to respond to the extreme poverty and homelessness of single men.

The number of veterans among homeless single men probably ranges as high as 50 percent. This corresponds roughly with the 41 percent of all adult men in the United States who are veterans. But only about a third of homeless vets receive any form of assistance from the Veterans Administration (Wright 1988b).

Most homeless veterans come from the poor or working class. They enlisted to obtain the economic advantages that military recruitment campaigns promise—job training, college benefits, and preferential hiring in civil service employment after leaving the service. But for homeless vets, these are false promises. For them, postmilitary experience consists of joblessness, periodic low-wage employment, poverty, and in-

adequate assistance from the federal government (Wright 1988b). Sam
and Henry's experiences are typical.

INTERVIEWER: You got some discharge papers there, right, Henry? You
   guys have both been in the military?
SAM: Right.
HENRY: I was. Seventeen years.
SAM: Nine years.
INT.: You did somethin' for them, right?
SAM: Them, who?
INT.: The military. This country. Your government.
SAM: This is my country.
HENRY: Yes, we did. We fought, both of us fought.
SAM: This is my country.
INT.: You both fought in wars?
HENRY: Yes. Only got three battle stripes. ...
SAM: But I got one silver ... good conduct medal.
HENRY: Fifth of Rhineland, Battle of the Bulge. Europe. I got eleven years
   in Europe.
SAM: I got a silver star. And that bleedin' heart there. Well, I got hit there.
   That Purple Heart ... I got hit in 'Nam ... I got hit one time ... that's all.
INT.: What'd the military give you back?
SAM: Nothin'.
HENRY: It gave me a hard time. I had to pay my own. ...
SAM: Now I'm on the streets. That's the bottom line right there. And I go
   to the VA anytime and I got to go through all that administrative stuff
   and then they want to do somethin' else and ...
HENRY: You even have to pay for your own stamps to send anything out.
SAM: You can't get nothin' for free. That's bullshit. You think a vet can get
   somethin'?
HENRY: You got to pay for your own stamps.
SAM: We don't get nothin'.
INT.: You ain't got nothin' from the VA?
SAM: We live on the streets.
HENRY: You got to pay for your stamps.
SAM: Damn right. If I go to apply for food stamps, they want to know
   where I'm workin'. Am I disabled? I can work. But yet and still they
   don't consider this. Is this disability? This here. That hand operate
   when it want to. I can't use it when I need it at all time. Like the
   weather bad now. It aches. Well I can't get a grasp. ...
HENRY: The Veterans Administration is a bunch of bullshit.
SAM: Yes it is.
HENRY: They are.

SAM: The U.S. government right now we're livin' in because we have to. If I could live in another country, I'd rather be there ... I don't care if lightning strike me dead ... I'd rather drink wine with ... communists.

About the only group that the American welfare state may have assisted is elderly homeless men. As noted earlier, the average age of the homeless in general, and homeless single men in particular, has been declining. In fact, among single homeless men, the HCH study reported above found only 3 percent to be over sixty-five (Wright 1988b). Twelve percent of single men in the United States are over sixty-five years old. Older single men, then, are actually underrepresented in the homeless single male population. It is not coincidental that this is the group that is eligible for Social Security payments and Medicare health coverage. Over the past thirty years, these entitlements have worked to bring about a significant reduction in the poverty rate of older Americans. When the welfare state is present, it makes a difference.

In the Great Depression, the New Deal established the welfare system. Although this system was designed in the main for mothers and their children and the elderly, work was provided for single men through programs like the Civilian Conservation Corps (CCC) and the Works Progress Administration (WPA). But this work is no longer available. Single homeless men must create their own work since the labor market provides only irregular and low-wage employment, welfare state assistance is meager, and public job creation is no longer a function of the federal government.

Shadow Work

Since both wage labor and the welfare state prove themselves unreliable sources of income, homeless men turn to "shadow work"—panhandling (is there an urban resident who hasn't been asked for a quarter?), scavenging (working the dumpsters), selling blood, drugs, or even sex, and theft. Homeless men appear to have varying degrees of commitment to this sort of work and earn varying amounts of their total income from it (Snow and Anderson 1993).

Another part of the stereotype of the "old" homeless on the streets of American cities today, again grounded in the stereotype of the "old" Skid Row resident of a previous era, is that they are a particularly criminal group. Available data do not confirm this. One study of Skid Row in Chicago found that only 3 percent of the city's felony arrests occurred there (Vander Kooi 1966). Studies of the contemporary "old" homeless indicate that they are less violent than housed males of the same age. The homeless arrest rate for violent felonies is only about one-half of the housed rate. Homeless single men are arrested for theft more often than their housed counterparts, but nearly half of these homeless arrests are for shoplifting cigarettes, small quantities of food and drink, or calculators or other small items that are sold on the streets or in pawnshops. Petty theft is engaged in to acquire the most basic necessities and survive the day. It is also important to see here how the arrest rates of the homeless are no doubt inflated by the way in which life on the streets makes them subject to increased police scrutiny (Snow, Baker, and Anderson 1989).

Sam's plan for shadow work is more typical than serious crime.

SAM: If we had a reel and rod, we'd go fishin'. We'd bring some; I've seen a guy bring some stuff out of there. Would you help us get a reel and rod?

INTERVIEWER: A reel and rod, huh?

SAM: Yeah.

INT.: And you'd fish out of the river?

SAM: Doggone right.

INT.: You got some place to, uh, do you ever cook? Do you cook out on the street?

SAM: You damn right. We'd make a little grill or somethin'. Bricks and somethin' out of the refrigerator like that. All we got to do is clean the fish.

Extreme Poverty

Wage labor, welfare state, and shadow work together fail to lift homeless single men out of poverty and into the housing market. Researcher James Wright summarizes Rossi, Fisher, and Willis's (1986) findings in Chicago:

> The Chicago survey contained a number of questions on income, employment status, and means of support. Median income from all sources for the month prior to the interview was just under $100; mean income for the same period was $168. The 1985 poverty line for single persons under 65 was $5250 (annual income), 2.6 times the mean income and 4.4 times the median income of Chicago's homeless. The homeless are thus among the poorest of the poor, surviving on less than 40 percent of a poverty-level income. (Wright 1989:71)

The data above are for the homeless population in general. There are indications that the statistics are even worse for single homeless persons, since poor single people got poorer throughout the 1980s at a rate surpassing that of other kinds of poor households (Burt 1992).

The connection between the homelessness of single men and their extreme poverty is easy to demonstrate. In 1985, the average monthly rent in Chicago SROs (single-room occupancy hotels), among the cheapest housing in the city and, as we shall see, traditionally the kind of housing most often sought by single men, was $195. This was $27 more than the mean income in Rossi, Fisher, and Willis's (1986) Chicago homeless sample. An average homeless person could devote all of his or her income to housing and still not have enough and be on the street (Community Emergency Shelter Organization and Jewish Council on Urban Affairs 1985).

Alcohol Myths

"The Old Homeless Were Alcoholic"

Skid Row was associated more than anything else with alcoholism. The media portrayed nearly all of the men who lived there as alcoholic, and the public assumed that this was true. This stereotype has also been applied to the "old" homeless single males of the present era.

The problem with this view of both contemporary homeless men and the men on Skid Row who preceded them is that it is not true. Every sound investigation of Skid Row drinking found only a small minority of residents who were alcoholic (Hoch and Slayton 1989).

The overwhelming majority of men on Skid Row were working men, not alcoholics. One of the reasons this was overlooked was that middle-class researchers were often unfamiliar with working-class social life. Like other working men in the cities, particularly single men, most residents of Skid Row did go to bars and did drink. But for most, drinking was a social activity and they did it in moderation. In places like Chicago, working-class taverns served as neighborhood social clubs as well as meeting places for working-class and union solidarity and politics. The role that these saloons played in the development of working-class social and political life, unions, and working-class solidarity was not lost on the middle-class Temperance Movement, which was intent on shutting them down. None of this had been any different on the Main Stem and was no different on Skid Row. Even Skid Rowers who were not heavy drinkers, or drinkers at all, went to the bars with their friends (Harris 1956; Duis 1983).

Bogue (1963) found only 17 percent of the men on Skid Row alcoholic. Vander Kooi (1966) asked Skid Row men how much they had drunk the day before he interviewed them. Fifty-nine percent said none. Twenty-two percent said one or two glasses of beer or wine or a single shot of whiskey. Contrary to the ongoing stereotype that Skid Row bums and now the "old" homeless were and are *old* alcoholic men, research on Skid Row indicated that it was younger men who tended to be the heaviest drinkers. Older men were more likely to be light drinkers or even teetotalers. Also contrary to popular notions, being "on the dole" was not always associated with Skid Row alcoholism. One study found 55 percent of the men on public assistance were either teetotalers or light drinkers. And perhaps most important as we look at Sam and Henry's use of alcohol below, heavy drinkers on Skid Row were found to be most prominent among the unemployed, "spot job" workers, and those working in service jobs (Hoch and Slayton 1989; Bogue 1963).

Another early Skid Row researcher, Howard Bahr, concluded that "most skid row men are not problem drinkers, and they are not on skid row because of their drinking" (1973:103).

"Alcoholism Causes Homelessness"

During the 1980s it became conventional wisdom that alcoholism was one of the primary causes of homelessness, particularly the homelessness of single males, of the "old" homeless. Much social science research claimed to show or prove this connection. This research, however, has been seriously flawed in at least four ways.

First of all, it is not entirely clear that problems with alcohol are any more prevalent among the homeless than they are among the non-homeless. The General Social Surveys undertaken by the National Opinion Research Center between 1972 and 1987 indicate a rate of "problem drinking" among the adult population in the United States of about 27 percent (for the derivation of this estimate, see Wright 1989). This figure lies well within the estimated rates of alcohol abuse found in studies of the homeless, many of which are about a third. The homeless, then, even though they may have very good reason to, do not drink considerably more than the non-homeless.

Second, it is assumed that if alcoholism is more prevalent among the homeless, then alcoholism causes homelessness rather than the other way around. For example, in an attempt to determine what distinguished the homeless from the "extremely poor but housed," sociologist Peter Rossi and his associates compared the incidence of alcohol-related problems in these two groups. When the investigation found much higher rates of alcoholism in Rossi's sample of homeless persons in Chicago (and in fifteen other studies of the homeless done in other places) when compared to domiciled samples of extremely poor Chicagoans on General Assistance or AFDC, Rossi and his researchers concluded support for the contribution alcoholism makes to homelessness (see Rossi 1989:156–157). But it is just as logical to conclude from these sorts of data that homelessness contributes to alcoholism. It is every bit as logical, and indeed more sociological, given the devastating and disorienting experience of being homeless, to interpret these kinds of studies as empirical support for the way in which homelessness causes alcoholism.

Third, the putative causal link between alcoholism and homelessness ignores the way in which both may be the result of other factors. For instance, both problem drinking and homelessness are related to labor market marginality. We have already seen how the heaviest drinkers on Skid Row were jobless, working at irregular or seasonal "spot jobs," or working at low-wage service jobs. The experience of Sam Sheldon and Henry Walsh confirms this among contemporary homeless men. As he explained above, Sam identifies the origins of his alcoholism with a dozen years of off-and-on seasonal, "spot" and "scab" employment and the periodic or sustained homelessness that accompanied it. After seventeen years in the military, unable to find secure employment, and too ill to perform some kinds of work, Henry began to drink heavily. But his condition was not permanent. He went to the Salvation Army, lived there five years, and was sober—did not drink at all—for three. Leaving "Sallies," however, more disabled with emphysema and unable to work and without adequate public or VA assistance, Henry returned to the bottle.

Sam seems to understand the real causal links between the labor market, the welfare state, alcohol, and homelessness better than most social science researchers:

SAM: If I could get some money and get me some shelter, I wouldn't have to drink in public. I'd have me a place to go then. I'd work and everything'd be taken care of. Me and my partner, we could take care of business. 'Cause I could work. And he'd take care of the place. Damn sure could.

Finally, any research, media, or public official support for the "alcoholism causes homelessness" line, consciously or not, focuses public and political attention on the homeless themselves as the cause of their situation. If they are homeless because they are drunk, it is their own fault. They are personally responsible. This view not only fails to recognize the myriad socioeconomic sources of homelessness but effectively

removes any public or government obligation to alleviate it. Homelessness ceases to be a public policy issue. Sam understands this too.

SAM: Who'd wanna give me a job? If I go to get, uh, uh, sign an application, who in the hell's gonna, uh, say, "Look. That guy there, he done
wasted food all over his body. And he drunk. And he don't need no
help. He's a drunk. He's an alcoholic. So spit on him. Kick him in the
ass. Get away from here and call the law." And that take care of that.
That's social life in America as far as I know.

The Demise of the SRO

The homelessness of single males, like all homelessness, is at bottom
line a housing issue. We have seen how unskilled single males have been
growing more marginal to the labor market, have found always meager
public assistance decreasing still further, and thus have been getting
poorer. But it does not necessarily follow that this should lead to a vast
increase in the numbers of the "old" homeless. The reason it has is that
both the private housing market and the public sector have failed to
make available the kind of housing these homeless men need and can
afford. In fact, the market and the government have often conspired to
destroy the housing that has best served homeless single men.

Once the typical housing for poor single people, SROs dotted neighborhoods in cities large and small from the 1920s through World War II.
SROs were particularly prevalent in the Main Stem and on Skid Row.

For the first time, however, the New Deal made federal funds available
for the demolition of "deteriorated" SRO districts. Housing for the poor
began to disappear, most times without replacement. This process was
accelerated in the 1950s and 1960s when massive federally supported urban renewal programs cleared "slums" and "blighted areas," usually
paving the way for large public institutions or middle-class commercial
and residential developments that took their place. The demise of the
SRO continued and reached its zenith with the redevelopment of downtown areas during the 1970s and 1980s. As city after city transformed and
expanded its downtown to accommodate the change to a service economy, many adjacent SRO areas and districts became office towers, park-
ing lots and garages, upscale shops and restaurants, and gentrified
apartments, condos, and lofts (Adams 1986).

The ultimate loss of SRO units that had served the men on the Main
Stem, and to some extent those on Skid Row, was phenomenal. Chicago's stock of residential hotel units dropped by nearly 70 percent be-

tween 1973 and 1990—from 28,226 to 8,810 units (Gillis 1991). During the 1970s and 1980s, New York City lost as many as 100,000 units; at least 40 percent of its stock of these kinds of units has disappeared. Between 1970 and 1985, more than half the SRO units in or near downtown Los Angeles were demolished. In the same period, Boston lost 94 percent of its rooming houses and Seattle lost half of its downtown rental stock. Denver had 45 SRO hotels in 1976, but no more than 17 by 1981. Studies have revealed similar figures in San Francisco, San Diego, and even in smaller cities such as Cincinnati, Portland, and Nashville (Burt 1992:33–34).

Here the contradiction highlighted throughout this book takes the following form: Unskilled and younger single males are more marginal and poorer. The welfare state has failed them. They are more "at-risk." More and more of this group run up against the urban housing crisis—in this case, the decline of the SRO. This is the institution that once supplied affordable housing and a community for the men on the Main Stem and to a lesser extent for those on Skid Row.

The result has been unparalleled increases in the number of single homeless men in American cities during the 1980s and into the 1990s. With the trends that produce these increases left unchecked, it is a sure bet the numbers will continue to rise. Indeed, the single poor in urban America are now so poor that they are unable to afford the cheapest housing available in the city. Extreme poverty does not even allow entry into what is left of the SROs.

Sam, Henry, Housing, and Homelessness

Sam Sheldon and Henry Walsh's understanding of their own homelessness surpasses that of many of the bureaucrats, professionals, experts, academics, caretakers, and advocates who have studied the problem. They underscore not only how homelessness is fundamentally a housing issue, but also how housing is integral to all that most of us believe is most important in our lives—employment, health, property, and safety:

INTERVIEWER: Start listin'. What are the things you need right now?
SAM: A home. Shelter first.
INT.: You need that first?
SAM: I guess first. I guess shelter, then I could earn money and I know everything I put there is gonna be there. And because everything I, I earn today, I put it one place, I go back lookin' for it, it's not there.
HENRY: I was gonna say that.

SAM: You can't stash nothin' on the streets. We need shelter. I need shelter. I know Henry needs shelter. I ain't no magician. That's what we need is—if we had shelter right now, we wouldn't worry about no food or clothes or nothin' like that because I could work. I'm able. I ain't Cain or Abel like in the Bible but I'm able to work a little bit, you know. And if I got shelter over my head I know I can, I can put a pair of clothes here, I can go back and that's it. It's gonna be there. Where I'm crashin' now, there ain't nothin' when I go back. …

HENRY: We, one day, soap and every darn thing else. Washcloths and everything in one place. And we come back. I say, "I'm gonna get washed off. Get cleaned up," and went back there. Ain't a damn thing there.

SAM: It was gone, brother. It damn sure was gone. We weren't …

HENRY: Wasn't even a washcloth.

SAM: We just wanted to take a bath.

HENRY: Wasn't even a drinkin' cup.

SAM: They took every fuckin' thing. And that's the way it is on the streets. You can't leave a, a, I tell you what. I throw my cap down there. When I come back, I'll betcha it won't be there.

HENRY: Within an hour it won't.

INT.: Anything else on that list?

SAM: A job. A constant job. A job that I can handle. See, I'm a painter. Interior and exterior. Professional. It really don't matter if it's outside or inside or whatever. But I ain't got the tools and I ain't got the shelter and I ain't got the work so I can't get that back together. And that ain't no, what you call, a joke. That's what I need. I need my tools, I ain't got no rollers, no brushes, no cutter, no scrapers or whatever, you know. And no square and this and that and the other. But I need shelter before I can gain that. I can't earn until I have a place to stay. … This is what I'm saying: I ain't got no roof over my head where I can say, "Well, I live here. And I want such and such a thing here." And when I come home I got a key to unlock that. Open it and lock it again or whatever. See, because once I have that, I can get myself established. I can accomplish something. Like a bank account, see? And then I can talk shit. A nigger like me, with nothin', on the streets. It's hard.

4

Work Versus Welfare—A False Choice: Sue Jackson

Sue Jackson is a thirty-seven-year-old single black woman who has lived in Chicago all her life. She is the mother of five children, including twins, who range in age from seven months to nine years. Four of these children are in her custody; a three-year-old son is currently living with his father. Interviewed in a shelter for women and their children on the South Side of Chicago, Sue talked of her extensive job history and her experience as a welfare mother.

Villains of the 1990s: Welfare Moms

Welfare has become the political weapon of choice. Social problems ranging from poverty and crime to drug abuse and dropouts are blamed on the welfare system and welfare recipients. One specific program, Aid to Families with Dependent Children (AFDC), has gained the dubious distinction of becoming synonymous with public aid and is deemed the specific culprit of much that troubles America.

The welfare system was once a convenient "enemy" for Republican Presidents Reagan and Bush. As the Soviet threat faded from the international scene, taking with it the sense of a common foe, a domestic threat was defined to take its place. (Recall Reagan's diatribes against "welfare queens" and Bush's re-election campaign of 1992, which attempted to gain votes by replacing 1988's successful Willie Horton image with that of nameless welfare recipients.) Democratic President Bill Clinton has joined in this politically popular derision of the welfare system. Clinton's call for "reforming welfare as we know it" includes limiting AFDC payments to two years, after which "able-bodied recipients" would be required to find employment (Nicodemus 1993c).

Welfare, and particularly welfare mothers, have become America's scapegoat. Placing the blame on welfare recipients, stereotypically defined as irresponsible black women with a horde of kids, produces a polarizing ideology that pits hard-working "us" against lazy "them." And in its extension, this polarization becomes "suburbs versus city. Workers versus welfare. Taxpayers versus tax-eaters. And, by inference, white versus black" (Jones 1993).

The Facts on AFDC

The cost of AFDC to federal and state governments reached $25.5 billion in 1991. The amount appears staggering and is used repeatedly to rally antiwelfare forces. But this sum is deceptive. In 1991, AFDC accounted for less than 1 percent of federal and 2.2 percent of state expenditures (Sklar 1993a:26). "Reforming welfare as we know it," even doing away with it entirely, would neither make a massive dent in the federal deficit nor save cash-strapped states from fiscal difficulties.

The number of families receiving AFDC has grown from 3.5 million in 1976 to over 5 million in 1993 (*Chicago Sun-Times* 1993). This number includes approximately 4 million women, half a million men, and 8.5 million children. Of the 13 million persons currently on the welfare rolls, two-thirds are under the age of eighteen.

Unlike the "entitlement" of Social Security, AFDC payments are not indexed to inflation or protected from cuts by a politically powerful interest group such as the American Association of Retired Persons (AARP). Median monthly AFDC benefits for a family of four dropped 44 percent between 1970 and 1991, from $777 to $435 in constant 1991 dollars (*Chicago Sun-Times* 1993). The Reagan administration cut the federal AFDC budget by 14 percent ($1 billion) in 1982, resulting in an additional billion-dollar loss in state matching funds. Another $85 million was cut from the federal AFDC budget in 1983 (Sidel 1992:86).

Added to these 1982–1983 cuts in AFDC funding were federal provisions limiting eligibility and reducing grants. Some of these provisions were mandatory if states were to receive matching funds, whereas others were optional. Included as mandatory were changes in the way eligibility was calculated for working parents so as to reduce the number who could receive assistance. Optional provisions for the states included requirements for recipients to participate in work programs—the infamous "workfare" (Sidel 1992:86–87). In the decade since these provisions were enacted, millions of families have seen an outright reduction in their grants or have been removed from the AFDC rolls altogether.

Though the total number of families receiving AFDC has risen, the percentage of those in poverty who receive AFDC has fallen precipitously. In 1979, 88 percent of all poor families were receiving AFDC; five years later, that percentage had dropped by over twenty-five points (Sidel 1992:87). The number of AFDC recipients under age eighteen as a percentage of those in poverty dropped from just over 80 percent in 1973 to 60 percent in 1990 (Sklar 1993a:26).

In addition, the amount AFDC provides relative to the federal poverty line continues to plummet. In 1960 the average AFDC benefit provided 63 percent of the poverty threshold for a family of three. By 1991, that number had dropped over twenty points, to 40 percent. An AFDC family of three qualified for a maximum grant of $367 a month in 1991—$4,404 a year—much less than the official poverty threshold of $10,973 for that year (Sklar 1993a:26). The official poverty line itself is generally agreed to be far too low to meet basic human needs, and no state provides benefits up to that level. Recent research reports that an urban single mother of two preschoolers must earn $20,052 a year to cover expenses (Baurac 1993).

Stereotypes regarding AFDC recipients' race and number of children are simply untrue. Approximately equal percentages of AFDC families are white and black (roughly 40 percent each), 17 percent are Latino, 3 percent are Asian, and 1 percent are Native American. People of color are disproportionately AFDC recipients since these people are disproportionately poor. And contrary to common perceptions, women on AFDC do not have larger families than do other women. Forty-two percent of families on AFDC have only one child and another 30 percent have two children (Windishar 1992).

Sue Jackson's experience with AFDC is in many ways typical but in other ways unusual. Sue begins her story:

SUE: We were raised real poor. It's eight in my family and my mother raised us on welfare. She got a job and went off Aid when my youngest brother was around ten. Her and my father been separated thirty-one years. So they been separated since my youngest brother was born. When she brought him home from the hospital, my father left.

Sue was raised in a family that received welfare for about ten years, and she herself went on to receive welfare. This is *not* the typical case. Most daughters in welfare families do not become welfare recipients as adults (Sklar 1993a). Also unusual is the size of Sue's own family; as the mother of five children, she is quite atypical. Fewer than 10 percent of AFDC families have more than three children (Sklar 1993a:26). More characteristic is Sue's negative response to being on welfare. Dispelling the myth of the greedy "welfare queen," she has avoided AFDC whenever possible.

SUE: I been off Aid three or four times since I had kids cause I don't even want to be bothered with it if I got some other means of income or somebody to help me. I've had one job since I had him. [Her oldest son Shawn, who is nine.] I don't even apply [for Aid] until my shit just really get down and stuff. I don't even want to be bothered with it.

Occupational Segregation of Women in the Low-Wage Economy

The public generally assumes that those on welfare have no high school degree, employable skills, or work record. But Sue Jackson is a high school graduate. And she has an extensive employment history.

SUE: I didn't have Shawn until I was twenty-eight. I had always had a job since I was sixteen. Up until, you know, I got pregnant with him. I've had one job since I had him.
INTERVIEWER: What was that job?
SUE: My brothers had a store. I worked in there about two years. But that's only one. I've worked bars. I've worked every department store downtown. Most of the banks. A lot of offices. Sometimes I had two jobs at once.
INT.: Good jobs?
SUE: Not for me. You know, other people might've thought they were good. You know, good-lookin' jobs. White-collar jobs. You know, where you look good but you don't be makin' shit. You end up runnin' up all sort a bills on clothes for your good-lookin' job.
INT.: What kind of work were you doing in those offices?
SUE: I did a little light typing and adding machine and microfilm, you know. I'm tryin' to think. Some of everything. Just general clerical work.

Sue Jackson's work experience exemplifies occupational segregation by sex in the American labor force. Almost half of all working women are employed in occupations where more than 80 percent of their fellow workers are female; 71 percent of men work in jobs that are more than 80 percent male (Coontz 1992:265). Two of Sue's past jobs—secretary and bank teller—are among the most sex-specific of all women's occupations. Over 99 percent of all secretaries are women, as are 91 percent of all bank tellers (Sapiro 1990:25).

Women are more heavily concentrated in fewer job categories than are men. These "women's jobs" tend to be in clerical or personal service areas, where women's supposedly "natural" abilities in caring for others can be put to use. As the economy shifts from industrial production to service work and information processing, more of these jobs have become available. By 1990, women constituted 45.4 percent of the civilian labor force; this percentage will increase as de-industrialization continues (Rothenberg 1992:129).

The consequence of this labor force segregation is a major wage gap between working men and women. Since women's employment is primarily in the service and information processing economy, where pay tends to be low and benefits few or nonexistent, women earn much less than men. In 1991, all men, working year-round full time, were paid a median salary of $29,421 a year. All women, working year-round full time, were paid a median salary of $20,553 per year. Putting this another way, women were paid $.70 compared to each dollar paid to men (Baurac 1993).

Differences in educational attainment do not explain this wage discrepancy. In 1985, both women and men had a median educational level of 12.8 years (National Committee on Pay Equity, quoted in Rothenberg 1992:133). Female high school graduates working year-round full time in 1988 earned a median income of $16,810 as compared to the $17,190 earned by fully employed men with *less than eight years of formal schooling* (Baca Zinn and Eitzen 1993:188).

The cause of the wage gap is discrimination. The greater the proportion of women employed in an occupational category, the lower the pay. A 1986 National Academy of Sciences study found that "each additional percentage point female in an occupation was associated with $42 less in median annual earnings" (National Committee on Pay Equity, quoted in Rothenberg 1992:133).

This discrimination is not only by sex but also by race. A 1987 study in New York State found that "for every 5 to 6 percent increase in Black and Hispanic representation in a job there is a one salary grade decrease. (A one salary grade decrease amounts to a 5 percent salary decrease.)" (National Committee on Pay Equity, quoted in Rothenberg 1992:133). Women of color face a double burden of race and sex discrimination. In 1991, the median income for full-time, year-round workers was $16,244 for Hispanic women, $18,720 for black women, $19,771 for Hispanic men, $20,794 for white women, $22,075 for black men, and $30,266 for white men (Sklar 1993a:27).

Two out of three minimum-wage workers are women. Full-time work at $4.25 per hour adds up to an income below the poverty line for a family of two. Is it any wonder Sue Jackson and other black women heading families with children under eighteen experience just under a two-out-of-three chance (60.5 percent) of being in poverty? (Sklar 1993a:27) (The comparable figure for white women is 39.6 percent.) To be employed, particularly if you are female and black, does not mean you will avoid poverty.

Child Care for Working Mothers

Add to this low-wage reality the lack of available and affordable child care. The United States is distinct in that it has no comprehensive child care system.

> For decades, other countries have recognized that children are valuable so-cietal resources, and they have provided families with a broad base of sup-port. Sixty-seven countries, including all developed nations except the United States, provide family or child allowances in the form of cash bene-fits to supplement the incomes of those raising children. In addition, most European countries guarantee jobs, seniority, and pension entitlements to parents who leave work for an average of six months to one year at the time of childbirth. Most also provide some cash benefit through the social secu-rity system as wage replacement during the leave period. All now provide additional unpaid leave from six months to three years. (Lubeck and Garrett 1983:31)

After much political haggling, the Family Leave Act, twice vetoed by the Bush administration, was passed by Congress and signed into law February 5, 1993. This act, which guarantees workers up to twelve weeks of unpaid leave a year for births, adoptions, or the care of sick children, spouses, or parents, also guarantees workers the same or an equivalent job upon their return. But the act covers only 40 percent of all workers, and low-wage workers in particular cannot afford to take unpaid leave, even if offered. The Family Leave Act does nothing in regard to the provi-sion of day care for the children of working parents.

The government's basic strategy is to offer parents tax deductions for child care expenses and to provide modest sums of money to the states for subsidizing day care fees. Neither of these "solutions" is sufficient for low-wage workers, because the costs of care are so high relative to in-come earned. Sue Jackson recognizes this fact.

INTERVIEWER: How about now? Do you need a job now?
SUE: Yeah. I need one. You know I need one. But it doesn't seem practical to me. It don't seem practical to me to get a job now.

INT.: How come?

SUE: I got four babies all right close to each other. Who's gonna keep 'em? And how am I gonna pay 'em? Nobody's gonna keep no four kids, you know, four little kids not in school. The going rate for a babysitter—for small kids—is like thirty-five dollars a week while you're working. But that's for one. Maybe if you got the family plan ... they might charge me a hundred for four. So that wouldn't make, you know, much sense to me. You know, to pay all that money in child care. If your kids aren't old enough to be in school—and even those goin' to school—you still payin' somebody for those few hours after school. Unless I was workin' somewhere where it was really payin' good. If it pays decent enough, you know, where you could afford a babysitter. But not those office jobs. It wouldn't be payin' nothing. They all be payin' shit, but four to five dollars an hour. You know, the only kind of job I could get, would be a bootleg job. Where I'd stay on Aid and they wouldn't find out about it. Like workin' somewhere like a bar or somethin'. Or at night. That's the only way you can really make it. Shit, a job that ain't makin' no money, you got a bunch of kids and you still be poor. Or you get off Aid and ... you know, either way, shit.

Child care costs are significantly higher than Sue estimates. A Bureau of the Census study released in September 1992 reported an average weekly child care cost per U.S. family of $54 per week in 1988, up from $40 per week in 1984 (Dubin 1992). Parents and child care experts criticized these figures, saying they were much too low. The Children's Defense Fund recounted figures from its 1990 survey of four cities, where the average weekly cost for a one-year-old in licensed day care ranged from a low of $75 to a high of $127 per week (Kreck 1992). Using the Children's Defense Fund's lowest estimate of $75 per week, paying for care for even one child eats up almost half of the pay earned in a minimum-wage job. Infant care, such as Sue Jackson would need for her seven-month-old baby, is considerably more expensive and more difficult to find.

Sue Jackson is correct in assuming that it is "not practical" for her to get a job right now. If she did find and take a low-wage job, she would forfeit all or part of her AFDC grant. She would also lose government-paid health benefits for herself and her children. And she would have enormous child care costs—on top of the necessities of food and housing. These latter two expenses take 85 percent of a typical poor family's income (Sklar 1993a:26). There is simply no money left for the "luxury" of child care.

Insufficient Subsidized Housing

Nationally, less than one out of four AFDC families lives in rent-subsidized or public housing (Sklar 1993a:26). Most AFDC families must therefore attempt to find affordable housing in the same private housing market as those with considerably higher incomes. Sue Jackson lives in Chicago, where only 80,000 assisted units exist, compared to 600,000 poor people needing rent subsidies (Holleb, as quoted in Henderson 1993).

Sue Jackson's monthly AFDC grant for herself and four children is $450. Though it cost her two-thirds of that grant, Sue was elated when she found a large apartment to rent for $300 a month, not including utilities. She thought her housing problems were over.

SUE: It was a big apartment. Eight rooms. I was really happy when I found the apartment. It was what I had been lookin' for. It had like four bedrooms, a living room, dining room, kitchen, back porch. You know, he [the landlord] was workin' on it, but it still looked better than anything else I had been stayin' in. And it had a lot of room. But after I moved all my and the kids' stuff in, I found out I couldn't get the lights and gas turned on. The bill was in the name of the person that had been in the apartment before. There was a problem there, so the light company wouldn't turn on any lights. [A relative of the landlord had been in this apartment, but hadn't paid the utility bills. The landlord refused to divulge the whereabouts of this relative to the utility companies, so they refused to turn the electricity and gas back on.] The landlord had ran an extension cord and I was usin' his lights in one room. He knew he couldn't get those lights turned on. You see that's why he wanted me to get in there and use that address for Aid. 'Cause usually they will let you get your green card and get the lights and stuff turned on. And, see, he didn't have any gas either. He probably figured, you know, that if I got the gas turned on, that he could connect all the apartments to it.

INTERVIEWER: You and the kids were in this one room. ...

SUE: We're in this one room and we think we hear a rat. But I don't see him, 'cause there's no lights back there, you know, back in the kitchen. Then I see him, so I know. It's a rat. So I just get the kids and left. And we stayed in the hotel for awhile. You know, not planning on staying there that long, but we ended up staying there 'cause every time I would go back to the apartment to see if the rat was around, you know, I always thought he had been there. I'd see stuff that was tore up. At first when he was in the kitchen I thought it would be alright, 'cause I wasn't gonna go back in there. But then I saw that he had been in the room that we was in, you know, and I had come back in there and see he had tore up stuff. He tore up bags and pieces of paper. Or been in somethin'. So I would never sleep in there.

Avoiding the rat cost Sue $33 a day in hotel charges. In the midst of this turmoil, her welfare checks were cut off entirely for three months. The local Public Aid office was investigating her case because of confusion regarding the children in her custody. Sue's three-year-old son had begun living primarily with his father, who applied for AFDC. After a cross-check of the records, his application was denied since the son's name appeared on Sue's grant. In the meantime, Sue's youngest child, Samantha (now seven months old), was born but had not yet been added to the family's AFDC paperwork. This mix-up in names and numbers resulted in Sue's check being temporarily suspended. Her only support now came in the form of $242 worth of food stamps per month. When almost all her money was gone, Sue turned in desperation to her brother.

SUE: I spent all my money in the hotel. Almost all of it. And I had got cut off Aid. Then I called my brother and we went over there. We stayed over there for a few days.

INTERVIEWER: Why didn't you stay there longer?

SUE: Because the kids kept gettin' into every damn thing. And tearin' up his, you know, messin' with all his stuff. Pushin' buttons, you know. He got a lot of stereo equipment and VCRs and stuff to fascinate them. And whenever I tried to go to sleep it was pushin' buttons and gettin' into everything. So he was gettin' really pissed off—he was really mad. He didn't really go off or somethin', you know, but when I be around people, I know they be mad about somethin'. You know it. I just went out and left.

INT.: What about the rest of your family?

SUE: What about 'em?

INT.: You couldn't stay any longer with your brother because you could tell he was getting irritated with the kids. What about the rest of your family?

SUE: Well, like most people in here [the shelter] ... if you could stay with your family, you would. Rather than to be here, you know. Especially when you have a lot of kids. Most people don't want to be bothered with a whole bunch of kids and stuff. If I didn't have any kids, then I would be welcome. I'd go stay over a boyfriend's house 'til he got sick of me, then go over another one's or somethin'. But you bringin' four and five kids with you, you ain't gonna be welcome too many places.

INT.: You don't feel like you could go stay with your mother or your brothers or sisters?
SUE: No. Definitely not.

Sue's housing problems culminated in her family's current residence at St. Martin de Porres, a shelter for women and their children on the city's South Side. She and her children arrived at the shelter on a sweltering 100-degree day in early July. She had ten dollars in her pocket. Since then, her Aid checks have been restored. But for the period of time she lived with her brother, and continuing now at the shelter, she does not receive food stamps. As Sue explains:

SUE: If you're livin' with a parent, brother, or sister, you won't get any stamps. And you won't get any stamps in the shelter. Because you're not cookin' and buyin' your own food. And, see, I have to buy Pampers for three babies, you know. When I get through buyin' the Pampers and the washin' powder and goin' to the laundromat and stuff, that takes almost all the money I have. 'Cause you got to put up sixty percent, you know, seventy percent, whatever, when you live in this shelter. [The shelter requires its residents to surrender 70 percent of their AFDC grant, which is held in a savings account until the family leaves the shelter.] Then you be owin' everybody. 'Cause you got to borrow some Pampers and stuff all month long.

Given the lack of affordable housing and Sue's meager income, her chances for improving her housing situation are slim.

INTERVIEWER: How much do you need to rent the kind of apartment you need for your family?
SUE: The kind of apartment I would need for my family would cost at least around four hundred dollars. I'd like to have my other son back home with me. I got five kids. Three boys, two girls. A three-bedroom apartment in Chicago—heated—would cost around four hundred and fifty dollars, you know. I could get one unheated for around three hundred and twenty-five dollars. This is what that apartment I'd moved into was rentin' for. It was rentin' for three hundred twenty-five but I was supposed to be gettin' the bargain. Plus you had to furnish your own utilities. Without utilities is around three hundred twenty-five. But heated, you know, four hundred and fifty dollars; four fifty and up. That's why the CHA [Chicago Housing Authority] is usually the only option if you're on Aid and got a lot of kids, and need more room.
INT.: So that's your option now, the CHA?

SUE: Yeah. The only thing I could afford with my four hundred and fifty dollars a month and not be in the CHA would be a one-bedroom apartment for between two hundred and fifty and three hundred dollars. The CHA is the only place where you could get enough bedrooms, you know. There's not much room in those, either. But the rent is the only thing that you could afford and have some money left to buy some clothes or somethin'. Four hundred and fifty dollars is nothing.

INT.: So now you're on the CHA waiting list?

SUE: Right.

INT.: And that's your ticket out of here.

SUE: Yeah. I had my interview. Now I'm waitin'.

Sue Jackson's rent in a CHA-subsidized building would be roughly 30 percent of her AFDC grant of $450, or $135 per month. She applied for a three-bedroom apartment in a high-rise development near Lake Michigan and 43rd Street and was added to its lengthy waiting list. Shortly thereafter, however, those buildings were closed for major rehabilitation.

Waiting lists of eight, ten, and even twenty years exist for low-rise CHA housing, which is preferred by most women in the shelter for its perceived safety. Though she would like to be out of the shelter as soon as possible, Sue is concerned about her children's well-being and carefully weighs the benefits of affordable rent in CHA housing with the possible danger to her family.

SUE: I didn't want to be up in a high-rise if I could help it. 'Cause the elevators don't never be workin' and you gotta walk up and stuff. I don't like the projects with a lot of buildings together. You know, if it's high-rise and there's maybe one or two buildings, then it's okay. But I would move in one, you know, 'cause I'm not afraid to live anywhere.

INTERVIEWER: You'd move into any project from here?

SUE: I wouldn't move into any of 'em. No. But it's not too many of them that I would be afraid to live in.

INT.: What are they?

SUE: Robert Taylor. I don't really want to move in any of those ones on State Street. You know, nothin' up on State Street.

INT.: Have you ever lived there before?

SUE: No. But, you know, you don't have to be out on the corner to know you don't want to be a hooker. Shit. You ain't got to experience everything to know that's not it. I know what's happenin' up there.

INT.: What's happenin'?

SUE: It's so many people up in there. On this block, nobody might not get killed for a year. Now this neighborhood here is just as bad as Robert Taylor. Or worse. But maybe one person might get killed every six months. But in Robert Taylor, six people might be killed every week. I want to decrease the odds. It's not that it's any worse people. But there's so many of them. More shit be happenin' up in there. I would never move nowhere like Robert Taylor or Cabrini Green, which they be tryin' to get you to go to.

INT.: That's where a lot of people who leave the shelter are going?

SUE: Right. Because they don't have a long waiting list. They don't have a long waiting list 'cause don't nobody want to move up in there. They know if you're here, you're desperate.

Work Versus Welfare: No Choice

Sue Jackson's situation highlights the absence of any realistic options for poor black women and their children. If she works, she will likely be employed in the low-wage economy. With few or no health benefits, she will have to trust to luck that she and her children remain healthy. She will not be able to afford child care and will be unlikely to find an apartment that is both affordable and of sufficient size.

Welfare presents its own problems. At current AFDC funding levels, Sue Jackson and her children remain poverty stricken. With no guarantee of subsidized housing and insufficient funds to enter the private housing market, Sue must apply and wait for openings in public housing. She must weigh the advantage of lower rent (if, in fact, an opening occurs) against the danger to her family. And Sue Jackson must bear the public's humiliating depiction of her as lazy, irresponsible, and personally to blame for her own impoverishment.

Work or welfare? Sue Jackson is poor either way.

The Role of Mental Illness

Sue Jackson's life has been difficult. That she has had bouts of depression should come as no surprise.

SUE: I was havin' a lotta problems in my life and I didn't really have anybody to talk to, you know. You be thinkin' people betray you and all that shit. You get paranoid. You tell somebody somethin' then everybody will know it and there's a lotta arguin' and stuff. I just wasn't dealin' with things like they were supposed to be dealt, you know. Lettin' things build up. Shit, I just went off. They sent me to Jackson Park.

INTERVIEWER: Who sent you?

SUE: The police sent me. They said it was either jail or the hospital. I was beatin' on my sister. I'd had a knife. When the police came to the apartment and were gonna arrest me for assault, my mother and my sister started talkin' bout, "Oh, she's crazy, she belong in the crazyhouse, she be crazy, she needs help, take her to the crazyhouse." So the police said okay and took me to Jackson Park. I stayed two weeks and walked out. I couldn't stand it. That was eighty-two.

INT.: Did that help any?

SUE: No. Not really. It was a lot like in here [the shelter]. We have group therapy. I can say anything here, you know. I know I'll never see these people again unless I choose to. But when you're around people that you know and family and close friends you keep a lot of stuff hidden. You don't want the word passed among your close group about stuff that be happening. Or might be troublin' you or somethin'. People in there really no crazier than other people. Just like people in here, you know. Just sort of depressed.

Sue Jackson was admitted to mental wards on two other occasions. In 1977, she spent two days in Cook County Hospital's psychiatric ward. In 1984, while at the same hospital for physical problems, a doctor suggested that she "needed help" and admitted her for psychiatric evaluation.

SUE: I didn't want to go. I was pregnant and I didn't have any money. I was depressed. They kept me at County a few days and then transferred me to Jackson Park. I was there about forty days.

In Chapter 2, we have criticized the popular notion that mental illness is a cause of homelessness in American cities. Sue Jackson is homeless and does have a history of mental hospitalization, but that does not mean that one has caused the other. Sue's homelessness is clearly related to her poverty rather than to her depression. And her depression seems reasonable—in fact, normal—given the circumstances of her life. A recent study of the homeless in New Jersey supports this conclusion (Gioglio 1989). Those judged mentally ill were compared to those with no "mental health factor" in their background; no differences in the two groups' primary reasons for becoming homeless were found.

Sue Jackson and her family are poor and homeless. Her high school diploma, extensive work experience, and delayed childbearing did not spare her this fate. What Sue needs is affordable housing, health care, child care, and a good-paying job, not moral exhortation or a lecture on personal responsibility.

5

The Economic Marginality of
Young Families:
Sara, Dave, Elizabeth, and Joshua

Sara and Dave Smith left high school after their junior year. They are now both twenty-six years old. They have two children: Elizabeth is seven and Joshua is twenty-one months. Sara, Dave, and their children are from Rochelle, a small industrial city in north central Illinois. At the time Sara was interviewed, the four of them were living in a shelter for homeless families in Tampa, Florida. They had come to the Sun Belt looking for jobs. Two years earlier they had moved to Texas to look for better employment and housing. Both proved elusive, so the family returned to their midwestern home, only to find its industry closing down and leaving town.

In addition to the large and growing homeless population in the United States, there is an even larger and faster growing *near-homeless* population. Many on the edge of hopelessness are presently living "doubled up" or "tripled up" with others. Many are paying far too great a proportion of their income in rent.

It is estimated that by the mid-1980s, in New York City alone more than 300,000 persons were living doubled up in public and private housing. By 1986, at least 50 percent of families entering New York City shelters for the homeless had previously been doubled up. It has been estimated that across the country there are now more than 3 million families living doubled up (Kozol 1988c).

Generally, housing has been considered affordable if its cost does not exceed 25 percent of household income. In 1985, nearly one of every four renters paid more than half of their income on housing. Eleven million families in the United States now spend more than one-third of their income in rent; 6 million spend more than one-half; and 4.7 million pay 60 percent or more of their income on rent. At least 2 million homeowners pay half or more of their income on their mortgage. There is a shortage of approximately 4 to 5 million affordable housing units in the United States for households earning $7,000 a year or less (Appelbaum 1989; Kozol 1988c). It is not surprising that some government agencies have now decided that the definition of affordable housing should be raised from 25 to 30 percent of income.

Neither is there much public assistance available in the United States for low-income families facing this affordable housing shortage. Six to 7 million low-income families receive no housing assistance of any kind and are at the mercy of the excessive rents of the private housing market. Only one in four persons living below the federal government's official poverty line has any kind of publicly subsidized housing. That is one of the very smallest percentages anywhere in the industrialized world (Appelbaum 1989). In a large city like Chicago, only 16 percent of AFDC recipients live in subsidized housing (Stein 1990).

Today's *near homeless*, if present trends in both public housing and the private housing market are allowed to continue, will become tomorrow's homeless. Within fifteen years, according to MIT professor Phillip Clay, "the gap between the total low-rent housing supply (subsidized and unsubsidized) and households needing such housing is expected to grow to 7.8 million units" (quoted in Appelbaum 1989:7). This would entail the loss of affordable housing for roughly 19 million people.

The Near Homeless and a "Precipitating Event"

The near homeless are often only a precipitating event—a personal catastrophe—away from being priced out of the housing market and on the streets or in a shelter. For Sara and Dave and their children the catastrophe was threefold: An injury to Dave coupled with the lack of union protection led to the loss of his job, abuse by an employer involved in a government-sponsored job training program, and medical expenses for a handicapped child.

SARA: OK, my husband had looked for work and he had kept looking and looking and finally, um, he heard that FDL Foods, which is a meatpacking company, was hiring. So he went over and put his application in and they recommended to go get a physical but didn't guarantee that he'd get a job. So he went over there and got his physical at Dubuque [Dubuque, Iowa, the company's headquarters] and they did the thorough checkup. And he had had a hernia operation two years ago, but ... they knew about it 'cause like he didn't lie about nothin' on his application. He just, you know, told the truth. So, um, after that he kept waitin' and waitin' and he'd call 'em every day and then they finally called him into work. So he was working second shift. And, um, the job went great ... but that lasted for three weeks. And, uh, he was at home and he had some time to do some odd and end things at home just before he went in and he was going down into the basement with some antique corner shelves and he had fell down the stairs and he had called me from the hospital where I work and told me to call his boss to let him know that he would not be in to work because he was in the emergency room. And so I called his boss and his boss said, "Fine. Don't worry about it as long as you have an excuse, you know, verifying where you was and wrote up by the doctor and everything. And if you cannot report to work Saturday to call us and let us know." Well, um, the doctor said that he needed to have a three-day weekend to lay back and take it easy. And he put him on Darvons and stuff we'd think could be dangerous workin' under that—with that kind of medicine. So I called back where he worked Saturday and told 'em that he will not be in to work 'til Monday and he'll have that written excuse from the doctor and everything verifying what happened and explainin' how it happened and all that. So he went in to work Monday night and he showed the excuse and it was written on the excuse that Dave Smith could return back to work ... that we would like him to be put in a different, um, department because of the hernia operation.

INTERVIEWER: The doctor was saying that?

SARA: Yes, the doctor wrote it—it's on the excuse—that it was too heavy lifting for him from that department. So he asked—showed it to his boss and he told him he was temporarily laid off. And I feel and Dave feels that it's from, we're afraid that he thinks that Dave's responsible that he got hurt, they think that he got hurt at work, which he didn't. He got hurt at home.

INT.: Was that a union job?

SARA: Yeah. But he wasn't in the union yet.

INT.: Because he hadn't been there long enough?

SARA: Long enough and plus he wasn't there long enough to draw unemployment either.

INT.: So when he was laid off, they didn't have to pay anything.

SARA: No, they didn't have to pay nothing.

INT.: What were you doing at the time?

SARA: I was working at a day care center as a teacher's aide for two-year-olds and it was very hard supporting a family of four on the income that I made. It was very hard makin' ends meet plus puttin' my child through school and buying school clothes for her.

INT.: What were you trying to support a family of four on?

SARA: Four hundred and thirty dollars a month.

INT.: Four hundred and thirty dollars a month?

SARA: Right. When you're talkin' you got to pay your lights, gas, and pay your rent.

INT.: How much was your rent?

SARA: My rent was a hundred eighty a month and in the winter time my gas bill was ninety-eight dollars a month, and my light bill was sixty-nine dollars every two months. It was kinda hard, very hard.

INT.: Before Dave got the job, the three-week job at the meat-packing plant, what was he doing before that?

SARA: He was working through an on-the-job training program. They had found him a job 'cause we were considered as low income. They had got him a job as a Nortown Subaru car mechanic and he worked every day he was supposed to.

INT.: Under the training program?

SARA: Underneath the training program which you had to be there—work under that program, I think, for three months and then the probation was up. And Dave had one week, one week left of his training program and his boss let him go, which he's done it to, excuse me, quite a few other people too.

INT.: Why was the Subaru dealer doing that? Why did he do it to Dave?

SARA: So he wouldn't have to pay—OK, when you go through on-the-job training programs, the JTPA [Job Training Partnership Act, a government/business–sponsored employment training program initiated by the Reagan administration], they pay you low wages at three thirty-five while you're working on your training and then after your probation time is up, they will—you will go by what Nortown will pay you, which would be higher wages. So instead of payin' higher wages, they let the person go. So they won't have to pay higher wages.

Finally, all of this and the added burden of young Joshua's medical treatment lead Sara and Dave to fall behind in their rent payments and they are evicted.

SARA: We were very behind on our rent. We were tryin' to work an arrangement out with our landlord as far as, um, you buy the paint, we'll paint the place. Um, we offered to do all kinds of work to help catch up on our rent. And it was to the point that she had just served us with a five-day eviction notice and we had to move, you know. I mean, we were, you're talkin' maybe three, four months behind because we'd been tryin' to be caught up on, on our bills where we'd lived before. Because of the income, we didn't have enough, you know, to stretch to pay the utilities. It was really hard. Plus makin' trips to Rockford to Crippled Children's Hospital for Joshua to get treatments done and things checked out on him. So that got to be expensive, too.

Sara and Dave are unable to maintain their housing when a series of "personal catastrophes" or "precipitating events" strike. Their situation illustrates how the near homeless become the homeless when afford-able housing is not a right guaranteed to all citizens and its supply is di-minishing.

The Declining Economic Status of Young, Non–College Educated Parents and Their Families

But why are Sara and Dave and their children so vulnerable to the pre-cipitating events that made them homeless? The answer lies in a num-ber of economic trends and forces that have made more and more young, non–college educated parents and their children more and more marginal in American society over the past two decades.

Poverty

The median income of young families with children—defined as fami-lies with children headed by persons under age thirty—declined by 26 percent between 1973 and 1986. That kind of income drop compares to the overall 27 percent drop in per capita income in the United States that occurred between 1929 and 1933 during the Great Depression. With this kind of drastic income drop, it is not surprising that the poverty rate for young families, like Sara and Dave's, nearly doubled between 1973 and 1986—soaring from 12 percent to 22 percent. By 1986, *one in every eight* of these families was poor. Nor is it surprising that three-fourths of this in-crease in poverty among young families took place during the 1980s, when Reagan administration budget cuts tightened eligibility require-ments and reduced benefit levels for a vast array of social and economic programs and supports for the poor (all figures cited from Children's Defense Fund 1988).

The increases in poverty for young families occurred in every region of the country. The rising poverty rates also affected nearly every type of young family. White, black, Hispanic, married-couple, and single-parent young families all experienced increased poverty. The largest increases in poverty during the 1973–1986 period, however, occurred among young white families, young married-couple families, and young families headed by high school graduates. Sara, Dave, Elizabeth, and Joshua fit, of course, two of these three categories. Between 1973 and 1986 almost half of the increase—47 percent—in the number of young families living below the federal government's poverty line was the result of the increased number of young white families living in poverty (all figures from Children's Defense Fund 1988). Sara and Dave's circumstances are not peculiar or unique. Their situation is clearly part of the impoverishment of families *like theirs* in American society.

Earnings and Income

Increases in poverty for young couples and their families are caused by declining earnings and income. Declining earnings, or wages, for non–college educated heads of households under thirty over the past two decades have been caused by sweeping changes in the labor market. Declining household income (household income defined here as the earned wages of all family members plus any disability, unemployment insurance, welfare, or Social Security benefits received by the family) for these young families has occurred as the result of both labor market transformations and the cuts in government assistance noted above.

Between 1955 and 1985 unemployment of young males in American society rose significantly (Rossi 1989). In 1968, the unemployment rate for young men under thirty-five years old was under 5 percent. By 1980, it had risen to 15 percent and had declined to only 13 percent by 1984 (Easterlin 1987). Workers over thirty-five did not experience these rapid increases in unemployment over this time period. Adjusting for inflation between 1968 and 1984, the earnings of workers under thirty-five declined to approximately 80 percent of their 1968 level. As a comparison, the inflation-adjusted wages of workers between forty-five and fifty-five increased during this period to about 125 percent of their 1968 level (Easterlin 1987). Among young employed males heading young married-couple families with children, "more than 90 percent of the drop in their annual earnings between 1979 and 1986 was a result of lower hourly wage rates (adjusted for inflation)" (Children's Defense Fund 1988:viii).

And the younger the young family, the more severe the drop in earnings and income. Since 1973, families headed by persons under age twenty-five have seen their earnings and income plunge the farthest. The median earnings of young family heads under twenty-five with children declined 60 percent between 1973 and 1986. By 1986, more than one-half—54 percent—of all children living in these families were poor. One in three poor children under the age of six now lives in a family headed by a person under twenty-five (all figures from Children's Defense Fund 1988). Because of declining wages and incomes for young workers and their families, the poor and the homeless are getting younger.

The falling wages and incomes of young workers and their families have their source in the de-industrialization of American society and the rise of the service economy. This means the loss of millions of relatively good-paying, "well-benefited" union manufacturing jobs and their replacement in the American economy with relatively low-wage, "poorly benefited," non-union employment. The development of this low-wage economy has been facilitated by a federal minimum wage of, until 1990, $3.35 an hour. The current $4.25 still remains the lowest minimum wage in the Western industrial world and virtually assures poverty for those working for it.

Younger workers have been particularly hard hit by the development of the low-wage service economy. As a result of the post–World War II baby boom, the past two decades have seen an increase in the proportion of Americans between the ages of twenty and thirty-five. What these two trends lead to is a relatively large number of younger workers seeking a shrinking supply of *decent* jobs.

Here again, Sara and Dave are immersed in national economic trends, Their labor market experience is that of younger workers, and they are part of the "youngest of the young" just described. Dave is unemployed in the Midwest, moves to the Sun Belt, and unemployed in the Sun Belt returns to the Midwest, where he finds low-wage employment in a business/government–sponsored job training program. Terminated by this program, and after a prolonged job search, he goes to work in a packinghouse, where he is soon laid off. He returns to the Sun Belt, this time living in a homeless shelter and making $5.15 an hour for a non-union tile maker. Sara, for her part, is making $430 a month as a teacher's aide in Rochelle and is unemployed in the shelter in Tampa.

Education

For the young families described here, a high school diploma is no longer a protection against economic loss and poverty. The median income of young families headed by high school graduates fell by one-sixth between 1973 and 1986. Their poverty rate doubled during this period. By 1986, more than one in every five American families headed by high school graduates under the age of thirty were living below the federal government's poverty line. These kinds of families account for 58 percent of the total increase in the number of young families falling into poverty between 1973 and 1986 (all figures from Children's Defense Fund 1988).

But Sara and Dave have not even graduated from high school. And it is young families headed by persons who have not finished high school who have experienced even more severe income losses and increases in poverty than those young family heads described above who have a high school diploma: "The median income of young families headed by high school dropouts fell by 35 percent between 1973 and 1986, while their poverty rate jumped from 29 percent to 46 percent" (Children's Defense Fund 1988:viii). In other words, nearly one-half of all young families headed by persons with Sara and Dave's educational background are living in poverty. As relatively good-paying unskilled manufacturing jobs in the United States have disappeared, undereducated and unskilled younger workers and parents must turn to the poorer-paying unskilled service economy jobs that have replaced them. And often even these jobs are unavailable, punctuating the economic decline of these young families with the kind of periodic unemployment that Dave and Sara have experienced.

It can be argued that the antidote to dramatic income loss and poverty increases for these young families is college education and training. The median income of young families headed by college graduates increased between 1973 and 1986. In 1986, only 2.5 percent of these kinds of families were poor (Children's Defense Fund 1988). But Sara and Dave and all of the other less-educated young families are caught in a trap: More and more education is needed to assume income stability and gains and to avoid poverty, but the declining incomes and increasing poverty of those families makes the education less and less affordable and attainable. Viewed from their room in a homeless shelter in Tampa, college training can be no more than a fleeting fantasy for Sara and Dave.

Health Care

The number of Americans without any kind of private or public health insurance shot up from 30 million in 1982 to 37 million in 1986. This resulted from a combination of employer cutbacks in employee health insurance benefits and the growth in low-wage, non-union, temporary, and part-time service-sector jobs much less likely to include the health care coverage that the unionized manufacturing jobs they replaced had provided. As outlined above, shifts in the labor market toward low-wage service-sector employment have had an impact on young workers the most. It is not surprising then that people like Sara and Dave have been the group most likely to lose private health insurance since 1974. "Young people between the ages of 18 and 24 are the least likely of any age group to be covered by private health insurance and suffered the largest decline in insured status of any age group from 1974 to 1984" (Children's Defense Fund 1988:ix). This has consequences well beyond "usual" medical costs for many young families:

SARA: When Joshua was born he was born with a birth defect. As far as, um, he's missin' two toes on his right foot and a finger's missin' on his right hand. And they told me he'll never walk. They told me that ... his shoes would run about a hundred dollars every time I needed shoes for him. And so then I made my last trip up there [to the Children's Hospital in Rockford, Illinois] and they told me that from what they could see that they were very, very surprised that he is walkin' 'cause they told me they didn't think he'd ever walk with him missin' the ball of his foot—the main balancing [thing].

By 1986, more than one in five children in families headed by persons under thirty years old had no health insurance coverage at all, and the share of young pregnant women who received either late or no prenatal care of any kind rose from 1976 to 1986. Although Medicaid has been expanded in many states in recent years to provide prenatal care to the poorest of poor women, *four-fifths* of all the states do not extend Medicaid-financed prenatal care to "near-poor" women. These "near-poor" women account for approximately one-third of all uninsured pregnant women in the United States (all figures cited in Children's Defense Fund 1988). Lack of adequate prenatal care, of course, is related to birth defects, low birth weight, and infant mortality.

Sara gave birth to Elizabeth when she was nineteen and to Joshua when she was twenty-five. Both of her pregnancies occurred when she was in the age group least likely to have private health insurance (nineteen to twenty-four years old). Part of this time she was poor, and for another part of it she was "near poor," thus making her part of that group of women in American society *least* likely to receive prenatal care. Joshua was born with a birth defect.

Sara and Dave are also a part of that group of American workers and parents, aged eighteen to twenty-four, who are most likely to suffer acute health conditions and lose the most days of work because of their illnesses. The injury that kept Dave out of the packinghouse is a case in point. And again, although young workers and family heads are more likely to be sick and more likely to miss work because of it, they are also the least likely to be privately insured and the least likely to have a regular doctor (Children's Defense Fund 1988).

Increasing numbers of young families in American society, like Sara, Dave, Elizabeth, and Joshua, are unable to afford regular medical care as well as specialized medical treatment, which both parents and children need. Often the choice is between food and health care or often between housing and health care. In Sara and Dave's case, the decision to use their limited resources to provide medical care that would allow their son to walk meant there was not enough rent money.

Housing

Because young families led by those like Sara and Dave are more likely to be poor, more likely to have low-wage or no employment, less likely to have the resources for education and health care, they are also less likely to be able to own or even rent a house or an apartment and more likely to be homeless.

The median price of a new single-family home in the United States was $69,300 in 1982. In 1990, it was about $120,000 (Dreier and Appelbaum 1990). Adjusted for inflation, the average price of a house rose more than 40 percent between 1973 and 1986 (Children's Defense Fund 1988). During this same period, mortgage interest rates also increased substantially.

In 1973, it took 23 percent of the median income of young families headed by persons under thirty with children to pay the monthly mortgage payment on an average-priced house. In 1986, this kind of mortgage payment took 51 percent of the young families' median income. For young families with children headed by persons under twenty-five the situation was even worse. In 1973, the mortgage on an average-priced house took 30 percent of their median income; by 1986 it took 90 percent of their income (all figures from Children's Defense Fund 1988). As the price of owning a home escalated, income for these young families with children, as we have seen, shrank. Needless to say, by the mid-1980s banks and savings and loans were qualifying fewer and fewer of these young families for home loans.

Since 1980, the home ownership rate in the United States has steadily declined. This has been particularly true for young families with children. For those young families with household heads between twenty-five and thirty-four, home ownership rates dropped from 52.3 percent in 1980 to 45.1 percent in 1987 (Dreier and Appelbaum 1990). For families headed by persons under age twenty-five, the ownership rate dropped by more than 25 percent between 1973 and 1987 (Children's Defense Fund 1988).

When it is not economically feasible for families to own their housing, they must rent. Over the past two decades increasing numbers of young families with children have had to enter the rental market. Rents have skyrocketed. More renters are competing for available rental units, driving up their price. This has been especially true in urban areas with extremely low apartment vacancy rates and critical shortages of affordable and low-income housing.

Over the past decade and a half, rental costs have increased rapidly as a percentage of young families' incomes. This has happened both because rents have risen—adjusted for inflation, by 16 percent between 1981 and 1987—and the incomes of young families with children have declined. Defining *rent burden* as "median rent as a proportion of median income," this burden increased by one-third for households headed by persons under age thirty-four between 1974 and 1987 (Children's Defense Fund 1988). Higher and higher rents for young families with lower and lower incomes means not only that fewer and fewer of them are able to save for down payments for their own home, but that more and more of them are unable to even stay in the rental market. Tens of thousands of these families, like Sara, Dave, Elizabeth, and Joshua, have become homeless. Young families with children have recently become the fastest-growing segment of the homeless population in the United States.

Shelterization Is Not the Solution

So now that Sara and Dave and their children are homeless, how does the temporary shelter for homeless families respond to their situation? Sara reports that Dave has found a job:

SARA: He makes tiles for your bathrooms, you know, your wall tiles. He makes those. And he makes five fifteen an hour.

And as for herself:

SARA: I talk to my counselor every day about goin' and starting GED classes right now. And then after I get my high school diploma, which'll be within a month, in a month I'll have my, hopefully, my diploma. And then I'll go into, uh, looking for a job. And then he's gonna, this, the guy that's helpin' me get my, get arrangements made for my GED, he's gonna check into seein' what I have to have for qualifications for a CNA—licensed Certified Nurse's Aide in Florida. And then I might get back into that kind of work again. I'd really like to get into that, back into nurse's aide work and bein' a teacher's aide, ... the place, which ... but that, that specifically right now is ... my goal is to get my GED. I'm workin' on gettin' it. And gettin' past that and that'll help a lot, a diploma will. And then I'll see about gettin' a job to help out. The more money the easier it'll be to make it, uh, especially with the way rent is, you know, how high rent is here in Florida.

This kind of shelterization offers two solutions to homelessness—more low-wage employment and a high school diploma—both of which, we have already seen, are related to *declining* economic status in American society. This puts Sara, Dave, and their family, along with thousands of other young couples and their children, in a "homeless trap"—where the original sources of their poverty and eventual homelessness are supposed to be the solution to these problems.

Low-wage jobs with few or no benefits and marginal education only ensure the continued poverty and periodic or long-term homelessness of young families like Sara and Dave's. To the extent that homeless shelters promulgate the causes of homelessness as its solution, we can add shelterization itself to the list of those things contributing to poverty and the inability of many to secure decent and affordable housing.

6

Left Behind in a De-industrialized, Low-Wage Economy: Bob and Nancy Shagford and Their Children

Bob Shagford, age thirty-three, and Nancy Shagford, age thirty-five, have been married for three years. The three children with them at the Metropolitan Ministries Shelter for Homeless Families in Tampa, Florida, ages eight, ten, and eleven, are Nancy's from a previous marriage. She has one other child, who lives with a grandparent in Missouri. Bob has two children, who live with their mother. At the time of the interview they had lived in the shelter for three weeks.

Before moving to Florida, Bob and Nancy lived in a town of 3,000 in Missouri, where Bob was a machine operator on a quilting machine in a mattress factory. He had worked there for twenty-one months at $4.50 an hour with no benefits and had never received a raise. Bob's brother from Illinois visited them and said that he was moving to Florida, where there were plenty of jobs, and why don't they join him? As Nancy described it:

NANCY: We felt like we were gettin' farther and farther behind all the time. So then here comes his brother, you know, "The land of opportunity in Florida. There's lots of jobs there. They pay good money." You know. We said, "What have we got to lose?" You know. 'Cause we had been, you know ... for several weeks before that we had been talkin' about how we just seemed to be gettin' farther and farther in the hole, you know, and really gettin' strapped financially. So we decided to take a chance. So in a week we sold everything we had or got rid of it and packed up everything we had left in a station wagon and a small pick-up truck and headed for Florida.

They left for Florida joining Bob's brother's family in a caravan. Their destination was Naples, where a friend of Bob's brother had worked every winter; the friend claimed that there were lots of jobs that paid good money. Upon arrival they did not find jobs but they did find out that housing was very expensive. A church, St. Vincent de Paul, put them up in a motel for two days. While there they met two men working in construction who told them that there were plenty of good jobs in Tampa.

The Shagford caravan moved to Tampa, where, they found, jobs were few and poorly paid and housing was expensive. As a result, Bob's brother decided to return to Illinois, leaving Bob and Nancy on their own. Bob searched for a job and the family slept in the car or on the ground next to the car. After several weeks, they asked the Salvation Army for help and were referred to the Metropolitan Ministries Shelter for Homeless Families. They will be able to stay there a total of eight weeks.

While living at the shelter, Bob found a job with a construction company for $5.00 an hour. The company, according to Bob, deliberately miscounts hours worked (there are no time cards), so the actual pay amounts to about $4.25 an hour. Also, there is no job security. Bob recounts what happened to the man who informed him of the job:

BOB: Charlie, the guy that told me about the job, they let him go. The same day that they hired me and he come home without a job. He didn't know why he came home without it.
NANCY: The only thing they can figure is that his daughter had been in the hospital that week and he had missed a day of work just because of that. ... But he called in, you know, and, uh, they had told him that his work was fine just a couple of days before they fired him. So the only thing he can figure is that it was because of the day he missed.

Bob is resigned to his powerless situation at work. "There ain't much you can do about it." There is no union. There are plenty of desperate people needing jobs, including Bob. It's a buyer's market with labor cheap.

The problem is compounded by the cost of housing. Bob and Nancy paid $175 a month to rent a house in Missouri. They make the same wages in Florida, but the cost for an apartment is double. In Bob's words:

BOB: You can't find nothin' for under $350. That's the rent. That's not deposit and lights and gas. Maybe making a dollar more an hour [for work] but we're talking double rent.
NANCY: It doesn't equate.

The insecurity is taking an emotional toll on Bob and Nancy. Nancy describes their desperation:

NANCY: The insecurity is making me a nervous wreck, you know. And I'm just—I'm almost to the point where I just feel like cryin' all the time, you know. He got up grouchy this morning when I started cryin' all over the place, you know. And, just security, you know, and I don't—I really don't know if we're gonna find it here. You know, 'cause the way jobs are, they don't pay from what we have been able to get, they don't pay enough to balance out the expenses. And I really don't know if we're gonna make it here, you know. And like, this was the promised land, you know, and, uh, where do we go from here?

The jobs that Bob has had pay low wages and are without benefits and offer no hope of advancement. The housing situation for Bob's family became acute when they moved from a low-rent situation to one double in cost yet they had similar wages. In Nancy's words, "It doesn't equate." The real story, though, behind Bob and Nancy's plight and millions of others in a similar situation is an economy that keeps them perpetually on the brink of financial failure. The U.S. economy has changed in the past two decades, placing millions at economic risk with less and less hope. To understand Bob and Nancy's adversity, we address two issues regarding the changing economy: (1) What has happened to jobs and wages in the U.S. economy? and (2) Why is the situation worse now?

What Has Happened to Jobs?

Fundamentally, there are three important trends regarding jobs in the United States. First, the character of jobs is changing as the United States moves from an industrial society to one characterized by services. For example, between 1981 and 1991, a time when the population sixteen and older increased by 19.4 million persons, *the number of manufacturing jobs shrank by 1.8 million* (Barlett and Steele 1992:xi).

A second trend is that the U.S. economy is disproportionately generating low-wage jobs. While manufacturing jobs have declined, other jobs have been added to the economy. From 1979 to 1989, for example, 13.6 million full-time jobs were added. But mostly these new jobs pay less and are not as desirable as the jobs created in the past. Nearly 5 million of these jobs paid less than $250 a week, which is below the official poverty level for a family of four (O'Reilly 1992a:62). A 1990 wage of $6.10 an hour for a person working forty hours a week for fifty weeks earned $12,195 a year. In 1990, 18 percent of full-time workers made less than this, compared to 12.1 percent in 1979 (Usdansky 1992). Using a slightly different measure, the Census Bureau determined that 18.9 percent of full-time workers had low-wage jobs in 1979. In 1992 the proportion of low-wage jobs was up to 25.7 percent (O'Reilly 1992a:62). "Although young workers, minorities and women were disproportionately represented among these low-wage workers, nearly three-fourths were non-Hispanic whites and had graduated from high school" (Moberg 1992:7) The kinds of jobs where wages like this occur are in the very occupations that the Labor Department predicts will be the fastest growing in the 1990s: retail sales, janitors, maids, waiters, receptionists, hospital orderlies, and clerks (reported in O'Reilly 1992a:65).

The trend toward lousy jobs is seen in the decline of wages over the past two decades: "Between 1973 and 1989, the median wages of hourly workers (adjusted for inflation) fell by 17 percent among women younger than 25, 19 percent among men ages 25 and older, and a stunning 29 percent among men younger than 25" (Children's Defense Fund 1991:24). Put another way, a study by the Economic Policy Institute found that a high school graduate with up to five years' work experience in 1989 could expect to make nearly 27 percent less than his or her counterpart ten years earlier (reported in Moberg 1992:7). And while wages declined, the cost of housing, utilities, clothing, transportation, and other goods and services increased, making life more difficult for those on the economic margin. One example is that in 1973 it took seventeen weeks of earnings for a median-income family to buy a new car. In 1992 it took that same family twenty-four weeks of earnings (Quinn 1992). Another example: In 1952 it took a store clerk two hours of work to pay for 100 postage stamps. In 1991, a store clerk had to work six hours to buy 100 stamps (Barlett and Steele 1992:20).

Another indicator of the substitution of "bad jobs" for "good jobs" is that in 1979, 43 percent of new jobs had pensions and 23 percent had health benefits. By 1988, only 38 percent had pensions and just 15 percent included medical benefits (O'Reilly 1992a:63).

The third trend regarding jobs is that unemployment is relatively high. The official unemployment rate in the United States since 1980 has varied from a high of 9 percent in 1982 and 1983 to a low of 4.8 percent in 1988. This official rate, however, understates the magnitude of unemployment in two ways. First, persons who have not actively sought work in the four weeks prior to being interviewed are *not* counted as unemployed. There are several million such "discouraged workers." Second, the official definition of unemployment excludes the 6 million Americans who work part time because they cannot find full-time jobs.

Even the decidedly understated government figures on unemployment reveal that there are many millions who want to work but do not.

In June 1992, for example, the official rate of 7.8 percent meant that there were approximately 10 million persons out of work. When the millions of discouraged workers and part-time workers who want to work full time are added, there is clearly a huge surplus of labor. According to Levitan and Johnson:

> [Since World War II] the demand for labor has failed to keep pace with the supply of job seekers. No doubt, some portion of this unemployment is inevitable in a democratic society, as both employers and workers freely choose to accept or reject work situations. Yet the bulk of unemployment is neither frictional nor voluntary. Due to whatever combination of structural barriers and governmental policies, the economy, though it has continued to expand, has failed to generate sufficient numbers of jobs in the aggregate or to produce a reasonable match between the skills of unemployed workers and the emerging demands of labor. (Levitan and Johnson 1982:55)

In addition to the unemployed, there are the underemployed (i.e., those working at jobs *below* their qualifications). One estimate is that "as many as 10 million to 15 million people who have lost their jobs since January 1990 are now re-employed at lower wages" (Dentzer 1992:26).

Why Is the Economy Changing?

There are a number of pressures on the economy that have changed and continue to change the conditions of employment and wages.

De-industrialization

Manufacturing, the backbone of the U.S. economy in this century, is no longer dominant. In 1947, employment in the service sector of the economy—everything from banking to retailing to janitoring—reached 50 percent and is now 78 percent. The biggest industrial corporations, which generally pay the best wages and provide the best benefits, have been cutting their work forces dramatically: "The *Fortune* 500 industrial companies employed 3.7 million fewer workers [in 1991] than the top 500 firms did in 1981, a loss of about one job in four" (O'Reilly 1992a:65).

The shift to service industries has led to a more unequal wage distribution. Goods-manufacturing industries tend to employ factory and construction workers in a middle-income range. Services, in contrast, employ disproportionately high numbers of low-paid clerks, custodians, and guards.

New Technologies Based on Microelectronics

The computer chip is the technology that is transforming the U.S. toward a service economy. Microelectronic-based systems of information allow for the storage, manipulation, and retrieval of data with speed and accuracy unknown just a few years ago. Parallel processing with supercomputers gives machines the ability to reason and make judgments. Computer-aided design (CAD) permits engineers to design and modify an incredible array of products in three dimensions very quickly. Computer-aided manufacturing (CAM), or the industrial robot, is replacing conventional machines and workers to weld, paint, assemble, package, and move products.

Globalization of the Economy

Because of the size of the domestic market, the relative insulation of the Pacific and Atlantic oceans, and superior technological expertise, the U.S. economy throughout most of this century has been relatively free from competitive pressures from abroad. This situation has changed dramatically in the past twenty years. Now steel and steel products are produced cheaper outside the United States, chiefly in Asia. Clothing, electronics, automobiles, and other consumer products are manufactured in other countries and sold in the United States in great quantities, primarily because of cheaper labor costs. These imports eliminated many relatively well-paid manufacturing jobs.

The Relocation of Businesses

In the search for greater profits, corporate administrators may decide to move their business to another locality. Such decisions involve what is called plant migration or, more pejoratively, runaway shops. Corporations invest in a new place and disinvest in a place where they had been operating because the economic climate is conducive to greater profit. Corporations within the United States move their plants into communities and regions where wages are lower, unions are weaker or nonexistent, and the business climate more receptive (i.e., there are lower taxes and greater government subsidies to the business). Typically, moves within the United States have been from the Northeast and Midwest to the South and Southwest.

As significant as plant migration within the United States has been, plant migration outside the United States is even greater. Multinational corporations have moved especially to Mexico, the Caribbean nations, and Asia because labor is cheap, labor is not unionized, and local regulations are not as strict as in the United States (regarding pollution controls, worker safety, and product standards). One example of the magnitude of this migration of plants and jobs outside of the United States: In 1965 every color television set purchased in this country was made by an American-owned company in a domestic plant. In 1992 not one color television set was made in the United States (Barlett and Steele 1992:35).

Mexico has the largest number of U.S.-owned plants outside of the United States (1,540 factories with 530,000 workers in 1990). This is the result of the Maquiladora program, in which U.S. companies establish assembly plants on the Mexican side of the border with workers paid wages very much lower than those paid to comparable workers in the United States. The products are shipped to the United States for sale, with a low tariff established by the government. The obvious consequences of such an arrangement are cheaper products for U.S. consumers, a loss of jobs in the United States, lower wages within the United States, and greater profits for U.S. multinational corporations. The North American Free Trade Agreement, which the leaders of Canada, Mexico, and the United States agreed to in 1992, will reduce restrictions on trade among these countries. The fear is that cheap labor in Mexico will depress wages in the United States and Canada and increase the likelihood of domestic corporations moving even more of their operations to Mexico.

Corporate Debt

During the 1980s, U.S. corporations accumulated $1.5 trillion in new debt to finance new acquisitions, the building of skyscrapers, and lavish office buildings.

> The debt required companies to divert massive sums of cash into interest payments, which in turn meant less money was available for new plants and equipment, less money for research and development. During the 1950s, when manufacturing jobs were created at a record pace, companies invested $3 billion in new manufacturing plants and equipment for every $1 billion paid out in interest. By the 1980s, that pattern had been reversed: Corporations paid out $1.6 billion in interest for every $1 billion invested in manufacturing plants and equipment.
>
> Similarly, during the 1950s, for every $1 billion that corporations paid out in interest on borrowed money, they allocated $710 million for research and development. By the 1980s, corporations spent only $220 million on research and development for every $1 billion in interest payments. (Barlett and Steele 1992:18–19)

Robert Reich, Secretary of Labor under President Clinton, argues that the huge business debt accrued during the 1980s will have negative consequences for workers: "The 1980s will go down in history as a time when financial capital overwhelmed human capital. Business debt will continue to be the most troublesome constraint on corporate America, and the workers are going to pay the price" (cited in Baumohl, Hequet, and Shannon 1991:55).

A common ploy of corporations in financial difficulty is to declare bankruptcy. Under the bankruptcy laws, corporations are able to restructure to reduce costs. Thus, they may terminate all workers and hire new ones at lower wages and benefits or eliminate or reduce health insurance, pension, and other benefits to their workers.

Takeovers, Mergers, and Leveraged Buyouts

A major reason for corporations taking on so much debt during the 1980s was a buying binge by them to merge with competitors or to buy companies in unrelated industries. One method of acquiring other companies was the leveraged buyout. In this instance, investors purchase a company mostly with borrowed money (often with very high interest "junk bonds"), using the assets of the purchased company as collateral. The problem with these deals is that the interest payments due were often enormous. This meant that sometimes companies that had miscalculated went bankrupt or that they had to sell off assets to meet the interest payments. In either case, jobs were eliminated. Moreover, the concentration of capital through mergers and acquisitions increases the power of the huge organizations over workers. As a result, workers often had to make concessions to management.

Loss of Union Strength

The existence of cheap non-U.S. labor gave management the threat of moving operations overseas. Therefore, "workers, fearful of losing their jobs, accepted pay cuts or freezes, worked longer hours and shouldered more expenses management once assumed, especially health care" (Moberg 1992:22). As an indirect indicator of this, the U.S. Labor Department found that in companies with 100 or more employees, the percentage of those employees with fully paid health coverage for themselves and their families fell from 50 percent in 1982 to 31 percent in 1989 (Barlett and Steele 1992:126). The major unionized industries such as automobiles, faced with foreign competition and possibly losing jobs, rolled back conditions. Thus, workers lost their collective strength in facing management and wages and benefits declined.

Having unemployed people who are willing to work keeps the employed relatively docile out of fear that management will replace them with cheaper labor if they become too militant. Thus, even unionized labor cowers when unemployment is high. Feagin has summarized the argument of capitalists regarding unemployment:

> The ... unemployed are essential to the operation of the capitalist system because they put downward pressure on wages and provide a reserve labor force that can be drawn back into employment when profit and investment conditions require it. Not only the officially unemployed, but also other groups make up this reserve labor force: discouraged workers, part-time workers, immigrant laborers just over the border, and housewives who might enter the market in the future. (Feagin 1982:89)

Decline in the Defense Industry

During the 1980s, under President Reagan, the United States built up its defense through huge expenditures. Many jobs were created, especially in the Sun Belt states. But with the breakup of the Soviet empire in 1990, and because of the huge national debt (much of it a result of defense spending during the 1980s), the defense industry faces reduced spending. This, of course, means the loss of jobs.

Moreover, the military is cutting back significantly in personnel. They have fewer openings for new recruits, and career military are encouraged to retire early. This adds pressure on domestic jobs, as people formerly in the military or who would have volunteered to be in the military no longer have that option.

Permanent Layoffs

During the 1980s, with the decline of manufacturing, huge corporate debt, and foreign competition, many companies have cut back their work forces. Corporations accelerated worker layoffs during the early 1990s with the decline of the defense industry and economic recession. General Motors, IBM, and other major corporations have downsized by tens of thousands each in jobs. Most significant, many of these jobs are permanently lost. As banks, retailers, computer makers, defense contractors, and other firms from Boston to Burbank slash their payrolls in the face of falling profits, experts predicted that half the jobs lost in 1990 would never be restored (Baumohl, Hequet, and Shannon 1991:54).

Conclusion

Bob and Nancy Shagford and millions of others like them are caught in the middle of an economic transformation. These structural forces have changed the nature of occupations, eliminated jobs, and reduced wages for many workers. There is a ripple effect as workers from executives to engineers to factory workers to nonskilled workers seek jobs in this environment. The problem for those, like the Shagfords, who are at or near the bottom is that there are more and more people competing for marginal work, making their jobs even less secure, their pay meager, their job benefits nil, and their chances not very hopeful. In Nancy's words:

NANCY: 'Cause the way jobs are, they don't pay from what we have been able to get, they don't pay enough to balance out the expenses. And I really don't know if we're gonna make it here, you know. And like, this was the promised land, you know, and, uh, where do we go from here?

7

Eviction:
Debbie Jones and Her Children

Debbie Jones is thirty years old, black, divorced, and has five children ranging in age from six to thirteen. She is a high school graduate. Debbie and her three youngest children have been living in the St. Martin De Porres Shelter for homeless women and their children, in Chicago, for two and a half months. Her two oldest children went to live with their grandmother when Debbie and the other children entered the shelter.

Debbie became homeless when she was evicted from her apartment.

DEBBIE: I wasn't paying the rent, that's why I got evicted. Plus, I took him [the landlord] to court. [He] wasn't, uh, repairing. OK. I would have to go to the bathroom with a umbrella. The roof was leakin', ceilin' was leakin'. ... We had mices, rats, cockroaches. They went into the garbage and the garbage was right at the back entrance of our kitchen. And, uh, holes in the walls where the kids could have got lead poisoning and he wouldn't even come repair it, nothin'. ... I had pictures [which I presented to the Housing Court] that showed the way things wasn't bein' fixed which it was promised that they were going to be fixed. ... And, once my refrigerator went out and they wouldn't give me a new one. And, oh, I had—this one'll shock you—all my meats got spoiled. And, uh, I told him about it several times and he wouldn't do nothin' about it. So I took action and took them to court. And, then, you know, I wasn't paying rent 'cause I told 'em I was just gonna hold my rent and I holded the rent. And, uh, by me not paying the rent he took me to court. And finally he was able to evict me. ... I had seven days to move. And when the seven days were up, well, I stayed there [anyway] and the Sheriff served the papers and said that I had twenty-four hours.

Eviction, the legal expulsion of a tenant, occurs fairly often. In New York City in 1988, for example, 21,000 households were evicted, almost always for nonpayment of rent. In the past, eviction did not doom one to homelessness because other low-cost housing was available.

There was a time when eviction simply meant moving to another low-rent apartment—one with rats and broken pipes, perhaps, but housing nonetheless. But now, in a city with an almost nonexistent vacancy rate, eviction can lead to homelessness. The percentage of homeless people in New York City who have lost their apartments through eviction is not known, but one study in 1986 by the City Human Resources Administrator estimated it was 26 percent. (Rimer 1989:1)

Debbie's situation reveals four harsh realities for the poor and near poor. First, the demand for low-cost housing far exceeds the supply, which means, among other things, that owners can charge excessive rents and they do not have to maintain the housing adequately. Second, the poor pay an extraordinary portion of their income for their housing, even lousy housing. This places low-income renters at a high risk of eviction. And, third, the poor do not have power either through political mobilization or through powerful allies to change their situation. Let's examine each of these.

Housing Demand for the Poor
Is Greater Than Supply

The dominant theme of this book is that *homelessness is a housing problem*. People do not have permanent shelter because they cannot afford whatever is available: "The past ten years have witnessed a virtual decimation of the low-income housing supply in most large American cities. During the same period, the poverty population of the cities has increased substantially. Less low-income housing for more low-income people predestined an increase in the numbers of those without housing" (Wright and Lam 1987:48). Since 1980 or so several trends have converged to account for this shortage. First, the vast amount of newly constructed rental units are at the high end of the rent range. Second, federal expenditures for subsidized housing declined by 80 percent from 1981 to 1989.

Today [1991], 27 cents of every tax dollar are spent on defense; only half a penny on housing programs. Money targeted for Section 8 housing has been cut by 82 percent [since Reagan assumed office]; the Section 202 program (elderly and handicapped loans) has been abolished; and Section 235 (homeownership program) has been eliminated. ... New construction for all HUD lower-income housing programs dropped from 183,000 units in 1980 to 28,000 in 1985. HUD hopes to sell or demolish 100,000 public housing units during the next five years, and previous commitments for about 250,000 low-income units have been cancelled. ... Currently, it is estimated that only six percent of the households who qualify for low-income supplements get assistance from the government. (Gilderbloom 1991:31)

Third, many low-income housing units such as SROs (single-room occupancy units) were destroyed or remodeled for either upscale apartments or office space. Fourth, the high cost of home ownership (in 1991, 57 percent of all owners and renters could not afford to buy a median-priced house with a conventional, thirty-year mortgage) meant that hundreds of thousands of middle-class renters delayed purchasing a home, thus driving up the cost of rentals for the working class and the poor (Downey and Taylor 1991). And fifth, the number of low-income and very poor families is large and growing.

The result is that in 1989, for example, some 9.6 million low-income renters were competing for 5.5 million low-rent housing units (Associated Press 1991). Put another way, according to Harvard University's Joint Center for Housing Studies, the number of privately owned, unsubsidized apartments with rents of less than $300 a month (in constant 1989 dollars) had dropped 50 percent to 1.4 million between 1974 and 1989 (cited in Pacelle 1991:B1).

This situation likely will worsen, given the strong tendency to let market forces rather than a progressive public policy guide decisions. According to MIT professor Phillip Clay, "by the year 2004 the gap between the total low-rent housing supply (subsidized and unsubsidized) and households needing such housing is expected to grow to 7.8 million units [representing an affordable housing loss for nearly 19 million people]" (cited in Appelbaum 1989:7).

There are four major consequences that result from the demand for low-cost housing far exceeding the supply, as is and will be the case into the near future. First, there will be rent inflation. This has occurred as the housing supply has dwindled while the demand increased. For example, rental costs for the 3.2 million poor families not receiving government aid increased 49 percent from 1974 to 1987 (Miller 1990). Put another way, low-income households have experienced rent increases from 34.9 percent of their incomes in 1974 to 58.4 percent in 1987 (Apgar 1989).

A second consequence is that spiraling rent inflation means that fewer and fewer tenants can pay the rent. This means, of course, increasing eviction rates and homelessness.

A third consequence of the tight rental market for low-cost housing is that owners are not motivated to maintain their apartments. One in five poor households lives in housing classified by the Housing and Urban Development Department as substandard (Dionne 1989). One study of government data found that the distribution was skewed on the basis of race/ethnicity: 33 percent of poor black households were in substandard housing, compared to 27 percent of Latino households, and only 14 percent of white households (reported in Dionne 1989).

The fourth consequence of the low-cost apartment shortage is that owners are more apt to discriminate against racial/ethnic minorities. HUD conducted a survey in 1989 of twenty-five metropolitan areas and found that African Americans and Latinos face discrimination when they seek to rent an apartment: blacks 56 percent of the time and Latinos 50 percent of the time (reported by *New York Times* 1991). Presumably, if there were many more housing units than available renters, owners would be more willing to stifle their biases and rent to whomever had the money.

The Poor Pay More for Housing and Other Services and Commodities

Debbie Jones and her five children receive welfare from three sources.

DEBBIE: I get a SSI [Supplemental Security Income] check which contains $336 a month and I get a regular AFDC [Aid to Families with Dependent Children] check which contains $450 a month and [I get] $191 in food stamps. ... [My son receives the SSI.] He's, uh, has a learning disability. He goes to St. Peter's School 'cause they have special classes.

Debbie's family of six, then, receives $786 in cash and $191 in food stamps. Is this enough for their housing, food, health, clothing, and other needs?

The common assumption is that housing is affordable if it takes no more than 30 percent of a family's income (in Debbie's case this would be rent of $246 a month, considerably less than she had paid). A joint report by the Center on Budget and Policy Priorities and the Low Income Housing Information Service reported that nearly half of poor renters (47 percent) spend at least 70 percent of their income on housing and 56 percent (about 10 million people) paid more than half of their income for it (reported in DeParle 1991). When the poor pay more than 30 percent of their incomes for housing they are unable to afford the minimum basic necessities—a condition known as "shelter poverty."

The relatively high cost of shelter is not the only reason why urban poor renters have difficulty paying their rent and thus risk eviction. Money does not go as far in the inner city. Food and commodities cost more since supermarkets, discount stores, outlet malls, and warehouse clubs have bypassed inner-city neighborhoods. During the late 1970s and early 1980s major supermarkets migrated away from the inner cities to the suburbs. This exodus meant that only small, independent grocery stores or "mom and pop" type stores remained. Since many inner-city residents do not have transportation to get to the supermarkets and warehouse stores, they must buy from nearby stores, giving them monopoly powers. As a result, the poor pay more. New York City Department of Consumer Affairs found that groceries cost 8.8 percent more in poor neighborhoods than in middle-class areas. Similarly, in Chicago a spot check of five items in 1991 found that the poor paid 18 percent more. The finance charges that the poor pay for furniture, appliances, clothing, and the like are extremely high. Alan Alop, director of consumer litigation for the Legal Assistance Foundation of Chicago, says that "it isn't uncommon for the poor to pay annual rates of 40% or 45%" (cited in Schwadel 1992:A1). The poor, because they are poor credit risks, pay 2 percent or so to have their checks cashed. Gas stations and convenience stores charge more in the inner cities than they do in the suburbs (*Black Scholar* 1990).

Once again, the problem is compounded for nonwhites. A number of studies have shown that African Americans and Latinos face discrimination in employment and housing. A 1991 study by the Urban Institute, for example, that used carefully matched and trained pairs of white and black men applying for entry-level jobs, found that discrimination against blacks is "entrenched and widespread" (reported in Sklar 1993b:54). Similarly, studies in Chicago, Tampa, Atlanta, Denver, and other metropolitan areas have found consistently that African Americans and Latinos face discrimination in housing—i.e., they are denied equal access to rental or ownership opportunities; they pay more than whites for similar housing; or they are steered in segregated housing markets.

Joseph Boyce has called the additional price in dollars that one pays as a victim of racial discrimination the "Black Tax" (Boyce 1992). This "tax" is, for example, the hidden charge in rents and mortgages blacks pay because of housing and lending discrimination. It is the higher expense of owning an automobile because, as studies have shown, car dealers give larger discounts to whites than to blacks. It is the greater cost of doing business in the black community because of higher insurance and security rates. It is the cost of transport to jobs at companies that have fled to the suburbs.

The conclusion is obvious: Not only do the poor pay more for commodities and services in absolute terms, but they also pay a much larger proportion of their incomes than the nonpoor for comparable items. This is especially harsh for the poor when the items are necessities such as food, pharmaceuticals, clothing, housing, and utilities. Similarly, when the poor pay taxes on the items they purchase (sales tax), the tax takes more of their resources than it does from the nonpoor, making it a "regressive tax."

The Relative Powerlessness of Low-Income Renters

Renters, especially low-income renters, are subordinate to property owners. There are several reasons for this power imbalance. First, the legal systems in capitalist societies are biased in favor of those who own property.

> Landlords face few restrictions on their ability to rent, sell, or otherwise dispose of rental units. In most jurisdictions, landlords retain the right to convert rental units to condominiums or nonresidential uses, to demolish units, and to make capital improvements that permit a retargeting of rental units from one market to another. *Landlords in non–rent controlled cities are free to evict tenants without cause, to raise rents by any amount, and to choose freely among various categories of tenants* (emphasis added). (Gilderbloom and Appelbaum 1988:61–62)

The evidence is found in legislation and court decisions. Debbie, you will recall, went before the Housing Court in Chicago with pictures to document that her apartment was not maintained to minimum standards. The court, however, ruled to evict Debbie for her refusal to pay rent until the apartment was maintained in a satisfactory manner. As another example, the Colorado legislature in 1983 turned down a bill designed to force landlords to assure tenants of safe dwellings, working plumbing and appliances, and adequate heat. The argument by the major opponent of the measure, the Colorado Apartment Association, was that any habitability problems will be solved voluntarily by landlords (McGovern 1983). In the lobbying that occurred before that vote there was not an organized effort in support of the pro-tenant legislation. Had there been, the imbalance would have still favored the well-funded and well-placed Colorado Apartment Association.

Second, tenants usually act alone rather than together to overcome common problems. Typically, their one option when dissatisfied with a housing situation is to move. However, in tight housing markets this becomes less of an option since tenants are trapped by the marketplace (Gilderbloom and Appelbaum 1988:68). Even if another apartment can be found, there are economic costs (moving, security deposits, connecting utilities) and noneconomic costs (the loss of community attachments and social relations, moving children to another school) that make moving an unattractive option. Moreover, the choices of tenants, especially low-income tenants, are determined by the availability of work, transportation, and affordable housing. Their choices are also limited by the discriminatory practices of landlords, who often refuse to rent to families with children, racial minorities, and the poor in general. The result is that low-income tenants are trapped within certain areas, conferring on the landlord a "virtual monopoly of power in the relationship" (Vaughn 1972:82).

Rarely have tenants organized successfully to make collective demands for reasonable rents and reasonable maintenance. In Debbie's case she was involved in a successful effort when she lived in another apartment.

DEBBIE: We got a petition for all the tenants that were staying in the building. And we took them [the owners] to court. ... We got a settlement. After that we got to be, uh, the tenants got to be the, uh, landlord. ... We had a committee set up [with officers]. We kept everyone's rent and then paid the rent and then we got the landlord to come around and fix whatever needed to be done. But then the building went into condemnation. And, then everyone [had to move].

Feagin and Parker (1990) show that tenants' groups have only occasionally been successful. Even low-income tenants' groups have achieved some common goals but these efforts usually have not worked.

Whereas tenants rarely are organized as a cohesive force, landlords often are. Research has shown that landlords often cooperate with one another in setting rents through several social networks (Gilderbloom and Appelbaum 1988:59). The objective of the social organization of landlords is to maintain rents above an established minimum. The local landlords' association often suggests minimum rents and minimum rent increases for its members. Informal networks among landlords also establish guidelines through conversations in which rents are compared and mutual determinations made.

The largest and most influential landlord organization in the United States is the Institute of Real Estate Management (IREM) of the National Association of Realtors. This organization provides instructional materials to educate landlords. One IREM publication urges property managers to "act together" and provides the following advice:

Here's a tip: When you raise rents, *send a notice to your competition.* It's the best mail they'll get all day. Everyone is afraid to be the first to increase rents. *Once your competition sees you doing it, they'll very likely follow suit, thus making the rent increase a fact of life for all tenants.* The need to make rent adjustments to restore or safeguard the return on your investment should be very clear. Your manager must be made aware of what *your goal is: it is not occupancy levels, but money in the bank.* (Reprinted in Gilderbloom and Appelbaum 1988:61; emphasis in the quote added by Gilderbloom and Appelbaum)

That same IREM publication also

recommends that rent increases be made on January 1, because the holidays and poor weather make it difficult for tenants to relocate. Further ... January 1 is desirable because "the news media spends a lot of time reporting spiraling costs toward the end of the year. This coverage will help substantiate the need for more rent." (Gilderbloom and Appelbaum 1988:61)

In sum, the asymmetrical relationship between owner and tenant, which is buttressed by the formal and informal organization of landlords and by the bias of the legal system, means that the supply and demand factors of the marketplace do *not* shape the urban rental landscape (see Feagin and Parker 1990:1–36). Thus, racial discrimination by landlords limits the options of renters; rents are arbitrarily raised; apartment buildings are renovated for a higher-priced clientele or demolished for some other purpose; and renters are evicted. These common practices, in turn, take permanent housing away from some former renters, leaving them, like Debbie and her children, homeless.

8

Social Service Bureaucracy and Homelessness: Diane Moore

Diane Moore is a white single mother. She is thirty-five years old and has always lived in or near Tampa, Florida. She left high school after completing her junior year. Eric, her only child, is eight years old and living with his mother in the Metropolitan Ministries Family Shelter just north of downtown Tampa. They had been in the shelter about three weeks when Diane Moore allowed us to interview her.

Unsuspected Sources of Homelessness: Social Service and Welfare Programs

We have already documented in other chapters and interviews the meager U.S. welfare state. Public welfare—programs run and financed by the government for poor people—fails to provide levels of income and housing support that would prevent a growing number of them from becoming homeless. But the level of support is not the only way social service and welfare programs fail poor people. The agencies and bureaucracies that administer these programs regularly abuse their recipients as they distribute the meager resources that are available. In some cases the way these organizations provide the "social safety net" actually becomes the immediate source of poor persons' homelessness. This is precisely what happened to Diane Moore and her son, Eric.

Ethnographer Elliot Liebow's recent study included considerable observations of homeless women's encounters with the welfare bureaucracy. He concludes that there is an underlying ideology at work in the providing organizations: "Whatever the form, it boils down to something like this: We mustn't make things too easy for them (mental patients in state hospitals, welfare clients, homeless people, the dependent poor generally). That just encourages their dependency" (1993:141).

Liebow believes this prescription against "encouraging dependency" makes the abuse of poor people easy and legitimate. The poor may be dealt with harshly because in the end it is "for their own good." They won't develop the negative characteristic of dependence.

> "For their own good" we may set welfare payments at a level below what is needed to live on or refuse a person a second bowl of soup. "For their own good" it is all right to make them wait in lines for hours, harass them with questions, demand unavailable documentation or otherwise make them jump through hoops for one or another entitlement, treat them discourteously if not with outright contempt, withhold a service product, "keep them on the move" with limits on the length of stay in a shelter, and so on. (Liebow 1993:142)

The backdrop for the presumption that we are at risk of giving poor people too much too easily, of course, is public policies in the United States that assume many of the poor are not deserving of any public support whatsoever. The end result is that many social service and welfare bureaucracies, administrators, and workers begin to tend more to their own needs than to those of the poor people they are there to assist. Says Liebow:

> Otherwise well-intentioned workers and administrators are encouraged to tolerate or ignore the needless hardships or the system failures that so often attend the day-to-day operations of our support programs. Beginning with the proposition that "you mustn't make things too easy for them," we end up with an array of support systems staffed by administrators, supervisors, and workers who sometimes forget why they are there, and who put organizational needs ahead of needs of the people they are supposed to serve. Examples abound. (Liebow 1993:142–143)

Diane Moore and her eight-year-old son Eric are one of these examples. The actions of a social service bureaucracy and one of its workers have made them homeless.

DIANE: Nineteen-eighty-four I moved into an apartment. I had a knee injury. I was AFDC. I was on County Section 8 where my rent was very, very low at the time. I paid six dollars a month. I was getting one eighty-five from welfare. I had a knee injury. I had surgery. I had food stamps. I had medical expenses taken care of on Medicaid. I was doin' pretty well. So I was on Section 8 for two years. Eighty-six I lost my Section 8 by not following the instructions from my worker that I had to get some kinda paper from Eric's dad to say that I was still married or divorced or got child support.

INTERVIEWER: They told you you had to have this documentation?

DIANE: Well, they told, she told me sometime last year, but she said that she would overlook it because his father wasn't here in Tampa. He was in California. And as long as I was on welfare then she knew I wasn't getting any child support. She knew it anyway. I don't know what the big deal was.

INT.: But you had to have this piece of paper?

DIANE: But I have to have it. I had to go down to the Legal Aid and either get a, uh, final separation totally or some kinda evidence. That's what I couldn't understand. But she never made it really, really clear to me. But because she had papers already from California, where he was supposed to pay child support, and he never paid one dime. And welfare, they had his last address. And they pulled him in. So what they did from there I don't know. So, I called the landlord and asked him would he work it out by the week because I was getting paid by the week. And he told me no, that I had to come up with two hundred and eighty-five dollars at once—all at once—or I would be causing big problems. He'd have the sheriff evict me. To avoid this when my month ran out, I had already moved on my own.

INT.: OK. So this is after you've lost your Section 8?

DIANE: Right.

INT.: The Section 8 worker, the Section 8 program, had told you, like a year or so ago, that you had to have this. But your worker told you she would overlook it?

DIANE: Right.

INT.: Did you hear from Section 8 again?

DIANE: No. What happened was I called her and asked her if I could renew my, my, um, papers. And she said no because I didn't have that particular paper. And she said if I did, I could reapply, reapply again but I'd be on a longer waiting list. So if I went down to Legal Aid this week and got the papers she wanted, then I could reapply. But I could … it sure was no guarantee that I'd be back on it. There was no guarantee and I'd have to be on a waiting list.

After losing her Section 8 rent subsidy, Diane looks for housing she can afford. She ends up in a trailer house in Land O' Lakes, north of Tampa, in lousy housing conditions. Poverty incomes may command housing, but rarely is it decent and livable. Diane moves out.

DIANE: I wasn't stayin' out there because there was rats in the ceiling. They were coming out and they, they were half the size of a cat because they're field rats. But see I didn't know all this until after I was out there and it started raining and they started rumbling through the ceilings and coming out when you could see 'em physically, you know.

You know we had some bad storms up there. These rats were stirred up. So when we found out there were rats, we tried to catch 'em and it just, it all fell apart out there. I mean I was scared, Eric was scared.

Diane then tries to find a place to live in Tampa, near her job, but she cannot afford it and she and her son finally land in a shelter for homeless families.

INTERVIEWER: So you're looking for a new trailer closer to the city ...?

DIANE: OK, the rent was higher. The rent there, she wanted, um, seventy-five a week, plus you had to pay your own utilities.

INT.: And with what you're making ...

DIANE: I couldn't make it. I couldn't a made it.

INT.: You can't get the trailer in Tampa?

DIANE: She wanted a hundred dollars right off the bat for a deposit and seventy-five for the first week. That's one seventy-five and I don't even—I didn't even have that then because I was already broke.

INT.: And then after that starts the two nights in the car?

DIANE: With my friends. I had to put my stuff in storage.

INT.: Over to the Dorcus House [another Tampa shelter], another night in the car.

DIANE: Right, And I went to a church the next morning.

INT.: And then here.

DIANE: Then here [Metropolitan Ministries Shelter in Tampa].

INT.: Have you ever been in a shelter before?

DIANE: No.

INT.: Have you ever been out, without a place to go before?

DIANE: No. It's not a very good feeling.

We inadvertently became aware of another example of a social service program and policy contributing to homelessness during the course of our research. At a forum on homelessness held at the Chicago Public Library, several women who spoke derided a program called Project Chance. This program, run by the Illinois Department of Public Aid, offered AFDC recipients job training and work experience while allowing them to retain their other benefits, including food stamps and Medicaid. If needed, the state also assisted the women with day care and transportation costs. The program was small in scope and could accept only some of those who volunteered for it. Those who volunteered to participate also were confronted with a host of program rules having to do, for the most part, with dates, times, and places. If any of those rules were violated by the women, Project Chance could cut, reduce, or eliminate benefits the women would have legally had and been entitled to if they had never agreed to participate in the program. This loss of benefits, the women at the forum testified, was pushing some women onto the streets or into the shelters.

Bureaucracy Meets the Urban Housing Crisis

Urban poor people like Diane Moore are caught in a trap: a growing low-wage economy with increasing and intensifying poverty on the one hand and a shrinking supply of low-income affordable housing on the other. The decision to take away Diane's Section 8 rent subsidy must be seen in the context of this contradiction. Only a small minority of the poor in the United States receive any housing subsidy—in fact, the smallest percentage in the industrial world. That she can reapply in reality means that it is highly unlikely she will be able to regain her housing assistance.

Section 8 is a federally financed program that determines how much a recipient can afford to pay in rent and then provides the difference between that and the "going market rate" to the apartment landlord each month. Section 8 certificates are not an entitlement; they are given out on an "as available" basis. And they are not very available. By the mid-1980s, only about 20 percent of eligible low-income renter households were receiving Section 8 assistance (Carliner 1987). Thus, in almost all cities, large and small, waiting lists for Section 8 certificates are very long. In the 1980s, waiting lists became so long in many cities, including Tampa, that local housing authorities simply quit taking applications.

The Section 8 program has at least one other serious limitation. Recipients are required to find, usually within two months, apartments that meet housing code and quality standards and are available for no more than what the federal government determines to be a "fair market rent." Few apartments satisfy both of these Section 8 criteria. The result is that even a majority of poor households who do qualify and actually receive Section 8 benefits end up forgoing them because they are unable to find housing that qualifies (Carliner 1987:121).

Elliot Liebow recently found, in the Washington, D.C., metropolitan area, that even the "most qualified" women living in a homeless shelter waited a minimum of two years for Section 8 assistance. Others waited indefinitely.

Eligible persons are assigned places on the waiting list according to a point-preference system: five points for living in a shelter or car or substandard housing, for being involuntarily displaced, or for paying more than half of one's income for rent; two points for living in the country; and one point for being a victim of domestic violence or for having a family member in foster care due to lack of housing. Even for the most qualified applicants, waiting time for an efficiency apartment ... is a minimum of two years. For eligible persons with less than the minimum preference points, however, waiting time is "indefinite." (Liebow 1993:317)

Clearly, if Diane Moore reapplies for a Section 8 rent subsidy it will not solve her immediate dilemma and allow her and her son to leave the shelter.

Homeless Shelters

During the course of our interviewing and ethnographic work we spent a considerable amount of time in two different shelters.[1] We used some of this time to observe the operation of the shelter, its staff, and the shelter experience of residents.

Both of the shelters in which observation was undertaken are "program"shelters. They do not simply feed and "warehouse" homeless persons and families overnight, returning them to the streets each morning. Rather, if compliance to shelter rules is satisfactory and residents convince the shelter staff they are diligently pursuing employment and housing, they may stay for an extended period of time.

Both of the shelters' programs tend to treat their residents' homelessness as a matter of values, more specifically as a matter of culture of poverty values (Lewis 1971; Banfield 1974). Homeless persons tend to be regarded as the culture of poverty in action. They are often perceived as irresponsible, unable to sacrifice the moment and delay gratification (drinking instead of job hunting or buying cigarettes instead of saving the money), valuing education or training very little if at all, and suffering from a low achievement drive or lack of initiative and aspiration, which is at once thought to be the cause of their homeless predicament and their inability to overcome it. As the director of one of the shelters said to one of us when explaining the majority of homeless families she has seen:

Families who just ... have missed it somewhere along the line. Somehow they just have never learned what they needed to learn to get along in this world. They have no sense of planning, no sense of reality, responsibility. A lot of them are just impulsive and childish and irresponsible. And it's like they're almost in a state of arrested development. ... If there was someone somewhere just to take the time with them and sort of hit them over the head and say, "hey, obviously this is not working, you know your current life-style is not working, these are the types of things that you're missing out on ... ," and really lead them through the process, and teach them. ... They are salvageable. They don't have to be on welfare and they don't have to be homeless. ... And that's what we want to do here. That's our major goal.

A counselor in the same shelter identifies the inability to manage money, the lack of financial management skills, as almost always contributing to the homeless crisis of the families on her caseload. The shelters attribute their residents' situation to individual or family traits, characteristics, and values, which are essentially similar to those of the culture of poverty and which might alternatively be identified as the "culture of homelessness" in this context. In this way, the shelter and its staff come to perceive homelessness as a matter of individual or family deviance. The individual or family traits, characteristics, values and the "deviant" behaviors based on them that have made the homeless homeless must be changed; that is an important, if not the most important, role for the shelter.

The underlying ideology of these shelters encourages the homeless person to take full responsibility for his or her situation and the solution to it. The promotion of this ideology, however explicit or subtle, is facilitated by the fact that shelter residents are in no position to challenge it. They must be and stay in the shelter since there is no alternative food or housing available to them. As a black pregnant welfare mother of two put it to us, "Shoot, where am I gonna go?"

But many homeless people do resist the shelter, even forgoing the necessities of life provided there. The seemingly inexplicable irony of increasing numbers of homeless persons juxtaposed with empty shelter beds speaks to this issue.

When bitter cold hit Chicago in late December 1990, the media reported in disbelief: "The homeless won't come in from the cold." The city's Department of Human Services publicized the fact that there were over 4,000 shelter beds available but 600 were not being used. Film crews followed department workers in unsuccessful attempts to coax the homeless into shelters. All this occurred amid the annual U.S. Conference of Mayors report of increasing homelessness in almost all American cities.

The media's interpretation was a *psychological* one: "These people are crazy. ... They want to be on the street. ... They won't take the help available to them. ... They want to be free to hustle." A more accurate *political* interpretation is that the homeless are resisting the control, threats to their autonomy and privacy, dependency, and victimization that come with shelterization (Talley and Timmer 1994).

As the shelter promotes the ideology of full responsibility or "victim blame," there is a tendency not to believe its residents, particularly when they blame the system.

Often the shelter staff does not appear to talk or interact much with the residents. Often the staff does not appear to know the residents' circumstances, the stories of their own homelessness. As one staff member said: "I really don't talk to these people very much. I really don't get to know many of them very well. I don't know if that's intentional on my part or not." But even if the residents' stories are heard, there is a tendency not to trust them—a tendency to interpret what they say as the "hustle" of a deviant. The shelter worker may become as guarded against the "con" of the homeless person as the correctional counselor is guarded against the convict's story, the youth counselor against the delinquent's, or the drug and alcohol counselor against the addict's or alcoholic's. Inclination to trust or believe a homeless person's story seems to occur only once there is some perception that the resident accepts the ideology being promoted by the shelter and its staff.

The ubiquitous promotion of middle-class values, mores, and behavior in these shelters is apparently designed as an antidote to the culture of poverty, to the culture of homelessness. Shelter residents often resent the middle-class standards of orderliness and cleanliness, middle-class moralisms about appropriate behavior, the official shelter rules and regulations, and the rigid daily routine. The resentment may grow when residents are officially cited for rule violations. Alternatively, Extra Mile Reports are used to reinforce exceptional displays of shelter-required conformity and responsibility. A thirteen-year-old inner-city black kid tells some other kids in the shelter that a female staff member who he doesn't like and is having a conflict with "sucks cock." Both he and his mother are disciplined, even though this is a very typical and normal "street" remark for kids who come from where this thirteen-year-old does. Nonetheless, middle-class morality had been violated. A mother and her daughter are scolded for "cracker crumbs" under their portion of a dining room table. An eight-year-old girl is given an extra work assignment after her chair left "black marks" on the wall behind her. The enforcement of middle-class morality can become extremely severe in the shelter. During the course of my observation, one of the shelters instituted a policy of not paying for children's drug prescriptions if their parents were spending money on cigarettes. In short, shelter staff expend considerable time and energy enforcing "middle-class order" around the shelter, enforcing both the written official shelter rules and regulations and other unwritten "middle-class standards" such as no swearing. All of this is often resented by residents, and more important, it is often perceived by them to be irrelevant to resolving their homelessness. This view is shared by some staff members as well. As a counselor in one of the shelters confided in me:

I had to kick a family out yesterday that only needed until the fifth. They were going to get paid and all three of them were working their tails off. But they've been smoking in their room. Well, I had warned them twice. Then I got the word I had to kick them out. They've got a little kid. ... And Ron [another staff member] put up the money for them to stay in a hotel so they wouldn't be out in the street.

Homeless persons are easily controlled in the shelter setting, which can be seen as analogous to the control of delinquents in juvenile institutions or prisoners in correctional facilities. The accounting of comings and goings, lack of privacy, and regimented daily schedules in the homeless shelter are evidence of this similarity in institutional function. It is seen as simply impossible to shelter large groups of vulnerable strangers without the tight restrictions and rule enforcement reminiscent of correctional facilities (Talley and Timmer 1994).

Of course the daily management of a shelter with 100 to 250 residents requires some organization, procedures, and rules and regulations. But it is very difficult for most residents and even some staff to appreciate the link between not smoking (or only smoking in certain places at certain times), never having a beer after work, going to breakfast each morning, and making your bed and finding permanent jobs, sources of income, and housing. The irrelevance of many of these rules and regulations is highlighted when the shelter makes their enforcement a higher priority than stabilization and support for the homeless (as in the case described by the shelter counselor above). When this happens, it is clear that the shelter is functioning more as an institution to manage and control a deviant homeless population than it is an institution to assist the homeless in overcoming their employment and housing problem. Indeed, the homeless shelter itself can be a source of homelessness. It can, as its homeless residents recognize, "put you out." For the extremely poor and homeless, the shelter is often just one more part of a meager and insensitive welfare bureaucracy.

"Class" Divisions Among the Homeless

In both of the shelters we observed that a distinction is drawn between the "deserving homeless" and the "undeserving homeless." The "deserving homeless" are persons and families who are "legitimately homeless." Through no or little fault of their own they have fallen victim to circumstances that have left them with nowhere to go. They are responsible and deserve and appreciate the shelter's assistance. The "undeserving homeless," or "bums," however, are those persons or families who are believed to be homeless by virtue of their own attitudes, values, and irresponsibility—in other words, by way of the culture of poverty or the culture of homelessness. The "undeserving homeless" may refer to single persons or families on the street or inside the shelter. They are not only undeserving but unappreciative of shelter assistance when they receive it. They are also generally regarded as manipulative in their attempts to gain the support and services of the shelter.

This "class" distinction among the homeless is made by the managers of the homeless population—the shelter administration and staff—and then passed on to the homeless residents of the shelter. The homeless residents are both directly and indirectly socialized to this distinction. The distinction is either directly communicated by the staff to the residents or it is passed on indirectly through conformity to the shelter's program and rules and regulations. Those who conform to the shelter's requirements and at least give the appearance of accepting its underlying ideology become the "deserving homeless." Those who do not are usually identified as undeserving.

The socialization of the homeless themselves to this kind of distinction was brought home by the experience of a family we interviewed soon after they had entered the shelter. Both parents had been laid off. Soon they were unable to pay their rent and were about to be evicted. They put their three daughters, their dog, and all of their possessions in a small pickup truck and a station wagon and moved halfway across the country. Running out of money and unable to find jobs or housing in their new locale, they lived for a short time in the station wagon. Frightened, desperate, and at wits' end, they finally found their way to the shelter. The shelter took them in, providing a roof over their heads, food, and medical care. The shelter staff soon began to regard them as a model family. To facilitate a more permanent solution to the family's crisis, the shelter employed the woman as a receptionist and switchboard operator and the man as a shelter maintenance man. The shelter provided a small wage for each of them and gave them a house across the street, owned by the agency that runs the shelter, to live in. Soon after this, in our frequent interaction with the man who was the husband and father, we would listen to him make the "class distinction": He referred to the "bums" on the street who lived in the neighborhood and lined up three times a day at a nearby soup kitchen and the unappreciative rule-breaking "bums," "jerks," and "assholes" who populated the family shelter. Never mind that most of these people were in the same situation he had been in only a few weeks earlier.

That the ideology of the shelter includes this class distinction is sharply reflected in those homeless residents of shelters who do not want to admit their homelessness. They do not want to be identified and stigmatized as "one of them"; they say, "I'm just in transition" or "I'm not in dire need." Or as a homeless black jazz trumpeter from New York City, out of work and living in the Loop shelter in Chicago, told one of us while blowing his horn in Grant Park, "I'm not one of those people ... I'm just down on my luck a little bit. ... It'll be alright later on."

This class division among the homeless, made by both the managers of the homeless and the homeless themselves, can function only to prevent the kind of solidarity that must precede the emergence of an effective homeless political coalition or movement. Only a unified, not a "class-divided," homeless population can begin to influence the social and economic policies necessary to reform the structural sources of homelessness.

One Woman's Experience in the Shelter

Diane Moore's response to our queries about her life in the shelter paralleled and reinforced much of our observation there:

DIANE: Rules and regulations? Well, they're a lot different than you would have at a home, I guess. I mean, I'm thirty-five and never been told you have to be in bed by eleven o'clock, OK? That's a little outrageous. You can't smoke in any of the rooms. You have to smoke out in the courtyard. You can't smoke in the dining room. I do what I did tonight. I cut hair. I don't know. When you live in the shelter, you live on, like on a day-to-day basis. You can't plan anything 'cause you never know what's gonna happen or who's got what goin' or, you just don't know. The rules are after ten o'clock you can't go out at night. If you stay out all night, it's an automatic eviction. If you can stay out at somebody's house, they figure you can stay at the same place permanent. So they don't allow you to go out after ten o'clock at night. The neighborhood we live in is kinda, it's scary to walk out at nights. It was just a couple weeks ago in broad daylight out in front of the center they had taken in a Spanish couple, or a Spanish family, and they lived in the motel part 'cause the house [the shelter] didn't have any rooms. And she was coming up to talk to a counselor and a black guy took her purse right off her arm in broad daylight and started running down the street. She lost all her ID, all her money, and everything, what money she had. The neighborhood's not too much to talk about. Its got too much winos. It is strictly almost black over here, this area.

INTERVIEWER: How do you feel about the way the shelter treats you?

DIANE: I mean its not like livin' in luxury. You have to like almost earn your keep if you stay here. You have to do odd-and-end jobs that you'd have to do in your own house anyway. The dishes have to be done by somebody, so it might as well be us because we ate. But if you come visit us tomorrow night, I probably won't be here.

INT.: How come?

DIANE: Because I'm up on channel 8. And I'm gonna call a couple of other people tomorrow. I've had it with this place. I was told if I come in tomorrow night after seven, I will not get fed. And I don't ask for lunch. And I ask for my supper when I come in. And I was told tonight by a few of the people that one guy came in after seven and he didn't get to eat and got bitched out about it. You miss supper. Supper's at five. They will not serve you after seven. You want me to really spill it, huh? People around here are exploding left and right. One of the guys exploded at the guard the other night. I don't know why, but he did. ... But this place is, is getting people upset because you can't do this, you get a brown slip. I got a brown slip for not havin' my beds made the other day. But Ron [staff member] told me to overlook it because he put on the brown slip that my room's always clean. I was told if you get three brown slips you're evicted. If you're caught smoking in your rooms, you're evicted. I'm sure if I called somebody tomorrow and have him check out this place, I'll probably be evicted. I was told if you don't follow the rules right to the T, you can be evicted. If you don't find a job, you can be evicted. If you don't do your chores, you can get in trouble. So I do my chores in the morning and I told Ron I have the dishes and the pots to do and I was not gonna mop the floor before I go to work. And I've looked. 'Cause there's other people in here they haven't asked to do any chores and they're not out lookin' for a job. And I told, uh, Huey [another staff member] tonight that I was not gonna do the floors in the morning. So Ron is supposed to make arrangements for somebody else to do the floors for me. So if I get a brown slip, I'm goin' right to Ron. ... The problem with this place is these people don't care how many problems you got. ... The counselors, the people that generally work here ... I'm gonna make a big stink about this place. Sure, the building is fine, the rooms are fine. The food ain't good. The way the staff treats you ain't good. ... The rooms are fine. It's the staff. I don't know what they're afraid of.

INT.: What about the hours in the place? When do you have to ...

DIANE: Alright, they changed the hours. Breakfast is from six A.M. to seven. After seven twenty, you do not eat if you miss breakfast. Eleven-thirty is lunch. Five o'clock is supper time. Anybody comes in after seven goes without a meal. I was also told that if you took a lunch, a sack lunch, you don't get a supper when you come back in. They figure two sandwiches is gonna hold you over for lunch and supper. You won't get a hot meal. ... You can go all day long but you have to sign out and sign in. So that they always know where you are. ...

INT.: You have to be in this building by ten?

DIANE: And you have to be in your room by eleven. You can't come back out and smoke a cigarette. You can't come back out to, to talk to anybody or anything. And if that's not imprisonment, I don't know what is. I talked to my boss that I worked with last year, as a friend. He said, "It sounds like a good place on TV," and this and that, and all the money that these people are getting for show, they should treat us a little bit better. With food, kindness, and not so many stupid little rules and tryin' to kick you, threaten to kick you out every two minutes because you didn't do something or you did something wrong. So I told him about it. I told him, "You know what I had for supper the other night? I ate string beans. String beans because the potatoes, scalloped potatoes, tasted sour." Said I was afraid to eat it 'cause I was gonna throw up my guts again. The bell peppers, the hamburger in the middle was just as raw, just like you put it in there. It wasn't even cooked. The rice was hard as pebbles. It wasn't even cooked. They took what was left over from last night and mixed it up with beans tonight and put it on top of rice. That's what I had for supper last night, string beans and a half a glass of Kool-aid that's like three days old. The milk this mornin' tasted sour. Four kids, four kids didn't go to school today, headaches, stomachaches, vomiting, and fevers. I thought I had food poisoning because of the taste that I had in my mouth. I had an awful ... matter of fact I ate at five. And at nine o'clock I was throwing up. That's six, seven, eight. Usually anywhere from three to four or five hours after you've eaten food that's not been prepared right, or food that's no good, you automatically get sick. They said it's the virus goin' around. So I'm lettin' 'em think what they wanna think. And I says you can call Poison Control and they'll tell you the same symptoms can tell you it's a virus as food poisoning.

The Myth of Family as the Solution to Homelessness

In August 1993, city officials in New York announced that in order to reduce crowding in city shelters, homeless persons would be allowed to stay in them only if they did not have friends or relatives to move in with. This, of course, effectively passes responsibility for a growing number of homeless persons from government to the families of the homeless themselves. Officials in New York, as in other cities, know that very poor families are already often doubled up and tripled up in both public housing and other run-down apartments. They also know that this over-crowding often precipitates homelessness.

Some social science experts on homelessness, like Peter Rossi (1989), see the alienation and isolation of homeless individuals from their families as having to do primarily with the personal "disabilities" of homeless persons. Families are unable to cope with the mental illness, drug and alcohol abuse, or other handicaps of their homeless members. The behaviors of the homeless themselves are the cause of separation and alienation from their families. In this way, Rossi blames the victim, but does so in a way that seems to imply that we will not be able to rely on family to solve the homelessness problem. We just can't expect these families to respond to the kind of desperate people who are homeless.

The reality is that most homeless persons are extremely poor and come from poor families that simply do not have the kinds of resources, like housing and income, that can support homeless members. Besides, it is increasingly the case that the whole family is homeless. How can extremely poor families and households assist extremely poor homeless persons? How can homeless families aid homeless family members?

Beyond extreme poverty and/or homelessness, homeless persons have many other reasons for not being able to rely on their families for shelter. David Wagner's (1994) recent research suggests that Rossi has it turned around. Isolation and separation from family are not caused by the problematic behavior of homeless family members, but more often by the problematic behavior of the family itself. Wagner's ethnographic work has found that, like Americans from all classes, homeless persons are often forced to escape their families. Often the victims of parents (natural, adoptive, or foster), siblings, mothers' boyfriends, uncles, aunts, or cousins, homeless persons have been physically and sexually abused by their families. Homeless women have been beaten and battered by their spouses or male partners. Homeless spouses and children become victims of family dissolution. These are the families that the poor and homeless are supposed to return to; these are the families that are supposed to be the solution to their members' homelessness. The housed or affluent, of course, are not expected or encouraged to return to these kinds of exploitive family circumstances.

In fact, Wagner found that many homeless persons resist any family contact and assistance even if it means continuing to live on the streets or in a shelter. Homeless family members are often fearful that the "help" they receive from hostile families will include their institutionalization, losing custody of their children, or being stigmatized as a failure. And their experience indicates that these fears are real.

In addition to all of this, homeless people, again like people from all other social classes, exhibit a strong desire for privacy and independence. As one young homeless street person Wagner interviewed said about his family, "I can't be a burden on them. I have to get out of this myself" (1994:66).

Although Wagner correctly points out how experts like Rossi blame the victim for the failure of families to support and care for their homeless members, he too ends up blaming another victim—the family itself. Although homeless persons are most times unable to turn to patriarchal, poor, hostile, or abusive families, these families must be put in a wider political and economic context. These families themselves are victims. Left vulnerable to the market and economic transformations, they are unprotected and unsupported by the state. Lacking most of the government supports provided by the social democracies and welfare states of Europe, a vast number of American families are left without income security, subsidized housing, guaranteed health care, access to quality education and training, and day care for their children. Rather than a solution to the extreme poverty and homelessness of their members, many American families, left to "go it alone" by the state, are often another source of these problems.

Diane Moore's family is an example. Once homeless, she and Eric had no family to turn to.

DIANE: So we got back in the car and we left. I went back uptown and seen my sister, couldn't stay with her. She lives in an all-adult trailer and she had a very small traveler's trailer. It's very old and it's not big enough room for three people, so—and they don't allow kids in the park at all. They, they didn't even like her watchin' him at nights. ... I think I went downhill also when my grandmother died, because my mother put me through so much hell when I took care of my grandmother the last month that she died. I don't, I don't have any other family but my sister. And now that I'm moved in here, she doesn't contact me or call me at all. I guess because I threw it up in her face last year. For six months I took her in my apartment without Section 8 knowin' about it and helped her out, fed her, bought things for her. We had holidays together. And I threw this in her face three weeks ago and told her, "This is the way it is, you know. I helped you and now you can't help me. Then you can forget about me." So we haven't called each other at all. And I won't call her. 'Til doomsday. I won't call her. Even if she comes lookin' for me, she won't find me.

INTERVIEWER: The only other family now is your mother?

DIANE: Yeah, which I have no use for at all. I wouldn't even call her my mother. She ran my grandmother into her own grave by expenses, worry, and neglecting my grandmother when she was dying. I guess she couldn't handle it. I don't know what her problem was. Because we had gotten into a fight, a big fight, about May ... and my grandmother got us back together about Christmastime. January of eighty-five, my grandmother was sick and she had just turned eighty-one. And she went to the doctors and March she had surgery. She had an implant. And then March they took it out and they did another surgery. And they found out she had a tumor in her stomach that was producin' fluid. The first part of April my mother took her home in her own apartment and my grandmother was there all by herself. And I called the hospital to find out if she was still here, if I could talk to her without my mom knowin' about it. And they said she went home. So I called her house on April sixth and she cried and cried on the phone, "Please come get me. Please come get me." So when I got there, before my mom got there, I just packed her up some clothes and I took her in a wheelchair and put her in my friend's car and took her to my apartment. I took care of her that whole weekend. And she didn't seem right. She was worried about my mom finding our, finding out that I had took her. So we called HRS [Health and Rehabilitation Services, the largest state Social Service agency in Florida] Adult Abuse. They came out and they asked my grandmother where she wanted to stay and who she wanted to stay with and if she knew where she was. And they thought she was in her right mind. And she said, "Yes." Well that Monday I took her to the doctors. Saint Joseph took her from me. It was like, "She's mine," you know. And I said, "No, if she has to stay, I'll come back and help take care of her." And she stayed a week. They released her back into my care, not to my mom's but mine. And my mom got bent out of shape and caused all kinds of problems. Came rambling and raging and callin' us all kinds of names and causing me problems with my apartment. The sheriff was aware of this.

INT.: You're still in the Section 8 apartment?

DIANE: Yeah. I took care of my grandmother the last year that I, before I had moved out. I mean this year before I moved out. She died last year. I think that's when everything went downhill. It was when she, 'cause I always called her for advice and I guess if she was here today I probably wouldn't be here at the shelter. She woulda either come up and gave me the money, or I woulda gone and stayed with her, or she woulda had some of her Eastern Star friends help me out in some kinda way. I just know she would.

INT.: So your grandmother's not here. You can't go to your mother or your sister?

DIANE: No. I wouldn't go to my mom anyway. She's nuts.

INT.: So that means there's no family?

DIANE: Right. It's just me and Eric.

No Culture of Poverty, No Welfare Dependency

Among the homeless women Liebow observed, he found nothing in the way of culture of poverty values or behaviors that would encourage welfare dependency. In fact, many of the women attempt to avoid the welfare system if at all possible. Many find it too uncertain, unpredictable, and arbitrary. They see welfare bureaucracy as "a world of hurry-up-and-wait, of double-binds and contradictions" (Liebow 1993:147). They have experienced the system's contempt and the myriad rules and regulations that prevent it from truly assisting those it is supposed to help.

Diane Moore is one of these women. She has gotten off AFDC even though it means less money and that her rent increases.

INTERVIEWER: But now you're working. When you had Section 8 and things were going well, you were on welfare.

DIANE: Right.

INT.: When did you get off welfare and start working? When you moved out of the Section 8 house?

DIANE: No, I was already off AFDC. I started working the first part of eighty-six.

INT.: While you were still in your Section 8 place?

DIANE: Right. You see my rent went from six to forty-six dollars a month.

INT.: When you're working?

DIANE: When I'm working.

INT.: What kind of work were you doing and how much money were you making?

DIANE: OK. I'm a waitress, two-oh-one an hour plus tips. As a cook there was four thirty-five. We took thirty-five cents out every hour for coffee, whatever. So actually it was four dollars an hour. I made, brought-home pay was like forty-six dollars. If I was a cook I brought home, like seventy-six, eighty-six dollar check.

INT.: A week?

DIANE: A week.

Many homeless women avoid the welfare bureaucracy out of their well-founded fear that their children will be taken from them and placed in an institution or foster care. Social Service providers are obligated to report cases of neglect to the welfare bureaucracy and other legal authorities. Being homeless and living on the streets or in a shelter comes very close to meeting legal definitions of child neglect—no matter how competent, caring, and loving the mother might be (Wright 1989:120). Only because she is sick and in a shelter does Diane reluctantly agree to go back on AFDC. She says:

Although I'm tryin' to keep from, I didn't want to go back on HRS [meaning back on AFDC]. I didn't want to go on that route again because of my mother had called them several times on false charges of child abuse. And that's why I'm hesitating about going back on welfare. But at this point right now I've got a real bad infection and my counselor here wants me to get feeling better before I go out and look for a job. And I already told her that I already applied for AFDC. For me to get the doctor bills paid now, I have to go back on so I can get the medical treatment that I need.

Notes

1. This section is taken in large part from Doug A. Timmer, "Homelessness as Deviance: The Ideology of the Shelter," *Free Inquiry in Creative Sociology* 16 (2) (1988):163–170.

9

Runaway and Throwaway Teens: Jeffrey Giancarlo

Jeffrey Giancarlo is white and nineteen years old. He grew up in a middle-class suburb of Chicago with his parents, one older sister, and a younger brother. Jeffrey and his parents do not get along. Jeffrey ran away from home at thirteen; after a brief period "on the street," his father brought him back. In and out of trouble with both his family and legal authorities, Jeffrey ended up in Chicago, homeless at age seventeen.

Youth Homelessness

One in every seven homeless persons is a child aged nineteen or younger, according to estimates from the National Health Care for the Homeless Program (Wright 1989:59). Of these, approximately one-third are on the streets by themselves, while two-thirds are in homeless families. Most of those who are alone are teenagers, perhaps as young as twelve and thirteen. Males and females are found in equal numbers (Wright 1989:59).

Most accounts attribute teen homelessness to runaway or throwaway children fleeing abusive or otherwise unacceptable family situations. In a study of homeless youth in Chicago in summer 1992, three-quarters of the teens interviewed reported having been hit or beaten by those who raised them. Seventeen percent reported being locked into closets or basements. One-sixth reported having been sexually assaulted by family members. Almost half reported they had lived with a person with an alcohol problem (Chicago Coalition for the Homeless 1993:12).

In Chicago, nearly 14,000 teenagers are reported as runaway or missing each year. National figures are estimated at 1 to 1.3 million (Voices for Illinois Children, as quoted in Chicago Coalition for the Homeless 1993:12). Seventy-two percent of the homeless teens in the Chicago study said they had run away from home, with most experiencing numerous episodes of homelessness. Most of these teens had left home at least once before their sixteenth birthday (Chicago Coalition for the Homeless 1993:8–9).

Jeffrey Giancarlo was thirteen when he first ran away.

JEFFREY: Everything wasn't straight with me and my mom. We were fightin' constantly. My mom didn't give a fuckin' shit, man. She was just like, hey, "I wish you were never even born." I think eleven years old I really started gettin' into drugs a lot. And I was smokin' cocaine and snortin' cocaine—you know, shootin' up. I was into marijuana a lot. Between the ages of thirteen and fourteen I was doin' that: sellin' drugs. That's when I first ran away. I hit the streets for about a month, or a month and a half. I was sellin' cocaine to survive. And my dad found me and beat the fuck out of me. Then me and my mom got into a big argument where I swore at her and I got scared of my dad because I was always scared of him. My dad is a real fuckin' prick. I was away from home as much as possible doin' more and more drugs. My friends and I got really sick on drugs and booze one day. I was really ripped. My mom hit me over the head with a pole because she couldn't control me. I went off. I pulled out a knife on her. She called my dad, he called the police, and they arrested me.

Jeffrey's poor relationship with his parents centered on his use of drugs and alcohol. Their conflict was, in Jeffrey's words, "Because of me doin' drugs, and my parents hatin' me for it." Jeffrey Giancarlo's substance abuse caused him difficulties not only at home, but also with legal authorities. By the time he threatened his mother with the knife, neighbors had made numerous complaints to the police about his drug use.

As a result of the knife incident, Jeffrey spent two weeks in a juvenile detention center in Chicago. This particular detention center, the Audy Home, holds up to 500 juveniles at one time.

The official purpose of the juvenile court system in the United States is to work on behalf of minors rather than simply punishing them for criminal behaviors. Troubled families are to be identified and assisted. But the reality of the juvenile court is often different than its ideology. In Jeffrey's case, the system's intervention failed. The Giancarlo family was never successfully reunited.

JEFFREY: I lived through a lot of shit going through there [the Audy Home]. I was raped. Never go there again. I'm not goin' back to jail. From there I went to a psychiatric ward, where I spent seventeen months. I went back home on court supervision, with my parents' consent. I couldn't leave the house without my parents. Well, I was with my dad one day at his restaurant and he had an emergency call and had to leave. My mom was sick and couldn't pick me up. So my sister drove me home. The neighbors saw me without my parents and they called the police. The police came. I went back to court. I went back to the psychiatric hospital for about four months and got put on five years' probation. The court said I had to go there or to the Audy Home, and I wasn't goin' back there. By that time I was sixteen. From there I went to a group home, where I finished my last year of high school. Seventeen. At seventeen I finished high school. I was emancipated from DCFS [the Department of Children and Family Services, the state of Illinois's child welfare agency]; I was put out on my own.

Jeffrey's case is quite unusual in that he did not have problems with his schooling. In the Chicago study of homeless teens, three-fourths of all males and slightly over half the females had been suspended from school at least once. Roughly one-fourth had been expelled, and a third had been held back at least one year (Chicago Coalition for the Homeless 1993:13).

INTERVIEWER: How'd you get through school in such good shape?
JEFFREY: Even with all that other shit goin' on, I wasn't missing school. Even when I was on the street selling dope, and in the psychiatric ward. It's weird to say, but it's the truth. School was always important to me. It was the best part of my day. It was great. I loved school. I want to go back. I want to go back to college. I graduated high school on the high honor roll—the top ten percent of my class. It was real great. From there I moved out on my own.
INT.: How'd you get the money?
JEFFREY: Saved it goin' through my last year of high school. I was workin' three jobs my last year. Just put all my money in the bank. I had a one-bedroom apartment. But I started gettin' into drinking again. And doin' cocaine. I lost everything. My furniture, my dishes, my apartment. I sold everything just so I could support my habit. Then that's when I really hit the streets.

Jeffrey Giancarlo was homeless at the age of seventeen for just over a year. He survived for a time by finding occasional odd jobs but finally resorted to prostitution. An Illinois Juvenile Justice Commission report states that 75 percent of homeless youth who live on the street without resources for more than two weeks become involved in prostitution or commercial pornography in order to survive (Chicago Coalition for the Homeless 1993:10).

JEFFREY: I just fell apart even more and more. To the point where I was wearin' holey shoes, holey pants, holey shirts, holey socks in the middle of winter, dead winter. Eatin' outta garbage cans, sleepin' behind a bush or sleepin' in a dumpster so I could keep warm 'cause I didn't have a blanket. I got into prostitution 'cause I had no money at all, man. No money at all. I got into prostitution. And it was the only thing that could help me out. It was the only thing that could put money in my pocket. Put food in my stomach and clothes on my back and a place to stay. Then I got tired of whorin' my body. So I quit and called my dad, 'cause I couldn't take it no more. I told him to come down 'cause I needed to talk to him. He saw me and he literally died. He put me in with my grandfather here in Chicago. I got a job at Wendy's workin' full time. My grandfather wanted me to get a job. Well, my hours were outrageous. He said they sucked. But he wanted me to get a job so bad. I said, "I gotta work the hours they give me." It was like nine to six in the morning. I was wakin' him up when I got home and shit. He kicked me out totally. Threw my bags out on the fuckin' lawn. So I said, "Fine. You don't like my hours, I'm gettin' the fuck outta here." I called up my probation officer and told her, "Look, it's not workin' out."

INTERVIEWER: What was your probation officer doing while she knew you were on the streets?

JEFFREY: She knew I was on the streets, but every program she wanted me to go to, I had refused to go. Because they're not the right kinda place. They're like foster homes. They're all really bad programs. I'd rather stay out on the streets and survive than go to those places. I wasn't a DCFS ward any more, only a court ward, so I had a choice of not going. If I was still DCFS, I'd have to go. I'd have no choice. But then when my grandfather kicked me out and I called my P.O. [probation officer], she suggested a place called Neon Street Center for Youth. They helped me out a lot. I figure it changed my head. I was tired of bein' tore down from my parents, tired of bein' tore down from people period. I got a job. Then I found a new job, a better-payin' job. That's where I'm workin' now. I got my head straight, and now I got an apartment.

The Myth of Dysfunctional Families
as the Cause of Homelessness

Teen homelessness is generally linked to runaways and throwaways. If parents abuse or mistreat their children until the children finally leave home, the analysis of the situation focuses on the runaway. If teens abuse drugs and alcohol or otherwise make family life miserable so that parents cannot cope with them anymore, the focus is on the throwaway. In either case, the family is blamed. The family's "dysfunctional nature" is assumed to have caused the homelessness of the child. If teen homelessness is to be remedied, according to this line of reasoning, it will be through programs that improve interfamily relationships.

But no such causal connection is necessary. Yes, some teens are difficult if not impossible to live with. Yes, some parents are difficult if not impossible to live with. But neither situation *causes* homelessness.

Otherwise insightful analyses of homelessness fall into the "dysfunctional family" trap. Snow and Anderson, authors of the ethnography *Down On Their Luck*, fail to question the policies and trends that lie behind the "absence of a helping familial hand" (1993:270):

> The difference between the homeless and the domiciled, then, is not just that the homeless have been the victims of impersonal structural forces or strokes of bad luck that have pushed them down the path toward the streets, but that they have not been the beneficiaries of the kind of familial support that most people take for granted in times of personal crisis. Some of the homeless have no doubt worn out their welcomes because of their burdensome disabilities. ... [For still others,] the path to the streets began in turbulent, often dysfunctional families that left them on their own to deal with the structural victimage and bad luck they would suffer later on. (Snow and Anderson 1993:270)

The "path to the streets" does not *begin* at dysfunctional families. Why are these families "dysfunctional"? What structural forces and social policies lie *behind* the difficulties experienced by parents with their children and children with their parents?

Antifamily Social Policy

In the United States, families are assumed to exist as independent, self-reliant units. The government takes a laissez-faire approach to child rearing, assuming that parents know best how to raise their children. Except for cases of visible signs of child abuse, the state does not interfere with internal family dynamics.

This right of family self-determination has negative consequences for parents and their children. Families are expected to serve all their members' needs but are not assisted in doing so. The care and nurturing of children, for example, is defined solely as each individual family's responsibility. The society or community does not assume a political obligation for the welfare of its youngest generation. One result, as we have seen earlier, is that more than *one-fifth* of all children in the United States currently live below the federal government's official poverty line.

This excessive individualism is particularly dangerous given the structural trends of urban and industrial decline. Increased joblessness, declining real incomes, and expanding inequality mean that some families will succeed at providing for their children while others are doomed to fail. Some families will experience relative stability and the comfort of a predictable future, but increasing numbers of others will live with uncertainty. As families attempt to piece together a reasonable standard of living in an economy that structurally denies it to more and more citizens, stress and frustration are bound to take a toll on relationships within the home. The connection between economic hardship and negative consequences within the family includes divorce, spouse abuse, child abuse, and alcoholism (see, for example, Brenner 1973; Trafford 1982; Horwitz 1984).

Rather than supporting parents and their children through hard times, antifamily social policies deny the basics of a decent standard of living—universal health care, income security, affordable housing, and improved public education. And while government refuses to provide these fundamental supports, it blames families for their supposed poverty of values. Families become the scapegoat for social decay. Whatever is wrong is blamed on a lack of "traditional family values," not on the failure of social policy to support families.

Healthy and strong families require social supports. Families *cannot* successfully go it alone. Yet the dysfunctional family argument continues, often in insidious form. In its 1992 study of homeless teens, the Chicago Coalition for the Homeless had interviewers ask these young people the primary reason for their current homelessness. The number one reason given (shown only in an accompanying chart) was *not enough money;* the text reports that "approximately half mentioned a conflict with family members as the cause. Other frequently mentioned causes were lack of work or shortage of rent money" (Chicago Coalition for the Homeless 1993:9). Each teen was also asked to name three wishes. The most frequent responses (again shown only in an accompanying chart) were *money, a job,* and *a place to live.* But the text again skews the teens' answers, reporting that "over and over the youth expressed concerns for their family of origin; they wished for new parents; and their parents returned happy and healthy. ... An underlying theme was a desire for close ties, for people to care about them, for relationships to share and cherish" (Chicago Coalition for the Homeless 1993:19). Relationships with other family members are overtly highlighted in each of these examples, implying that "good" parents would not have allowed their children to become homeless. Families are blamed even though the study's *own data* follow a different line of reasoning: That money, a decent job, and affordable housing are what teens need once they are homeless. For these teens to have remained with their families in the first place, those families (and all families) must be sustained by profamily policies rather than left to "sink or swim" on their own.

The Failure of Child Welfare Agencies

Under the current system, state-run child welfare agencies are supposed to assist troubled families. But in addition to simply being a reaction after the fact, these agencies are chronically underfunded and understaffed. The number of children living in foster care in Illinois has increased by 140 percent over the past eight years, for example, while the state's Department of Children and Family Services experiences cuts in its budget and staffing (Voices for Illinois Children, quoted in Chicago Coalition for the Homeless 1993:18). The total number of DCFS wards in the state now surpasses 32,000, and the average case worker in Chicago has over seventy-five children under supervision (Chicago Coalition for the Homeless 1993:3).

Many abused or neglected children never come in contact with child welfare authorities. Even when children are taken from abusive homes and placed in group homes, larger "homes" and institutions, or foster care, there is no consistent evidence that this alternative care is the solution. In the Chicago study of homeless teens, 44 percent said they had been DCFS wards (Chicago Coalition for the Homeless 1993:10). The present system fails, by failing to intervene or by intervening unsuccessfully. Jeffrey Giancarlo has been a ward of DCFS. He speaks negatively of the experience:

JEFFREY: The whole system, group homes, foster homes, ... it sucks. They don't give a shit about the kids, I can tell you that. They'd rather see 'em roamin' the streets, man. Emancipate a kid at sixteen or seventeen, just to get him out of their hair 'cause they got so many goddamn kids. They got so many that it doesn't matter to 'em. It's cheaper for DCFS if the kid's on the streets. If they're placed in a foster home and fuckin' run away, they run away. DCFS puts a warrant out for their arrest. So what? The police aren't gonna be checkin' every goddamn kid that walks the streets. That's bullshit, man. DCFS is cold-blooded. You hear about all this child molestation in the foster homes. How about child rape? How about child beatings? And everything else. DCFS needs to start gettin' more protection for kids.

Jeffrey's comments regarding the Illinois Department of Children and Family Services must be taken seriously. The federal court has ordered DCFS to correct many of the problems Jeffrey identifies.

Marginalization of Teens

Adolescence, the period between childhood and adulthood, is a relatively recent social construct (see, for example, Demos and Demos 1973). The concept of adolescence emerged in the last two decades of the nineteenth century along with industrialization. As production moved out of the home and into the factory, work and family became distinctly separate social entities. Children's relationship with their parents was restructured; prior to industrialization, children were "little workers," trained as apprentices and expected to contribute to the household. With industrialization, children were relegated to a dependent position. Instead of spending their days in productive labor, they were sent to school. Education was ideologically justified as preparation for the adult world of work; in reality, it kept children out of a labor market that could not absorb them.

As Donna Gaines writes in *Teenage Wasteland,* young people have been transformed "into a powerless age caste" (1992:240):

> For over a century, laws regulating the autonomy of young people worked to erode their autonomy. First, the child-labor laws took working-class kids out of the factories. Now made superfluous in the economic order, they were gradually locked away in public schools under the banner of mandatory schooling. To "protect" them further, their misbehavior was regulated by the invention of a "juvenile court" (*parens patriae*). Finally, through the notion of "adolescence" as a preparatory stage for adulthood, young people of all classes were reduced to complete psychological and economic dependency upon adults. With the hyper-credentialing of an increasingly postindustrial economy, this dependency can be extended indefinitely; "adulthood," a euphemism for economic independence and personal autonomy, takes longer and longer to achieve. (Gaines 1992:240)

Young people are marginalized; they are the "minority of minorities" (Gaines 1992:239). Their participation in the labor market is legally proscribed. Child labor laws prevent some teens from working at all. Other laws restrict daily and weekly hours. Their political participation is legally limited—they cannot vote or run for political office. Their rights as citizens are legally limited—they cannot sign contracts, they are required to attend school, and they must have parental permission to receive health care. Teens experience the lowest pay, the fewest rights, and the highest level of regulation of any group (Gaines 1992).

Adolescents are in both social and economic limbo, and their status in the 1980s and 1990s is more ambiguous than ever. They are not trusted to make good decisions—the drinking age has gone up, for example. The expectation is that they will behave irresponsibly. But when they do make bad decisions, they are severely punished. The age at which the death penalty can be applied has gone down.

Through the 1980s, media portrayals of material wealth and limitless consumption and the glorification of athletes, musicians, and the "yuppie" lifestyle, brought young people inflated expectations of personal success. Real opportunities, however, were diminished. De-industrialization and the growth of the low-wage, low-benefit service economy meant dead-end jobs for teens. These positions fail to offer any preparation for or promise of better jobs in the future; many teens continue working full time after high school graduation at the same position they held part time during their schooling. Whenever an increase in the minimum wage is suggested, a below-minimum-wage "training salary" for teens is proposed, which would further exploit and marginalize them.

Teens Who Don't and Won't Conform

Jeffrey Giancarlo, one of the "baby bust" generation and a self-described "burnout," experienced numerous conflicts with his parents over his right and ability to make his own decisions. Jeffrey defined himself as a young adult, but his parents saw him as a child. The more they attempted to control and regulate his behavior, the more Jeffrey fought back:

JEFFREY: I was startin' to becomin' a man and my dad's still hittin' me. He cracked me one last time when I was fourteen and that'd be probably the last time he'll ever hit me. Because I swung back. And I said, "Look, I'm a man now. You can talk to me like a man. You can't talk to me like a man without hittin' me, then, hey, we ain't father and son."

For teens who do not readily conform to adult expectations, one of three things tends to happen. These outcomes, rooted in race and class, transform nonconformist behavior into criminality, disability, or "craziness." Poor and minority teens end up in jail. Working-class white ethnic and minority teens are identified as having behavioral or emotional problems and shunted into special-education classes. And white middle-class and upper-middle-class teens are placed into private mental hospitals, where questionable psychiatric diagnoses such as "adolescent adjustment reaction" are blamed for young people's negative reactions to a lack of control over their own lives (Gaines 1992).

Jeffrey Giancarlo's two stays in psychiatric hospitals—one of seventeen months and the other of four months—support Gaines's contention of the increasing use of mental hospitals to warehouse and control "difficult" children. In-patient hospitalization of children under eighteen increased dramatically in the 1980s, even as the actual number of children declined. In 1980, approximately 17,000 kids were admitted to private psychiatric hospitals. By 1986, that number had swelled to 43,000 (*Newsweek,* quoted in Gaines 1992:127).

Declining Household Size

The combination of antifamily social policies and teen marginalization results in extraordinary pressure on families. One outcome of this pressure is the breakdown of family relationships. Parents and their children are alienated from each other. As mentioned previously, over 1 million young people run away from home each year. Most of these teens attempt, with varying degrees of success, to establish their own residences.

The breakup of families results in smaller households. This is indicated in U.S. census data: The average household size fell from 2.76 members in 1980 to 2.63 members in 1990 (Eitzen and Baca Zinn 1993:451). There are more households, even as the population of most American cities declines, because the size of those households is shrinking.

Since more households are created, there are more households competing for available housing units. Young people forming their own households have very few resources. If they can find work, it is generally part time and for minimum wage. Therefore, they join the increasing number of poor persons who seek shelter in the declining number of low-income and affordable housing units. Given the mismatch between demand and supply, many *must* be homeless.

Bad Trends and Policies, Not Bad Kids and Families

Antifamily social policies and the marginalization of youth lead young people to become runaways and throwaways. This is particularly true under conditions of urban and industrial decline. Families "break down," creating more households in the city that are chasing a shrinking supply of affordable housing units. Some of these new households are homeless teens on their own. To focus on "bad" kids and their "bad" families is to miss the socioeconomic and public policy sources of youth homelessness in American cities.

10
A Black Teenage Single Mother and Her Son: Michelle and Andre

At the time of the interview Michelle Archer is eighteen years old. She is black, single, and the mother of a son born seven days earlier. Michelle is a high school graduate. She has lived in a shelter for homeless women and children on Chicago's South Side for a month. She is about to become a welfare mother with the first welfare check due shortly.

Michelle is on her own and has been for the past five months or so. Michelle's parents wanted her to give up the child for adoption but she refused.

MICHELLE: When I was livin' at home my mom found I was pregnant. In my third month I told her. And, boy, there was a lot of problems then. Man, we'd just be arguin'. … And she be tellin' me that she want me to get my own place.

Michelle moved out, going to a home for unwed mothers in Wheaton (a Chicago suburb) that her doctor recommended. It cost $38.50 a week, which she paid from her work at a Burger King. In the later stages of pregnancy Michelle quit work, which meant that she could no longer afford to stay in Wheaton. She moved to her aunt's house:

MICHELLE: 'Cause I couldn't go home. And I stayed there for about, like five days. And it was alright there, but I know I couldn't stay there 'cause she wouldn't let me and then she called and tell my mama I was there and my mama she was so mad. … [She was mad] 'cause she didn't want nobody to know that I was pregnant.

Michelle went to a shelter, recommended by the same doctor who recommended the Wheaton home. She did not tell her aunt where she was going to live.

MICHELLE: I don't want her to know 'cause she probably gonna tell everybody. ... Probably tell my other aunties and uncles and cousins. And I
don't want them to know. ... Because, you know, people you say "a
shelter" then they can go lookin' down on you, you know, so a shelter—like makin' fun of you or somethin.' So I don't tell 'em.

Michelle's mother, however, did know about Michelle's living in a shelter.

MICHELLE: Yeah, she know I'm in a shelter. See, she wanted me to give the
baby up so she told me if I don't give the baby up I can't come home.
[After the baby was born] she told me we had to go back to the shelter.
I told her, "Well, I'm not scared to be my own woman." So I came back
here 'til I get me an apartment. [Later in the interview, however,
Michelle admits to being scared.] I'm real young. My family done let
me down and I'm on my own now. ... It's scary, you know, 'cause I
never, you know, been on my own. And now I know I gotta, you know,
be on my own and it is scary. But it's just somethin' I gotta take a
chance at ... bein' on my own—eighteen years old. I should be home
with somebody.

Michelle's estrangement from her mother has three major consequences. Foremost, she is deprived of the mother-daughter relationship
at a critical time in her life. As Hudson and Ineichen have put it: "The
most significant person in the pregnant adolescent's life is not always
the baby's father. It is usually her mother, whatever the overt nature of
the mother/daughter relationship, and the younger the girl, the more
dependent on her mother she will be" (1991:74). A second consequence
is that Michelle is thrust into an adult world with little preparation and
without her mother's counsel and support. "Teenage mothers are on the
whole totally unprepared for what lies ahead" (Hudson and Ineichen
1991:87). And third, Michelle's separation from her mother, coupled with
few resources, means that she will be homeless.

Michelle is truly on her own. The father of her child did not take any
responsibility—financial or relational—for Michelle and Andre.
Michelle does not like him. He does not even know where Michelle and
the child are living. Michelle's isolation is compounded by living in the
shelter, where she has not developed any relationships.

MICHELLE: Like the people in there [the shelter], they just so, I mean they
just so stupid to me. ... I'm not talkin' about the staff, you know, I'm
talkin' about the people in there. They just be beatin' on their kids like
they got a problem and they just be all—like they just, o-o-o be lookin'
all, mmm, depressed. And be gettin' nasty and take their problems out

on people. So I don't even talk to 'em. I don't say nothin' to them unless they say somethin' to me. ... [Also] you have to watch your stuff here. They just steal it.

Black Teenage Single Mothers

The details of Michelle's story differ some from the biographies of other young single mothers. Many have supportive parents and kin networks. Others may receive some financial support from the fathers of their children. Some are not disadvantaged by poverty. But many unwed mothers, like Michelle, find themselves alone, without resources, and without shelter. This section discusses the demographic facts concerning teenage single parents and the outlook for their children.

Demographic Facts About Single Parents

The percentage of American children living with two parents has declined from 85 percent in 1970 to 72 percent in 1991. For black children this proportion decreased from 68 percent in 1970 to 43 percent in 1991 (U.S. Census data, reported in *Rocky Mountain News* 1992b). Of the 5.8 million black children living with one parent in 1991, 5.5 million (95 percent) lived with their mother. The problem with this arrangement "is not the lack of a male presence but the lack of a male income" (Cherlin 1981:81). As Andrew Hacker has pointed out:

> Many of those [families] headed by single mothers get by at close to a subsistence level. In 1990 ... half such households had incomes of less than $14,000. Here is where the "feminization of poverty" takes its greatest toll. Some 38 percent of white single mothers and 56 percent of their black counterparts are trying to clothe and feed their children on incomes below the poverty threshold, which in 1990 stood at $10,530 for a family of three. (Hacker 1992:73)

The categories in the United States with the highest incidence of poverty are blacks, women, and children.

- In 1990 approximately 30 percent of all blacks were below the poverty line, compared to 25 percent of Latinos and 10 percent of whites.
- Two-thirds of impoverished adults are women. "Gender segregation in the workplace and wage discrimination against women are primary causes of poverty among women, especially those heading their own households" (Scarpitti and Andersen 1992:208).

- One out of every five American children under eighteen and 22.5 percent of children under six live in poverty. Slightly more than one-half of all black children under age six are poor, compared to 45 percent of Latino children and 17 percent of white children under six.

More specifically, what are the current facts about black teenage pregnancies?

- Forty-one percent of black girls become pregnant by age eighteen.
- More than 90 percent of births to black teens are to unmarried girls.
- Of single black mothers aged fifteen to nineteen, 99.3 percent keep their babies (Simons, Finlay, and Yang 1991:x; Hacker 1992:73–81).

Marian Wright Edelman of the Children's Defense Fund summarizes why teenage pregnancy is a crisis.

> Adolescent pregnancy is a crisis not because teenage birthrates are rising, as is widely believed. (In fact, both the proportion and number of adolescents giving birth generally has fallen since 1970.) It is a crisis because the society is changing and young parents are tragically unprepared to deal with the consequences of early birth in contemporary America. Both the number and rate of births to teenagers who are unmarried are rising, thereby increasing the likelihood of poverty for two generations of children—young mothers and their children. In 1950, 15.4 percent of these births were to unmarried teenagers. By 1970, the proportion had doubled. By 1986, it had doubled again—to 60.8 percent. (Edelman 1991:300)

Black Teenage Mothers: Myth and Reality

Although the facts concerning black teenage mothers as just presented are accurate, they present a distorted picture. They fuel negative stereotypes and faulty interpretations (the following discussion is dependent on the insights from Reed 1992; di Leonardo 1992b; and Sklar 1993a, 1993b). To anticipate the argument, the seeming epidemic of black teenage childbearing is viewed by many, including many social scientists, as evidence of a culture that keeps blacks disadvantaged. Put more strongly, blacks, especially young black mothers on welfare, are seen as the problem. Thus, these women often experience hostility in social interaction as well as being the object of punitive public policies.

The prevailing logic is that the very poor, especially poor blacks and Latinos, suffer from behavioral deficiencies. They are disproportionately criminals, drug addicts, and welfare mothers. Their behaviors are self-defeating, as seen in high rates of school dropouts, teenaged pregnancy, fatherless families, welfare dependency, and unemployment. In short, these people are locked into poverty, not just by their lack of opportunities but by their culture-bound behaviors.

There are problems with this argument. Most important, it ignores or diminishes the socioeconomic reasons for differences between the very poor and the more affluent. Instead of explaining unemployment or welfare dependency by the deficiencies of individuals, we should focus on the declining number of jobs in cities, the prevalence of low-wage jobs among those that are available, and the discrimination that racial minorities and women experience in the job market.

A second problem with this argument is that the deviant behaviors attributed to the poor *are found throughout the social structure.* As Adolph Reed, Jr., has put it:

> The behavioral tendencies supposedly characterizing the underclass exist generally throughout the society. Drug use, divorce, educational underattainment, laziness, and empty consumerism exist no less in upper status suburbs than in inner-city bantustans. The difference lies not in the behavior but in the social position of those exhibiting it. (Reed 1992:33)

To elaborate this point further, let's examine the facts regarding several forms of deviance. First, substance abuse rates are *higher* for white women than nonwhite women. Black youth are *less* likely to use drugs than white youth. In 1992 Louis Sullivan, secretary of Health and Human Services, said: "Our studies show that contrary to many misconceptions, these youngsters [African Americans] are less likely to use alcohol and other drugs than are kids from other ethnic groups" (quoted in Sklar 1993b:55). More generally, "If the irrational drug laws were applied equally, we'd see a lot more handcuffed white movie stars, rich teenagers, politicians, doctors, stockbrokers, and CIA officers on the TV news, trying to hide their faces" (Sklar 1993a:28).

Second, criminals, despite the selective attention of the media and politicians, are not exclusively from the lower socioeconomic stratum. To the contrary, much *more* money and property are stolen and lives threatened by white-collar criminals and corporate policies than by street criminals.

> While the corner mugger is terrifying and may physically harm us, white-collar criminals are just as common, and their financial damage to the commonweal is orders of magnitude greater. Doctors run Medicare mills, scientists fake their data, lawyers bilk old ladies, insurers transfer annuities to companies that go bankrupt, erasing thousands of people's pensions, car dealers defraud manufacturers and customers. ... So who's acting ugly? (di Leonardo 1992b:35)

Third, deviance is found disproportionately among some social categories, yet they escape negative labels. For example:

> We know ... that families whose members are police officers or who serve in the military have much higher rates of divorce, family violence, and substance abuse than do other families, but we seldom accuse them of constituting an "underclass" with a dysfunctional culture; more reasonably, we relate these problems to work stresses and other situational or structural issues. (Coontz 1992:247)

Fourth, welfare is handed out *more* generously to the nonpoor than to the poor. Farm subsidies, tax deductibility for taxes and interest on homes, low-interest loans to students and victims of disasters, and "pork barrel" projects are examples of government welfare and even the "dependency" of nonpoor people on government largesse.

Finally, out-of-wedlock births occur in all social strata. Although the rate is highest among those who are not high school graduates (48.4 percent), the sharpest increase from 1982 to 1992 was found among single women with one or more years of college (11.3 percent in 1992, compared to 5.5 percent in 1982). By age, the category with the most rapid growth was women in their thirties (U.S. Bureau of the Census, cited in Fulwood 1993:20a). Ironically, though, out-of-wedlock births are considered pathological only when the mothers are poor. Why is the stigma aimed only at the poor, especially poor black mothers? Clearly, the answer lies in race and class bias (Reed 1992:33–34).

These data show that the poor are not different from others in society. This is the linchpin for demythologizing the behavior of the poor. As Reed has said forcefully:

> It is imperative to reject all assumptions that poor people are behaviorally or attitudinally different from the rest of society. Some percentage of *all* Americans take drugs, fight in families, abuse or neglect children, etc. If the behavior exists across lines of class, race and opportunity, then it cannot reasonably be held—i.e., with some premise of generically different human natures—to be particularly implicated in producing poverty. If it does not *cause* poverty, therefore, we do not need to focus on it at all in the context of policy-oriented discussion about poverty. (Reed 1992:37–38)

A persistent myth concerns the dependence of black women on welfare. The stereotype is that these women have babies for the increased moneys they receive from welfare. Although it is true that black women are more likely to receive AFDC than others (in 1990, 40 percent of AFDC families were black, 38 percent were white, and 17 percent were Latino), this is because they are disproportionately poor (about one-third, compared to 28 percent of Latinos, and 10 percent of whites).

AFDC is not a lucrative scheme for several reasons. First, the average monthly payment for a family of three is much less than half the official poverty threshold. Second, AFDC benefits have been declining (since 1972, inflation-adjusted benefits have dropped by 43 percent). Third, AFDC payments are reduced almost dollar-for-dollar from outside income. And the working poor, in contrast to those on welfare, lose Medicaid benefits, which is a very strong disincentive to work outside the home.

The facts belie the stereotype of welfare dependency by these black single mothers: (1) The majority of women on welfare are white; (2) most daughters in families who received welfare do not become welfare recipients as adults; (3) black women receiving welfare do not have more children than those who do not; (4) the majority of women on welfare have only one or two children; (5) most families who receive AFDC do so for two years or less; and (6) "there is overwhelming global demographic evidence ... that raised standards of living, especially women's perceptions of rising social and economic opportunity lead to later births and smaller families" (di Leonardo 1992b:34). These contrary findings are all the more remarkable given the difficulties of poor black single women in the workplace. The jobs these black women get are disproportionately low-wage, dead-end ones with few if any benefits. As Sklar has pointed out, "Two out of three workers who earn the minimum wage are women. Full-time work at minimum wage ($4.25 an hour) earns below the poverty line for a family of two" (1993a:27). Moreover, entry-level wages for high school graduates fell 22 percent between 1979 and 1991. Moreover, low-wage workers are less likely than other workers to qualify for unemployment benefits; when they do qualify, their payments are only a portion of their already low wages.

These single mothers who work are further disadvantaged because the U.S. government does not provide or make allowances for affordable child care, parental leave, and other universal child supports common in other advanced industrialized nations.

In sum, again citing Holly Sklar:

> The stereotype of deadbeat poor people masks the growing reality of dead-end jobs. It is fashionable to point to the so-called breakdown of the family as a cause of poverty and ignore the breakdown of wages. ... For more and more Americans and their children, work is not a ticket out of poverty, but a condition of poverty. (Sklar 1993a:29)

What Is the Outlook for Michelle?

Given the facts, the probabilities for Michelle are not promising. She may want to work, leave welfare, and be independent, but her race and gender present a form of double jeopardy. Moreover, she is an adolescent, unmarried mother, which, given her class and race, are incredibly stigmatizing to potential employers, fellow employees, apartment owners, and neighbors. To whites she will be viewed as one of "them." She will be stereotyped in unfair ways and treated as such.

The Children of Teenage Single Mothers

What are the prospects for Michelle's week-old son, Andre? And, what of the prospects of other children raised by their poor, young mothers? Statistically, being born to poor, single mothers, especially black single mothers, means a disproportionate chance of being unhealthy. Andrew Hacker provides a summary of what is known:

> Compared with white women—most of whom are older and more comfortably off—black women are twice as likely to have anemic conditions during their pregnancy, twice as likely to have no prenatal care, and twice as likely to give birth to low-weight babies. Twice as many of their children develop serious health problems, including asthma, deafness, retardation, and learning disabilities.(Hacker 1992:78)

There are three reasons for the increased likelihood of health problems for the children of poor young single women: poor prenatal care, living in unhealthful conditions, and being without medical insurance. Each of these reasons is tied to poverty because poor people receive inadequate medical attention in the United States. The unhealthy consequences of teenage pregnancy are the result of poverty, not early fertility per se (Geronimus 1987). Actually the research by Geronimus (1987) shows that early childbearing among the poor has some advantages: "Given the accumulated physical stresses of extreme poverty, early childbearing may be better for the health of the mother and child, and [it] takes advantage of grandmothers' energies before they become too run-down to help out" (cited in di Leonardo 1992b:34).

If children from single-parent families are also homeless, the negative consequences for their development are compounded. For example, the infant mortality rate (deaths per 1,000 live births) in 1987 was ten. For births to low-income mothers the rate was seventeen and for births to homeless mothers the rate was twenty-five (Chavkin 1987). For those who survive birth there are a number of factors that work against their health (Mihaly 1991). First, living in makeshift settings or in shelters often exposes homeless children to extremes of heat and cold as well as unsanitary conditions. Homeless children often have chronic respiratory problems, diarrhea, and high lead blood levels.

Second, studies have found that homeless children, when compared to other low-income children, are more likely to have emotional problems and to be more anxious and worried. Third, homeless children do not do as well in school. As Mihaly has written, "All children really need stability and routine and security and safety to do well in school, to have good health, and to go get a job. When children are homeless, everything that is routine and stable about their environment gets completely turned upside down" (1991:9a).

Poor youngsters, especially African American and Latino children, have the cards stacked against them in at least two ways regarding school. First, they are commonly expected to do poorly, and these negative expectations of teachers and peers often result in a self-fulfilling prophecy. Second, through IQ tests and advanced placement tests, children are rated and sorted into ability groups, which is like a school caste system. Jeff Howard of the National Urban League has pointed out that "black students make up 16 percent of public school students, yet make up almost 40 percent of those placed in special education or classified as mentally retarded or disabled. They are even more severely underrepresented in the upper end of the placement hierarchy" (cited in Sklar 1993b:53).

Third, for the most part, schools in the United States are financed according to the wealth of the local district. The unequal funding of schools means that wealthier districts spend, on average, more than twice as much per pupil than do poorer districts. These extra moneys benefit students by luring and retaining the best teachers, providing better equipment, computers, and libraries, and by being more able to meet the needs of special students (e.g., those with learning disabilities, those with sight, hearing, and speech impairments).

The hard-headed reality for Andre and others like him is that "children born outside of marriage who grow up with single mothers are likely to be poor for most or all of their childhood" (National Center for Children in Poverty 1990:29). The problem, however, is not being born to a young single mother but to a *poor and black* young single mother.

The federal government has done little to meet the special health, educational, and housing needs of children. In 1990, for example, the federal government spent five times more on the elderly than it did on children ($354.5 billion compared to $68.6 billion) (Richman 1992:36). The results of these policies are dramatic: In 1990 the poverty rate among the elderly was below the national average (12.2 percent compared to the national rate of 13.5 percent). The poverty rate for children, however, was 20.6 percent.

Even when the federal government does provide a program, some children are neglected, especially racial minorities. Senator Daniel

Patrick Moynihan has pointed out that there are two ways in which the federal government provides benefits to children in single-parent families. The first is AFDC. The majority of children receiving this type of aid are African American or Latino. Since 1970, the government has *decreased* the real benefits from this program by 13 percent. The other form of assistance is Survivors Insurance (SI), which is part of Social Security. Most children receiving SI benefits are white, and these benefits have *increased* by 53 percent since 1970 (adjusted for inflation) (Baca Zinn and Eitzen 1993:167). Moynihan has written, "to those who say we don't care about children in our country, may I note that the average provision for children under SI has been rising five times as fast as average family income since 1970. We do care about some children. Majority children. It is minority children—not only but mostly—who are left behind" (1988:5).

In sum, the children of poor, single, minority women will face inadequate nutrition, housing, health care, and education.

Values Versus Structure

Michelle has hopes. She wants an apartment, a car, a job with benefits, and good day care for Andre. She wants to save money. She would rather work than be dependent on welfare. When asked about what type of job she wanted, Michelle replied:

MICHELLE: I wouldn't mind workin' at this, uh, company General Motors. You know, the car company. Make real good money. I wish I could start and find me a job. Start me off about, like, nine or ten dollars an hour. I wish I could some day. But if I could find a job startin' about five somethin' that would be good.

What are Michelle's chances for a job with decent pay and benefits? To her credit, she is a high school graduate and she believes in herself and in the American Dream. But, sadly, Michelle faces many negatives. Her only job experience is a minimum-wage job at Burger King. She is a black teenager and the jobless rate for black inner-city teenagers in 1992 was more than 50 percent (National Urban League, cited in *Rocky Mountain News* 1992a). As a black woman, she faces double discrimination (institutional racism and institutional sexism), which limits job opportunities, restricts types of available jobs, limits pay, and nullifies possibilities for advancement. Moreover, she carries the twin pejorative labels of "welfare mother" and "unwed mother," which likely will turn away many prospective employers. Whenever she finds a job, she must find and pay for child care for Andre, which will reduce her take-home pay substantially. Most significant, the labor market has changed in the past generation, making it especially difficult for single mothers to support a family. According to the Children's Defense Fund, "Jobs that don't require much education or specialized skills, yet pay enough to support a family, have all but disappeared. … A large fraction of young people, especially minorities, cannot find jobs at all" (Simons, Finlay, and Yang 1991:119). And, if they find work, single mothers find that it does not pay great dividends because the pay is so meager. After-tax income for a full-time worker at a minimum-wage job is about the same as if she were on welfare (actually less when expenses for transportation, clothing, and child care are deducted). And, as noted earlier, if one works, he or she will lose medical care through Medicaid.

Despite these constraints, Michelle does not want to stay on welfare. She wants a job and financial independence.

MICHELLE: A lot of people, a lotta, lotta people, you know, they think that bein' on the welfare and gettin' a check once a month is somethin' big but they just sittin' on their butts. They just don't know. They just don't realize havin' a job is the best thing.

The odds are that Michelle will not find a job that pays enough to make her independent of welfare and able to pay for child care. Moreover, she will be discouraged from working because AFDC withdraws a dollar of support for each dollar of earnings. Thus, she will try to make it on $250 a month in welfare and $100 in food stamps. Summarizing the situation, David Ellwood has said: "The system is totally stacked against single working moms. It's very difficult for them to survive, and the only alternative is welfare. The current welfare system only helps women when they've failed and reduces the support for them as they move forward in the workplace" (quoted in Dugger 1992:A1).

What about Michelle's hope of an adequate and safe apartment? Since her parents won't have her and she has little income, Michelle's options are limited. She can remain in the shelter a maximum of only four months. She can apply for Chapter 8 subsidized housing, where the Chicago Housing Authority pays half of the rent. The problem with this is that the waiting list is so long. According to a survey by the U.S. Conference of Mayors in 1990 the lists for public housing were closed in two-thirds of the twenty-seven major cities surveyed and for those with waiting lists. New York City's included 170,000 families; the length of Chicago's list was 60,000; Washington's was 17,000; and San Antonio's was 15,000 (Eleff 1990). A third option is to apply for a low-rent apartment through a church or other nonprofit organization. Again, the problem is that there are many more applicants than apartments. The final choice is to move into the projects, but Michelle refuses this option because of the physical dangers.

MICHELLE: I don't want no projects because they are too bad. ... They just be trouble. They tear up everything and fightin' and shootin.' I don't want my baby around that environment.

There is a high probability, however, that after her time in the shelter expires, Michelle will have no choice but to opt for one of the two worst options: to find another shelter or to move into one of the projects.

Finally, what are the chances of quality child care for Andre if Michelle finds a job? Three facts cloud the outlook for Andre. First, quality child care is in short supply. Second, the cost of quality care is high ($125 to $200 a week). Third, quality child care for infants is the most difficult to find and the most expensive (Hewlett 1991:50–52).

The child care options for low-income families are limited. Since day care centers with trained personnel are too expensive, most low-income families resort to family day care. This is, typically, an arrangement in which a neighborhood woman cares for several children in her own home. The good news is that the cost is relatively modest—$40 to $75 a week. The bad news is that only about 10 percent are licensed.

A second inexpensive day care option is a combination of relatives' time, neighbors' time, and paid help. "Many parents resort to this desperate juggling act when they cannot find or cannot afford decent family day care" (Hewlett 1991:51). This is not an option for Michelle, however, because of her social isolation. She is alienated from her family and does not appear to have close friends or neighbors whom she can trust with Andre.

When Andre is older—from three to five years—he will have another option: nursery school. About 35 percent of preschoolers attend nursery schools but they are mostly middle and upper class (90 percent of nursery schools are private and cost an average of $3,350 a year). Head Start provides the same early childhood education for poor children. Research has shown that this program provides a significant educational boost to low-income children. The federal government, however, provides only enough funds to serve about 40 percent of those eligible.

The outlook for Michelle and Andre is grim despite Michelle's sense of hope. Having the values of optimism, a work ethic, and independence are not enough for people in her very disadvantaged situation. The structural constraints working against Michelle are going to make it very difficult for her to meet her goals.

11

Battered Women and Homelessness: Barbara Evans

Barbara Evans is a single black woman with three small children. She is twenty-seven years old but looks much younger. Barbara's three children, all girls, are two, three, and seven. Interviewed at a homeless shelter in Chicago, Barbara recounts the years of physical and emotional violence inflicted by Thomas, the father of her two youngest girls. Barbara and her children escaped from Thomas's virtual imprisonment and have been at the shelter for two months. They hope that Thomas does not find them and that permanent housing will be available soon.

An Epidemic of Violence Against Women

According to the FBI's *Uniform Crime Reports,* a woman is beaten by her husband or boyfriend every fifteen seconds. This staggering figure is a gross underestimation of the extent of the violence, as most experts figure the actual number of cases to be ten times those reported (Bausch and Kimbrough 1986:ix). With over a million reported incidents per year, the 1988 U.S. surgeon general's report called domestic violence the number one health risk among women. A 1992 update by Surgeon General Antonia Novella specified that this violence was the leading cause of injury to women aged fifteen to forty-four (Ross 1992).

This high incidence of violence is not restricted to a small number of repeatedly victimized women. Twenty-five percent of all couples report at least one incident of aggression during the course of their relationship (Flanery 1993). According to another source, one in every five women involved in an intimate relationship with a man is beaten repeatedly by that man (Illinois Coalition Against Sexual Assault, quoted in Bausch and Kimbrough 1986). As many as *half* of all women will be battering victims at some point in their lives (Walker 1979:ix). With both reported incidents and estimates of the proportion of women victimized so high, battering may be defined as a common, not rare, event.

The almost routine nature of domestic violence against women is based in patriarchy. Men are expected to be the heads of their households and are granted a perceived "right" to exert control over "their" women and children. Only in recent decades has this authority been restricted, with physical force being outlawed as a method of coercion. Yet laws against battering do little or nothing to stem its occurrence.

Although battered women are found in every income category, they tend to be concentrated in households facing economic hardship. Ruth Sidel, author of *Women and Children Last,* reports a "clear correlation between unemployment and family violence" (1992:19). Research on married couples shows that violence against spouses appears to increase as income decreases (Dibble and Straus 1980:77). This may occur because

> low income husbands are less in a position to live up to their role obligations as providers than are middle-class husbands. Their wives are, therefore, less likely to recognize the male as the head of the house than are their middle-class counterparts. When such recognition and other resources are lacking, husbands may, in turn, use force to control their wives. ... In contrast ... high-income husbands have economic and prestige resources which let them control their wives without the need to use force. (Dibble and Straus 1980:79)

Given the high correlation between low income and minority status, it is no surprise that impoverished black households are overrepresented in domestic violence statistics. Barbara Evans, a poor black woman, is structurally at greater risk of victimization. She begins her story:

BARBARA: I was twenty when I met him. We went together for about a year, and I wound up getting pregnant. I was so blind in love. He had me move in with his mama. Then his ex-girlfriend Edna come back into the picture; she had had five kids by him. So I went back to my mother's, and had the baby. But I kept seein' him. He told me he had quit her. But he hadn't quit her. He come by one day, and told me he was gonna take me to visit his other kids. So I went with him to visit his kids and my two kids went along with me. But he wouldn't let me back out.

INTERVIEWER: He wouldn't let you back out of—

BARBARA: Right. Out of Edna's house. Her apartment. He said that I was gonna stay there, you know, of my own will. On my own will, you hear me? On my will, I was gonna live with another woman—him and his woman and five kids. I stayed in that lady's apartment for about two months, afraid to leave.

INT.: Afraid to leave?

BARBARA: Afraid to leave because he had a pit dog guardin' over me. And he [Thomas] never let me out of his sight. He stayed around with me twenty-four hours a day. I couldn't get away. When I went to pick up my Aid check, he went with me. I was too afraid to even yell for the police or anything else because he had my kids and I was with him. And I wouldn't, you know, chance it. So I stayed in that same apartment. It wasn't no problem with her [Edna]. She loved that man. Then Thomas started callin' me "bitch" and "whore." He said, "Bitch, you gonna stay with me." I took two months of that. One day I was tellin' him that I was gonna leave. And I was gonna get the police on him. That's when he beat me with a dog chain. I was pregnant [with her third child], and he beat me with a dog chain. Edna wasn't a help. She didn't have no power over him either. He told her what to do. For two weeks I was real sore. I'd get in the tub and soak. I says to him, "I'm gonna be nice. I'm not goin' nowhere. I'm not gonna trick you. I'm gonna do what you want me to do." And finally he trusted me. So he left one day and didn't take me. That was my chance out. Edna left, too.

INT.: So you were there by yourself.

BARBARA: I slipped a note to the apartment upstairs. I had the lady call my mother right away. Get the police over here because I wasn't stayin' on my own will. He had beat me with a dog chain. He was threatening me and my kids. My mother got my brothers. They came over with guns, but Thomas was home by then. They was knockin' at the door. And they said, "I'm lookin' for Barb. Is Barbara Evans there?" And Thomas said, "Who is this askin' for you? Another man? You been out doin' somethin?" I said, "I don't know who that is. I don't even know them." Finally he sent Edna to call the police. She called the police and my brothers seen the police car pull up. They ran off, 'cause they had guns. So the police came and knocked at the door. Thomas told me to get in the other room and hide. He had pulled a knife on me. He told me to get in the room. The police came in. He was tellin' the police different lies: "Everything's okay. Ain't nobody hurt here." And I came out. I said, "Here I am." I said, "He's threatening me. He put a knife on my throat." The police took me and my kids out the door. Thomas was sayin' "Don't take my babies. Please don't take my babies. Please, please!" And I said, "Get my babies, 'cause he's the type that would run off with 'em." So the police took me on down and put me in the police car. I told the police the whole truth then. About the dog chain. The police didn't lock him up. 'Cause I didn't really want him locked up. I just wanted to get away from him. I went home to my mother.

Many battered women trace the first instance of violence against them by their male partners to some time during pregnancy (Lips 1991:124). Barbara Evans's ordeal is not unique in this; the experience is amazingly common. Approximately one in twelve woman are beaten during pregnancy (Pollitt 1990:416).

Barbara Evans returned to Thomas within the year.

BARBARA: I stayed with my mother for three weeks. Then I moved to Ohio and stayed with my sister a while. I couldn't get over bein' beat with a dog chain. So I came back to Chicago after two months. I got my own apartment in Rockwell Gardens [a public housing project]. And my youngest was born. He [Thomas] came back in my life. He found out where I lived and he pushed his way back in. He persuaded me. Fakin' me with all that "Love, I love you," you know, "I didn't mean the things I did to you." So I fell for it. I was about twenty-four then. I fell for it. I took him back in my life. It was his child, after all, and he was glad to see us and everything. But the same thing went to happening all over again. He brought that lady back in my life again. When I got back he told me he was not goin' with her no more. Come to find out, he's still goin' with her. The next thing I know he was movin' in my apartment with his other five kids and her. I would get him to the side and I would say, "Hey, you know I'm not gonna play this game no more. I'm tired of this. I'm not goin' with you and her both. I don't appreciate you bringing her in my house to spend the night." And he would say, "You bitch" or "whore," you know, callin' me those names. The same problems again. I went through it for about seven months. 'Cause I didn't want to leave; it was my apartment. So I went through a lot of hell with him in that apartment. He just came and took it over. He was all set about bein' my man. He figured he owned me, you know what I mean? Nobody else can have me but him. No matter what. If I said I didn't want him and I would leave, he would get my kids and take them out, and call me and say, "Bitch, I will kill 'em. If you don't go back with me, I will kill 'em." He done that to me many, many times. One time I told him it was quits for good. He took my baby right there and ran out the door. I called the police, but they couldn't even find him. He stayed gone with her for about a week. And he called me threatenin' me, tellin' me what he would do to her. I believed it. Finally his brother called and said, "If you go back with him, you can have the baby back." I had to agree with that. I went back with him in order to get my baby back. Lovey-dove again. Lovey-dove. Then same thing happenin' all over again. Takin' over my house. Callin' me "bitch" and "whore" in front of the kids and everything. And you know, I accepted it. I accepted it and accepted it. He would threaten my life. I still accepted it.

I still believed I was in love with this man. It was like he owned me. I wasn't free. I wasn't free no type of way. And finally I got tired. His girlfriend and her kids was there and he was there. Finally one day I set him down. I said, "Hey, you gonna either change your way of life, or I'm gonna leave you. Because I ain't got time for this." He thought it was a joke. He laughed at me. I played my part; I was real nice so he trusted me, but I'm prayin' "Lord, help me to run away one day." One night he and Edna stayed out all night long. That morning I got up from bed around six o'clock and they still wasn't there. I got my kids and we left town. I went to Flint, Michigan, to stay with my auntie. I moved in with her 'cause I had nowhere else.

Barbara and her children stayed in Flint for almost a year. But Barbara felt lonely and unhappy and missed Chicago. She decided to go back and try once more to patch up her relationship with Thomas. As she reasoned, he was her children's father and deserved to see his kids. And by her own admission, she was "blind and in love." She felt that she owed him one more chance. Maybe he had changed. So she wrote him, and he drove to Michigan to pick them up. But she did not have a place to move into, since she had given up her apartment in Rockwell Gardens.

BARBARA: I didn't have nowhere to go when I came back here, so Edna offered me to live in her place. He was stayin' with her. But I had nowhere else to go, so I went. I moved in her house. I wanted him back. I was gonna save up money for a couple months until I could afford my own apartment, and then move out. At first it was okay, and then the changes come upon him 'cause I been there a while. He said "You can't move. You gotta stay here with me." I won't deny I made a big mistake again. Again, you know. I had come back to something that's not nothin'.

INTERVIEWER: He's not lettin' you leave again.

BARBARA: Right. He's doin' the same thing over again. "Bitch" and "whore." He was callin' us both "bitch" in front of the kids. He says, "You two bitches gotta do this." So now I was gettin' Edna to the side and I said, "Girl, you better wake up." I said, "'Cause I don't want that life. I done made three mistakes." Me and her both got together and we talked and we talked. How we both made mistakes, doin' wrong things. Lettin' these things happen around our kids. He never knew we would get together and talk. He never knew this secret about what we had. She got her Aid check one day, and she said, "Barbara, you ready?" I said, "I been ready. I been ready since April." So he left to go fishing that day. Edna said, "It's time now." I said, "I been waitin' on you." So we went to the store and got a newspaper. Found a number for the social worker at the Department of Human Services. And the lady told me to come there before five. So we went back to the apartment and got the things we needed to get ready so we can leave. But her mind wasn't made up then. I told her I thought she was ready. I said, "What we waitin' on? He's gone fishin'." She looked at the newspaper and said "I can't find an apartment." I said, "Hey, Edna, you gonna either make your mind up or what. 'Cause I'm gonna leave, even if I have to go to the shelter. You got me thinkin' you don't want to leave the man. You got me thinkin' you love the things he do to you or to me. I'm gone. Whether you like it or not. 'Cause those people are expectin' me at five o'clock to be there." So she tossed and turned a while. I said, "I'm gonna call a cab." I went and called a cab. I said, "The cab's gonna meet us around the corner." 'Cause I didn't want his family to see us. His family lived in the same building. And I didn't want them to see us leave because if they had a seen us leave, they woulda went to get him. So the cab picked us up at a store on California.

Barbara, Edna, and their children arrived at the Department of Human Services just after five. Their contact was gone. They called the police and were taken to the police station. After four hours there, Barbara and her three children were taken to a battered women's shelter on the north side of the city. Edna and her children were taken to another location; Barbara wasn't sure where. After a week at this shelter, Barbara thought she saw Thomas's brother while out shopping. The shelter's director decided to move Barbara to another location on the South Side, where she remained, waiting for permanent housing.

Battered women tend to be particularly isolated, often because of their partners' extreme jealousy. During our interview, Barbara spoke at length of her fear of Thomas and of his insistence that she devote herself entirely to him:

BARBARA: I couldn't have a friend. I couldn't go visit my mother. I couldn't visit my sisters and brothers. I couldn't talk to nobody. Nobody could say "hi" to me without him gettin' mad. He didn't allow me to go out the store without him followin' me. He didn't allow me talkin' to anybody without him there beside me listenin'. He didn't trust me. He didn't want me to be with nobody else. He said if I would do anything like that he would kill me first. He threatened my life lots of times. He told me before somebody else had me, he would kill me first. He pulled a rifle on me lots of times. He shot it at me lots of times. You know, clicked the gun on me. He told me that his friend killed his girlfriend. He shot her. He came home one day and he shot her twice in the head. Then shot himself one time in the head. Only two people that was left alive was his kids. And every time Thomas would argue at me and fuss at me, and make me mad, he would put his rifle up the side of the couch and he would tell me that "I'm gonna do you the same way he did his woman. I'm gonna shoot you and kill you. And maybe put you down in the basement, where nobody know where you at. Or maybe I might kill you and shoot myself in the head, too. 'Cause if you think you gonna go with somebody else and leave me and not be with me—you is my woman forever. Nobody can have you. I will have you for the rest of your life. Nobody else will have you." Sometimes he'd chase me through the house with the rifle. And pull the trigger. I'd get scáreder and scareder every day. Because he would bring it in my face what he would do to me. He would bring it in my face about what his friend did to this woman. I believed it. 'Cause I was fearful and scared because he done pulled that trigger lots of times. He was real serious. He looked like he meant it. Because that was his close, close friend.

Barbara Evans's fear was justified. A startling 40 percent of all women murdered in the United States are killed by their husbands or lovers (Illinois Coalition Against Sexual Assault and the Illinois Coalition Against Domestic Violence n.d.). Nine hundred thirteen wives were killed by their husbands in 1992 (Flanery 1993).

At one point in their relationship, Barbara's leg was broken as a result of Thomas's violence. Although she sought medical attention in a local emergency room, her injury was not brought to the attention of law enforcement officials. The Centers for Disease Control and Prevention issued a study in August 1993 estimating that as many as 30 percent of women who visit emergency rooms each year are victims of assault by husbands or boyfriends, yet most emergency room personnel are not trained to identify such injuries (Kritz 1993). Women like Barbara are sent home to face their attackers again.

Barbara Evans did not file formal assault charges against Thomas. She never sought a court order for protection. Would these steps have helped? Probably not. In an examination of 200 cases of assault occurring in a *single week* in 1992, 12 percent of the women attacked were seeking or had already obtained court orders of protection (Ross 1992). Susan Murphy Milano, an advocate for battered women in Chicago, suggests that the court system itself is part of the problem:

> Women come into Domestic Violence Court not knowing anything about what's going on, and a lot of times they leave not knowing anything. ... They're shuffled through, usually with inadequate representation. The men

get off too often, even if they've repeatedly violated an order of protection. And the darker-skinned you are, the more often you're treated unfairly. (Miller 1993:1)

Although Barbara feels safe in the shelter, she worries about Thomas locating her and the children.

INTERVIEWER: You don't think he knows where you are now?

BARBARA: No, he don't. He don't know where I am. He comes to my mother's and knocks on her door and says "Is your daughter back?" And my mama say, "No, and if she were, she don't want you."

INT.: So he's still lookin' for you.

BARBARA: Right. He comes to my mother and asks about me and says he wants his kids' pictures. He says, "Well, she better show up with my kids or I'm gonna kill her. They're my kids." I know he made 'em, but he's ain't supportin' 'em. He never did. But he ain't called her or showed up for a week now. I'm hopin' that he's forgettin' about me 'cause I don't want him no more.

INT.: Is that why you can't be at your mother's now?

BARBARA: Right. I'm not afraid to go to my mother's, but I'm not goin' 'cause I'm tryin' to keep down trouble. I was raised around the projects since I was eight years old. Them guys there, I know them all my life. They ain't gonna let nothin' happen to me. They'd kill him. They'd figure they was protectin' me. 'Cause he weigh 280 pounds. He was a body builder. I know it would be trouble. So I'm tryin' to keep away. He figure I'm scared of him, but I'm really tryin' to keep him alive.

Discussions of domestic violence invariably focus on the question "Why did she stay?" Women like Barbara Evans stay because they have no choice. They lack the material resources to change their situation. They need money and protection and have neither. They are afraid for themselves and for their children. They risk further violence—perhaps even death—by leaving. And agencies that are supposed to assist are of little or no help. Only very recently has battering been defined as a criminal offense rather than a domestic disturbance. Prior to grass-roots women's movements pressing for change, police departments and the judicial system treated this behavior as a minor infraction, not a serious offense.

Battered Women and Housing

Although Thomas's behavior was without question repugnant and criminal, his victimization of Barbara did not *cause* her present homelessness. Social problems experienced by homeless persons, such as alcoholism, mental illness, teenage prostitution, and battering, are serious issues and must be confronted in any society professing a concern for its citizens' welfare. These social problems are not, however, causes of homelessness. Barbara did need emergency protection when she first escaped Thomas and his abuse. She may need protection in the future, if Thomas discovers her whereabouts. But her continuing to stay in the shelter results from her poverty and the lack of affordable housing, not her experience as a battered woman.

BARBARA: I'm tryin' to get a place to live. Sister Corinne [on the staff at the shelter] is tryin' to place me in my own little house, on 103rd Street, I believe. I think that's far enough away to forget the past. I won't have to worry about turnin' my back, wonderin' who gonna shoot me down. Who gonna snatch one of my kids. And run off with 'em. And call me back and say, "If you don't go back with me, I'm gonna do this to my kids."

INTERVIEWER: Is this house run by the CHA [Chicago Housing Authority]?

BARBARA: Yes. I pray and hope that they'll find me a place to live. I'm not guaranteed, but I do know Sister Corinne said she would help me. I went downtown to interview, and they told me that I would have to go back to Robert Taylor [a high-rise public housing project]. But Sister Corinne say different. So I'm hoping her words will count, you know, and not theirs. Because I don't want to go back to Robert Taylor. I think I would leave town before I go back into that life. He would find me there. But I'm hopin' and prayin' I can go on a hundred somethin' because Chicago is where I lived all my life and I really don't want to leave it.

INT.: To get this row house from the Housing Authority—do you have a number on the waiting list?

BARBARA: Yes, I have a number. My number is 566351.

INT.: You even know your number. How long is the waiting list for a row house like that?

BARBARA: The waiting list for a row house is at least four to five years. And I never been on it, so I start from zero. But Sister Corinne says she got a little bit of pull. She promised to get me in there some way, somehow. I got my hope on her.

Barbara's optimism is likely quite unrealistic. Even if she does get into this row house, that means another family stays at the shelter or on the streets. There is simply not sufficient public and affordable housing for everyone who needs it. Barbara certainly cannot afford rent in the private housing market:

BARBARA: I get $385 a month in Aid and $187 in food stamps. I can't just rent an apartment, 'cause I don't get enough money. Apartments out here in Chicago, they want at least $300. I get $385. I got to pay my rent and utility bill. That's my whole check. But my kids ... I won't be able to buy them clothes. I won't be able to go places with 'em. I won't be able to buy myself nothin'. I can't move into a regular apartment, 'cause they are too high. They're askin' for too much money.

INTERVIEWER: Could you even find an apartment—a two-bedroom apartment?

BARBARA: You can find a two-bedroom apartment, but it's got rats. Big rats. Full of rats and roaches. It's just not a place to raise kids. It's damaged; it's pretty soon condemned. And the rent be entirely too high. And the utility bills be entirely too high. They give us a energy check to help pay the lights, but that still isn't enough, because you got to pay double security. It's just too high. It's just not right.

Barbara's comments refer to the devastation of inner-city housing stock wrought by slumlording. As briefly discussed in Chapter 2, slumlording occurs when unscrupulous real estate speculators purchase dilapidated apartment buildings in poor urban neighborhoods, never intending to spend any money on their upkeep or improvement. The apartments are rented out, but the owner keeps all money received, never paying for repairs or property taxes. The landlord continues to "bleed" the building for whatever can be gained until the property is condemned for code violations and all residents are evicted. At this point the building is abandoned by the owner and the city eventually takes over the property for nonpayment of taxes. Given the costs of boarding up abandoned buildings, much less their demolition, it is often years before the property is taken down, leaving a vacant lot. In the meantime, the building remains as a health and safety hazard to the community.

Barbara Evans lives in Chicago, where slumlording is a significant source of the loss of affordable housing. Using census data along with related statistics from the city's Housing and Demolition Court, a recent study found that during the 1980s, Chicago lost 41,664 housing units through the razing of condemned properties. Of those, 9,214 were demolished in 1989 alone. An additional 3,260 buildings are abandoned and awaiting demolition. More than 28,000 properties—5 percent of all the property in Chicago—are two years behind in property taxes. The comparable figure in 1980 was 2 percent. More than 11 percent of the city's land is now vacant. Predominantly black and poor communities on the city's west and south sides have been hardest hit. In some of these neighborhoods, as much as 40 percent of the land is vacant (Joravsky 1993; Nicodemus 1993b).

High Aspirations Meet Discrimination and the Low-Wage Economy

Barbara has a high school degree. She continued her education at both a community college and a specialized trade school after graduation. Her aspirations were high. A combination of inexperience and discrimination, however, resulted in her hopes for the future being dashed. Her additional credentials did not help her find a "good" job; on the contrary, her postsecondary education made her feel cheated and inferior.

BARBARA: I finished high school and went to City College. I went there for about a year. I was takin' up drama. I wanted to be a actress. I wanted to learn how to write. And act. I passed all my subjects. In the basic one [the acting class] we would read and act a little bit. But they was more interested in workin' with those that already knew everything. They wasn't interested in workin' with the new ones. So they made me feel left out. So I just finished the year up and I left. I didn't go back. Then I went downtown and signed up for a training school in computers. College of Automation. It was a computer school. I got a student loan and that's where I took computer. I went there a whole straight year. I got a diploma in that school. And you know what? They said "We guarantee you a job after a year." But they did not guarantee me a job. They didn't do nothin' for me. Nothin'. They helped the ones—I'm not bein' funny—they helped mostly those that was not my color. They got the majority of the jobs. There was some blacks, but not many. I felt it bad. That made me feel more left out 'cause it happened to me twice, you know.

INTERVIEWER: Did you ever find a job?

BARBARA: I worked at Burger King before I had Tawana [her first child]. They laid me off when I was pregnant with her. They laid me off 'cause they was afraid I would fall and sue 'em because I was pregnant. My payday was every two weeks. I made a hundred and sixty-somethin' dollars every two weeks. It wasn't much. But I didn't have no child then. I was livin' with my mama.

INT.: Is that the only job you've ever had?

BARBARA: I worked at a tape company after that. We made tapes. Recorded and labeled them. I worked there for about six months, maybe. I had to quit because my daughter got sick at home and my mother wanted me to be there with her. She couldn't take care of her no more.

INT.: What was the pay there?

BARBARA: Every week I was bringin' home at least a hundred and twenty-five dollars, maybe. But I had to stop to take care of my daughter. So those are the only two jobs I had in my life.

INT.: That's about the time you were twenty and you met Thomas.

BARBARA: Yeah, Thomas. My life … my life just went down. I guess that's part of why I gave up hope. It could be one of my reasons I gave up hope and went to havin' kids and this and that. I wanted to be somebody. I was gonna make something out of myself.

As a black woman, Barbara Evans faces discrimination on two fronts—race and gender. Even with post–high school specialized training, Barbara could not find a job paying an adequate wage. She was forced to leave the low-paying position she could find when her child became ill. Now on AFDC, Barbara cannot afford anything other than subsidized housing. But that housing is in dreadfully short supply. The shelter Barbara and her children are currently living in has a four-month maximum stay; Barbara has been there two months. As we conclude our interview, Barbara's optimism is at once both poignant and naive:

BARBARA: I'm a little bit happy. I'm not scared no more. I feel safe here. I been blessed with a lotta little clothes for my kids and me. And soon, I'm gonna be blessed with a place to live. I might even be blessed with more. A job. Back to school. You never know. I might come to mean somethin'. I might even get a chance to express myself to the world.

PART THREE

Conclusion

12

The Complex and Simple Reality
of Homelessness

Denise Moses has lived in Chicago all of her life. She and her three children have lived in a shelter for homeless women and children on the South Side of Chicago for three months. The shelter limits homeless families to a four-month stay. Denise is black, a single parent, and on Public Aid (AFDC). She is twenty-one years old. When she was sixteen she quit school because she was pregnant. At the time we interviewed her she was with her two daughters, ages three and five, and her son, a year and a half old. Five days after we finished our interview, she gave birth to a new baby girl in the shelter.

A Note on the Complexity of Homelessness

In each of the preceding chapters, for each of the persons or families interviewed we have highlighted and analyzed factors on both sides of the socioeconomic contradiction that is the source of homelessness in American cities. For each homeless person or family, trends and forces were identified that increased and intensified their poverty, making them more "at risk"; also identified were simultaneous trends and forces shrinking the supply of affordable housing in the urban United States. The way we have illustrated and identified these structural sources and contradictions that are involved in the production and reproduction of homelessness, however, does not always fully capture the individual's or family's *concrete* experience. In reality, most homeless persons and families experience a host of factors that put them more "at risk" and contribute to their extreme poverty, and they run up against the shrinking supply of affordable housing in multiple ways, *all at the same time*. In this sense, the concrete experience of homelessness is truly complex. To that end, in this chapter we present one of our interviews uninterrupted by our highlighting or analyzing any single or small number of factors that the personal account reveals to be a source of homelessness.

Most homeless people and families are inundated and overwhelmed by a wide range of the homelessness-producing factors we have looked at in the preceding chapters—by a wide range of forces that make them poorer and squeeze them out of housing in our cities. Denise Moses's story reflects this concrete reality. Many factors work to make her more at risk: meager welfare payments, a too-low minimum wage, the low-wage economy, bureaucratic social services that cut aid when a welfare recipient works, the lack of publicly funded day care, and her being unable to rely on a young black male, an "endangered species" himself, for support. The urban housing crisis meets Denise and her family when she rents an apartment without being given a lease so that the landlord can evict her and sell his property for the highest price to developers who want to gentrify the property and rent it to more affluent tenants, not having to bother with evictions themselves. "Doubling up," a bureaucratic public housing authority, unsafe public housing projects, and the homeless shelter itself all clearly work to leave Denise and her children without a place to live.

The Concrete Reality of Homelessness

DENISE: My mother died. That's, that's, that's the hardest part goin' through. There's a lot of changes, you know, after my mother dies.

INTERVIEWER: When did she die?

DENISE: She died November eighteen of eighty-three. So I was goin', you know, I was real hurt 'cause my mother was dead and I was like goin' through a lot of changes and stuff.

INT.: Were you livin' with her then?

DENISE: And bein' when she dies I was still livin' in her house and I was sort of scared and stuff, you know, I was, you know, goin' through a lot of changes and, and everything. So then I was with my kids' father and he was makin' it worse. You know, he wasn't makin' it any better. And then my mother had died, my mother had left the rent behind a month. And they wanted me to pay some money that I didn't have. I was stayin' in the projects. But my mother was payin' high rent 'cause there was, she had a lot of kids there.

INT.: They're still all with you after your mother dies?

DENISE: No. ... They with my sister now.

INT.: But what about right after your mother died?

DENISE: They was there.

INT.: Who was in the apartment with you then?

DENISE: My father. And my two brothers. My kids. And my other brother. My oldest brother. He was in and out.

INT.: Not your children's father?

DENISE: He was there too. But he was in and out too. You know. ... It wasn't, it ain't nothin'. So my father, OK, first he moved out but he was still comin' over. And I told him that they wanted me to pay all this back rent and I didn't have it. So he told me he was gonna bring the money over and he never showed up. He ain't never bring it over. And then, so my kid's father, he, he said that he was gonna help me pay the rent. And so I, one day I got mad. And I don't know if he had the money or not. He said he had it. But he asked me did I want it. And I just told him to stay out of my face and just stay away from me, you know. And I didn't accept it. I don't know if he had it or not. And, so then my sister started goin' over to the Housing Authority and telling them that I couldn't pay all this money and stuff and could they lower it.

INT.: There aren't as many people living there now, but they want the ...

DENISE: They want the back money. So then my sister kept asking them would they lower it. And it was like, no, 'cause this was gonna have to be paid. You know, and even though your mother died and your sister's in that apartment, she'll have to pay it. So I, my sister told, was tellin' 'em, "Well, she ain't have, she don't have the money to pay you all." So my sister kept goin' over there like every day she get a chance to. So when it got to about almost six hundred dollars, they lowered it to about four. And I still, still don't have enough money to pay that. So my sister was still goin' over there. Arguin' with them. Arguin', arguin', and arguin'. You know. And they still wouldn't do nothin'. Even like my mother's friend had came over here and she worked for CHA [Chicago Housing Authority] in the Robert Taylors [the Robert Taylor Homes, a high-rise public housing project on the South Side of the city]. And so she came on down and she was callin' herself and tellin' them you know they couldn't do that. And they were sayin' that they could do whatever they want to do. You know. So I moved out. And then I moved in with my friend. It was, you know, one of my friends I had went to school with, this girl.

INT.: But not in the projects?

DENISE: It was around the projects but it wasn't in 'em.

INT.: Alright. Now you're in, you're in an apartment. A flat or somethin'?

DENISE: Right. And me and her we were stayin', so we were stayin' together and everything. But she only had one bedroom. And I had, I had three kids. I had Tiffany, Tisha, and my baby was a newborn baby. And so, um, you know, everything was nice there and stuff. You know, I liked stayin' there with her 'cause she was nice. But it, it was gettin' so her boyfriend didn't like it. And every time he would come over he would say, you know, you know, just say crazy things and stuff, you know. And, um, and before I had moved over there, he used to be nice, you know. And then he just changed. So I had called my sister one day. 'Cause I had to tell her. I say, "Every time you leave the house, I don't supposed to leave." You know I say, "I want a key, you know, 'cause every time you go, you see what I mean, I want to go." You know. So then we got to arguin'. And so I called my sister and asked my sister would she come and get me 'cause I didn't want to stay, you know, with that girl no more. So then my sister say "Well, OK." And so she came over to her house and got me and took me over to my sister's house. And so my sister took me to a shelter.

INT.: Your sister's not in the projects?

DENISE: A HUD apartment that, you know, it's the same as the projects 'cause you still can't have nobody but who on the lease in your apartment.

INT.: In Section 8?

DENISE: Yeah, It's the same as Section 8 but it's HUD. It's up under a different agency like that. But it's the same thing. Low rent. Just in a, like, you know, a three-flat building like. I went, I went to my sister's house. And so my sister took me to a shelter. My sister took me to a shelter and I stayed there three days. I couldn't stand it and so I left.

INT.: Why couldn't you stand it?

DENISE: I, I just, I couldn't bear bein' there. It was Pacific Gardens Mission on State Street [the oldest shelter in downtown Chicago]. And it was, um, you know, they wanted you to be in by seven o'clock. Locked in at seven o'clock, no place for my family, drunks and winos be layin' out on the street in front of the place and be stayin' in the men's side of the place. And you have to go to church every night and you got to wear dresses while you in there. And you, you know, it, I just didn't like it. And so I, I stayed there for three days and my friend had called there with this other girl. And she said, "Denise, you can rent a room here, you know, if you like," And I was thinkin' about it. I didn't want to do it but I didn't want to stay there, so I went on and did that. And so while I was stayin' with her, you know, OK, at that time I didn't have no money or nothin'. And the girl she wouldn't …

INT.: You didn't have any money?

DENISE: No.

INT.: You didn't have a check?

DENISE: No.

INT.: Why not?

DENISE: 'Cause I hadn't got none. And 'cause, see, this was like in the middle of the month when I had already paid the girl's rent. The one who I had left at first.

INT.: But you are gettin' a check [a Public Aid check]? For you and the kids?

DENISE: Right.

INT.: And that's all, that's all the income you have?

DENISE: Right.

INT.: How much you gettin'?

DENISE: Three eighty-five.

INT.: For you and three kids.

DENISE: Mm hmm. So then, OK, I didn't have no money then when I moved with the girl. And the girl, she wasn't buying any food or anything to go in the house, you know. And her and her kids they would leave every day, you know, and I know they was probably goin' somewhere else to eat like. So then I called my sister and I told my sister what was happenin' so she brought us some food and stuff over there. And so then after that my check came and, you know, I bought some, you know, somethin' and stuff. But it go in the house. Then her brothers and them start comin' over and they were stealin' my clothes. And so I, you know, I kept tellin' her, I say, "Your brothers and them takin' my stuff." And, you know, she was sayin', "OK, I'm gonna tell my mother and my mother'll give them somethin'." But I never got my clothes back. Then they messes up my record player. So I say, "I can't stay here no more, can't stay here no more." So I left. Now where did I go? Let me see, OK I left and I went and stayed with this other girl. And I stayed with her for about three months. And, you know, it was alright. But then it was her man. You know, her man was livin' there. And he was, you know, talkin' a lotta stuff. So then I left there. And then my sister she took me to a shelter. Yeah. 'Cause then my sister took me to a shelter.

INT.: Not the same shelter?

DENISE: No. It's the shelter up on ninety-third and Cottage Grove. It's run by a reverend. His wife was talkin' stuff about him and the women in the shelter. She was jealous and didn't want nobody to stay up in there more than two weeks. I stayed a month, but then a young woman was stabbed to death in her room.

INT.: Why didn't you stay with your sister?

DENISE: My sister can't have nobody stayin' with her.

INT.: Because of the HUD restriction?

DENISE: Right. So I stayed there for a month. And so I had saved up my money and stuff. And, OK, when I came there I had gave them my money then and next month. ... Yeah, OK. So then, uh, I went to that shelter and I stayed there for a month. And I saved my money up so the next month I moved. Alright now I got my own apartment up north.

INT.: You got an apartment comin' out of this shelter?

DENISE: Yeah.

INT.: In the projects?

DENISE: I had, I had left the shelter. I went on the North Side in the projects. OK, and then I, and then I ran into my kids' father. He took me up north. You know, like Uptown [one of the poorest neighborhoods on Chicago's North Side]. He took me up there. Well, his mother lived there. So I stayed with his mother about four days. And I ...

INT.: How long did you stay in the projects when you got out of this shelter?

DENISE: I came there that day and left there that night.

INT.: The projects?

DENISE: Mm hmm. OK, I'm at my mother-in-law's house.

INT.: In Uptown?

DENISE: Right. And then I found me an apartment up there. And so it was in this nice—it wasn't really nice—an alright building. I liked it because it was mine, you know. So this dude, OK, the managers they was twenty-six, twenty-seven years old. And when I first, when I first came there to check it out he said, "Come back tomorrow afternoon and we'll talk about it." So I came back and he said, uh, "Do you want me to get this through the lease or do you want to just go through me and get it?" and I say, "Anything, it's the fastest way." "Well, if you go through me and get it, that's the fastest way you can get it." Alright, so then I ...

INT.: This is the manager of the building?

DENISE: Mm hmm. So I said, "OK." I said, "What do I have to do?" And he said, "You give me the money." I said, "Well, um, I don't exactly have all of it." 'Cause, ... OK, it was four hundred. I gave him three. OK. And so the manager said I could move in whenever I got ready to. So I moved in the next day. And, uh, he gave me a receipt then, you know. So, so the next month when I paid him rent, and I asked him for a receipt, he said, "I'll be back and I'll bring you a receipt." And I didn't never get that receipt. So then that next month, I'm sayin', "You know last month I didn't get no receipt from you." I say, "I want a receipt. I need it." You know, and he said "OK, I'm gonna get it to you. I'm gonna get it to you." But he never gave it to me. So then he said, um, also a new management bought the building. The old management knew what he was doin'. So they, you know, ... 'cause everybody in the building, he wasn't just doin' me like that. He was doin' the other people in the building like that. You know, gettin' the rent and not givin' them their receipts and stuff.

INT.: Why did you need the receipt?

DENISE: Why did I? Just proof that I paid my rent.

INT.: So they can't come back and say you didn't pay your rent?

DENISE: And so that's what happened. It was the new owners that did it. They brought a stack of books sayin' that they didn't show no, um, no receipts. You know, nothin' was sayin' that you had paid your rent.

INT.: This guy's got the money in his pocket?

DENISE: Right. 'Cause he, he definitely, he was livin' in an apartment on his own. You know, and the manager, the owner, I don't think he knew about it. So, um, so then they, I kept sayin', "Well I been payin' my rent and I been payin'." You know. So he kept sayin', the manager kept sayin', "Denise, we're gonna get this straight, you don't have to go nowhere." He kept sayin', "Denise, you don't have to go nowhere." So then after they kept on and kept on and kept on, the judge sent everybody in the building, um, a notice for to come to court. And so everybody who didn't go to court had to be out within like, five or seven days. And everybody who went to court, he gave them fifteen days to move.

INT.: Did you go to court?

DENISE: Mm hmm. I went and got fifteen days.

INT.: The judge says you got to move out in fifteen days, but you already paid your rent?

DENISE: Right. But I didn't have no proof showin' it. So, you know, and like I was tellin' them. I was sayin', "How do you think we got in this building? Well, we just broke out our way and took an apartment," you know. He sayin', "But you all don't have proof." So then I came in, I went with my sister and I stayed there for what was about two weeks.

INT.: You never had a lease with this guy. Because he said when he rented you the apartment, "You go through me"?

DENISE: Right. And I wanted to get it the quickest way I can.

INT.: 'Cause you had to. You didn't have a place to go?

DENISE: Right. Yeah. So I stayed with my sister for about two weeks. And so my, my sister she was alright you know. She, you know, it was, I wasn't supposed to be stayin' there. She letted me stay there, right. Then what happened? Because she let me stay at her house? And, uh, her daughter was gettin', her daughter, now when we came, her daughter moved out. But I wasn't realizin', you know, what it was at first, I think. And, um, let me see, OK, my niece she, she moved out. So I kept wonderin', I say, I kept asking my other niece, I say, "Well, where is Clancy?" She say, "She, uh, she over at her boyfriend's house." And then I say, "Will she always be stayin' there like this?" And Wendy said,

"No." I say, "Well, I wonder why she's been right now?" So then I asked my sister, I said, "Squeaky, is you leavin' 'cause of us?" I mean, I mean did my niece leave cause of us. Then she said, "Well, you know Clancy got bad nerves and she don't like it bein' around a whole lot of kids and stuff." You know like that. So that hurt my feelings. So then I had gone to my other sister and visit to the social worker. And I call her and tell her. I said, "Well, you know, I don't like it that my niece left because of me, you know. I don't want her to have to leave her own apartment, her own house because of us." So I told her that, um, did she know any shelter that I could go to. And then she said "Yes." and, uh, for a couple of days she had checked out a couple other ones. Then she said, she, you know, knew one. And she brought me here. And so then I stayed here, I stayed here for about a month. Then I got kicked out 'cause of bein' late.

INT.: When you were here? This is the third shelter you've been in?

DENISE: And the second time. That apartment up north is the only apartment I ever had.

INT.: How long were you there?

DENISE: I guess about six months.

INT.: What happened when you got here? The first time you came to this shelter?

DENISE: I didn't like it here. I was, I was cryin' every day and I didn't want to stay here. And my sister just kept sayin', "You just have to pray all the time. You just have to pray." 'Cause my sister, she said, "My landlord know that, you know, knew that you all was stayin' with me. And he said that he gonna report me to the people." And so I said, "Well, how he know?" You know, 'cause she said it was because my baby been hollerin'. But she got three kids. I don't understand how he know to make sure it's her kids. She said, "Well, he know I'm supposed to have no girls up here. You know, no little girls." And so then my sister she just kept callin' me every night, "Now you better not leave there 'cause they probably will help you. They can do somethin' for you." 'Cause she knew I was on the urge of just movin' out. Leavin' for to stay with another friend. So I kept on. Then there was these girls up here that I didn't like. They, you know, was messin' with me all the time. And talkin' stuff. You know they, they had, they bother your kids. So then I was really, I said, "I know I can't stay up in here." Then after a while ...

INT.: What kind of stuff were they talkin'?

DENISE: Like if my baby, if he get off the bed or somethin', they'll come in, throw him over, "Why don't you keep your child in," "You watchin'? You watch him." You know, stuff like that. Or either, "Go over there with your mother." And stuff like that. And my baby, he used to have it bad to go in this girl's, um, baby's bed and, and playin' with her baby. And she used to get real mad. 'Cause she hated for him to be around her baby. So I said I knew I couldn't deal with that. But then. ... When I started gettin cooler with other peoples up here, she started gettin' cooler with me. And started talkin' to me and stuff. And started, you know, tryin' to act like she was my friend. Even though I know she wasn't crazy about me.

INT.: Wait a minute. You were here for a month and you got put out. What happened?

DENISE: 'Cause, um, I was bein' late. I had got put out for I had been late a couple of times. But on Mother's Day I had went out ... and my sister had, um, kept my kids for me. And I had, I just went over to my friend's house, you know, for a little while and stuff. And when I thought about it, it was gettin' late, it was about seven o'clock. And I was up on the North Side. So I called my sister and I say, "You bring them to the shelter and I'll meet you there." 'Cause I know I wouldn't have time to go pick them up and they can't spend the night away from the shelter. So she said, "OK." But my sister made it here before I did.

INT.: With your kids?

DENISE: Right. She made it here about five or ten minutes before I made it there. But they was mad about that. They was mad about that. About my kids not comin' in with me. And for one thing I was late already. And so, see, they were sayin' that I had just put my kids off on somebody and left them. You know, like my sister had got mad and just brought 'em home. But that's not what happened. So then the next day, um, Yvette had ask me, she say, "Denise, do you have somewhere to go?" And then I say, "Why?" And then she say, "But do you?" I didn't understand that. So she went upstairs and she came back down and she said, "Now, do you have anywhere to go?" And I said, "Why, do you want me to leave?" She said, "Yeah." I said, "Well, I'll leave." Yvette is the assistant director [of the shelter]. And then I called my sister and I told my sister what happened. And my sister was goin' off: "You can't stay nowhere and you can't do this and you can't do that." You know, she was goin' off and stuff. But still, you know, people doin' that all the time. They be, you know, comin' in late and stuff and, you know, I never seen nobody get put out before. And so she, um, so Sister Theresa [one of the Catholic nuns working in the shelter] came up to me and say, "I'm sorry you chose to leave." I said, "She wanted me to leave." And Sister Theresa she didn't know about that. So anyways Sister Theresa said she wasn't gonna go over Yvette's head anymore. So I left. And my sister had come and got me and she was all mad and stuff. So I stayed with her for about four days. And I was tryin' my best. I was tryin' to keep them quiet. I was tryin' to make 'em lay down. I was just tryin to watch, make 'em watch TV. I was, you know, I was tryin' to keep 'em quiet. Me and my sister, I mean, I say, "You all go lay down." You know, they be runnin' around. So then she said, "Oh, you all kids too big and they do this, and they do that, and they do that." So at the same time she was arguin', Sister Paula called. Sister Paula say, "You got some mail here." And I say, "Sister Paula, could you talk to Sister Theresa for me and see if I can come back there?" And then she say, "I let you speak to her." So she got her and I ask Sister Theresa. And Sister Theresa say, "You can come back if you promise to obey by the rules." And I say, "Yes." And ever since then, I been late probably once since.

INT.: When, when you were put out, you said you were late a few times before. Like what? Late for what?

DENISE: Late comin' in. Like you have to be in at seven thirty. I probably had come in about eight fifteen or eight thirty. Maybe, I mighta came in at nine o'clock.

INT.: A couple of times?

DENISE: The only people who could come in at nine o'clock is people who don't have children. They come in at nine thirty if they don't have children.

INT.: When you were comin' in late, you were comin' in late but you were with your kids?

DENISE: Right.

INT.: So you come back in here a second time?

DENISE: Right.

INT.: How long ago was that?

DENISE: I came back about a week later after they put me out. When I asked Sister Theresa, it was about a week later.

INT.: You're still gettin' what? Three hundred and eighty-five dollars a month?

DENISE: Yeah.

INT.: What if somebody said to you, you got three hundred and eighty-five dollars a month just to rent an apartment?

DENISE: Isn't enough. I would say I needed some more money. I would say I needed some more money. But couldn't nobody tell me nothin' like that. I mean, 'cause I know even with a studio it costs, a studio costs too much now. I can't even get a studio. But I got too many kids for a studio. And a three bedroom is what I need and a three bedroom costs five something. Or close to five. And I, I don't near about get that much, shit. That's why I'm here. And I'm savin' up money and stuff. See, and what I'm planning to do is, while I'm here you save your money, right? So I intend to pay housing back.

INT.: The CHA? Then you can get in …

DENISE: Back in there.

INT.: Get a number, and be back on their lists. But not until you pay that money. Is that right?

DENISE: So I'm gonna, I'm payin' 'em back next month.

INT.: Life in the shelter? What makes it hard?

DENISE: For one things all the rules. You know, most people don't be used to abidin' by all the rules and stuff. I know I wasn't used to it.

INT.: Like what? What kind of rules?

DENISE: Like bein' in at seven forty-five and, OK, you know, doin' your chores. That's, that's alright. You know, 'cause everybody, even if you had your own apartment, that's one thing you gonna have to do, is do chores and stuff. You know. I could say that's the really, the only thing is, is the seven forty-five curfew. But, um, I, I know so everything just about happenin' at that time. And, you know, that's the time I just be wantin' to go outside when it be summertime. And they want you in by that time. And then they have the rule that you can't hit your children. But they can hit your children. That ain't the rule that they can hit 'em but they have hit them.

INT.: You can't hit your children but they can hit your children?

DENISE: Right. But as far as, Yvette said that I used to have a nasty attitude. And I, I always thought I was the same. You know, I said, "When I first came here maybe I was actin' kinda funny because I didn't want to be here." But I told her, I said, "I never knew that I had a nasty attitude." You know. And that was now since I been back, you know. And stuff, shit, everybody'll write down what, what they think their bad points were and their good points and stuff like that. And so I had said, "I don't think my attitude was that bad." She said, "Now it's not. But at first it was." I mean, I can't deal with it. And, you know, there be a girl up there now. And she always be, she jokes about it, you know. 'Cause she said, "Everything you do up in there's a rule for." She say just silly stuff like, if, if your child take, put her shoes on the wrong foot, you gonna get put out, you know, just crazy stuff. And it's a lot of rules but if there wasn't them it would be, you know, real terrible up in there. 'Cause everybody'd be doin' everything. There was this one girl who was there before. My friend had to take a, a axe out of her locker, 'cause she had it hid in her locker and stuff. You know, that's the only thing, they, they don't obey your privacy. But some people sometimes they should. 'Cause, you know, people might be bringin' things up in there and stuff.

INT.: Do you feel safe in here? Do you feel safe? Do you feel your kids are safe? Do you feel your things are safe?

DENISE: No. Not all the time. I don't leave my, I carry my purse everywhere I go. And even though, like, most of the people I'm cool with. But still, they still be takin' stuff. You know, they, they'll steal from you.

And, uh, that's, it's a couple of nights, OK, like now, this is about two or three weeks ago, and I had called my sister, I was scared and I didn't know why I was scared. I was just scared. You know, my, my sister said, "Girl, that's just, you know, you goin' through them changes and stuff. And you feelin' nervous and stuff." I said, "Huh uh. I am scared." And all of that night I slept sitting up. I tried to sleep standin' 'cause I was really scared. A lot of times I get like that. You know. But now the crazy folks are gone. There used to be crazy people in here. They wasn't mentally, they was mentally insane but they wasn't, you know, like they shoulda been in a crazy home or nothin'. But they was kinda crazy.

INT.: That's what you were scared of?

DENISE: Yeah. And I used to sleep right in between both of 'em.

INT.: And your things, they aren't safe?

DENISE: If you keep 'em, I mean if you put 'em where somebody could get 'em, they gonna get it. They gonna steal 'em.

INT.: How come?

DENISE: It just happen.

INT.: What do you think the reason for that is?

DENISE: I don't know. Like when my friend, her money came up missin' the other day. And she know it's, it got to be somebody that sleep around us. And all, all of us just sleep around each other supposed to be real tight. We be together every day. We go leave there and go eat. You know, it's just, you know. And, like I told her, I say, "We all supposed to be tight. But we really didn't know as much about each other before we got here. You know, we don't know what the other did before we got here." And so it's just like, "Yeah, but that's wrong." 'Cause, like she, like she done set off food to us. And bought us stuff and bought me cigarettes. And I have did it for them. And that's why I'd be real hurt if one of them took from me. So I try to keep my purse with me wherever I go. And make sure it don't happen. 'Cause I would be real mad. But, like, there was this one girl, before she left, I used to give her Pampers all the time. And she never paid me back. You know, she just acted like I hadn't did anything. And then another girl, one of the crazy people, they, she, um, was stealing my Pampers. And that, that was killing me, too. Because I was steady, you know, giving up my Pampers and they just stealin' 'em. And that hurted me. That's why I say I wasn't givin nobody nothin' else.

INT.: It's not always clear to me who's in charge of the kids, OK? Like, um, I've seen mothers of kids sittin' downstairs while kids are upstairs.

DENISE: Upstairs, where?

INT.: Talkin' to somebody else about something they did wrong.

DENISE: Oh, OK.

INT.: You see what I'm saying?

DENISE: Yeah.

INT.: Like sometimes I see the staff get between the mother and the ...

DENISE: Child?

INT.: Child.

DENISE: It be, it be like that sometimes. Like, OK, let's say if my kids do something wrong, I, before I could say anything to 'em fifty other peoples now hollered at 'em, maybe done cussed at 'em, done told 'em to get somewhere and sit down. You know, and I'll be like, "What is goin' on?" You know. And then they be, like, "Well she did such and such a thing, such and such." And like me and her, she holler all the time. Me and her could be talkin' or whatever, and I could say, "You ain't gettin' this or you ain't gettin this," 'n' she could probably holler. Before I can get her, maybe somebody else have done came and grabbed her and tell her to stand in the corner. You know, and it just be like that. But since, you know, like, OK, they try to tell you and they means, they say, "Don't," well they say, "Don't whip your kids. Just stare at 'em, or make 'em stand in the corner or anything." And I be tryin' that all the time. You know, and I, I try not to whip them and stuff 'cause I don't like it. It hurts me. I have a, it stays, it stays on my mind after I whip them, you know. It sort of hurt. And so I be tryin' that, but it don't all the time work. But still I feel like even while you here, if you can't discipline your kids, then they ain't gonna have no discipline. You know, if, if they be able to run wild up in here and you can't tell 'em, 'cause I know a couple of kids that told their mother that they know they couldn't whip them. You know, they knew they couldn't whip 'em and they were cryin'. They would talk back. They would, you know, 'cause they knew it. All the kids do. They know it, that they are not allowed to be whipped. And they show it. They talk back to their parents and everything. But see, I, I know, couldn't nobody hold me back if these talks back to me 'cause I am gonna be really mad. It just like, 'cause my friend, she's one of the girls up in there was whippin' her daughter today, and, uh, one of the sisters had came and grabbed her and stuff. All she had was a little dainty house shoe. Now how she, with no sole on it or nothin', you know. And the, the little girl was hollerin' and screamin' like she, it was killin' her. But she wasn't hurtin' her with that little thin house shoe. And the sister was still walkin' around sayin', um, she shouldn't of, she was whippin' that girl like that and all that stuff. But she wasn't hurtin' her. Shoot. These, these damn things they'll holler but they don't be hurt. But some, some of the mothers, you know, they will hurt their childrens, you know. See, that's one reason why they don't want you to whip them. Because they know you can get mad enough that you can hurt them. And, you know, of 'em, some mothers they, that might be the case, you know. That they just, they might have their child took from them because they done whupped 'em so bad and stuff like that. I'm not, I'm not gonna whup them bad. I'm not gonna hurt them. I'm not gonna put no whips on them. But I, I will spank them. You gotta have discipline, though. You know, some people today got their different ways, you know, people, some people be raised up their different ways. Some people they don't have to whip their kids 'cause there's somethin' else they could do. You know, OK, like them, they could say, they'll say, "Well, take away the TV." They don't watch TV. The bigger kids watch at night. But they be in the bed. You know, so there's not really nothing to take from them, you know. And what, what the little stuff that you can, like them, they ain't really interested in no TV. If I say, "Go in there and watch TV," I mean, "You can't watch no TV," they gonna go in there and play. They ain't gonna even think about it no more. 'Cause they ain't even that big to be really interested in it you know. So, it, it be other people, they, they act like your children. ... They do make me mad 'cause they be hollerin' at your kids, they holler at your kids like it was their kids. But they get mad when you say something to their kids. When you say something like ... "You all gonna have to wait a minute." They get really mad when you say something to their kids.

INT.: Is there anything else about the shelter? Life in the shelter? When do you want to leave?

DENISE: As soon as possible. I know by my bein' here and savin' money and stuff, even when I get out of here, there's a chance that I could find somethin', you know. But if I leave and go stay with somebody, my money gonna be messed up then. You know, it's gonna be like, if people know you have money they death on you, you know. I mean, just— I mean that, um, you gonna have to pay such and such a program, and everything.

INT.: Is there any place you could go right now besides here?

DENISE: No. I could, well, I could go to my sister's but I was, I would probably would spend the night and she would take me to another shelter. And that would be it. No, I don't have nowhere to go. Mostly, at first I thought I did. I used to say, "Hmm. I don't have to be here," you know. And then my friends they'd call me, "Girl, you, you must like it up in that place 'cause you just be, you know, don't be comin' out and you stayin' there and you just livin' there, you know." I say, "I'm just here." You know, then when I got kicked out, it was, I mean I was really hurt then, 'cause everybody was talkin' this stuff and then I can't get no help. I said, "Shoot, I got put out here and still don't have nowhere to go and everybody's sittin' around and talkin' all this stuff. I mean, I, uh, I'm gonna stay here 'til I'm better got myself together." The lady, my friend's mother, had said I could stay with her. She had a four-room apartment. She had it 'cause she had a lot of kids but they all done moved out. She ain't have but two there with her now. And she said I could rent out a room. She want two hundred dollars and all my food stamps. I said, "Huh uh. Ain't no way. That's too much money for one bedroom," and all of us to sleep in one bedroom, the same bedroom, and then she want all that much. So I just said no.

INT.: How many stamps do you get?

DENISE: One eighty-five. And like, my sister, she come over here, OK, like if I don't have money, my sister come over here and she bring money. You know, she'll give me money, OK. But if she, my sister don't get stamps, so most of the time I get my stamps, I give her some of 'em 'cause she don't have 'em and then she couldn't a gave me money, you know, all the time when I don't have any and stuff. So I just pay her back in stamps. It just all adds up with all this. And one thing about my sister's, it's crowded in her house. My sister got, OK, my two brothers, my two brothers are sixteen and eighteen. My sister's got three daughters of her own. She got a daughter nineteen, eighteen, and eleven. And the eighteen and nineteen got two, got a child apiece. You know, so my sister's a grandmother and stuff. And it's like, OK, she got three bedrooms. And it's kinda crowded, you know, and it's, especially a lot of grown folks be like, you know, stayin' at her house. I couldn't stay there. No way. 'Cause they all feel like they, you know, grown as you.

INT.: Have you lost all contact with the father of your kids?

DENISE: I can see him whenever I want to see him. But I'm not interested really 'cause he, he have, he cheats. He's stingy and he ain't no good. You know, he go to school. He a veteran. He go to school. And he make about at least six hundred dollars, I guess a month. 'Cause that's allowance for him. You know, he could be doin' something for his children. But he, he won't do nothin'. Now, now last week and I'm sayin' to him about it last week. And I told him, I say, uh, "I know you done got a check for school already, you know. Is you gonna look after the kids or what?" And he said the first check he had to pay some bills back or something but the second one he gonna make sure that he do all this and that, all this and that for 'em. So, but I'm not countin' on him 'cause I know he not. I know he not 'cause he, he gonna get high or hang out with the fellas and just show, you know, he just like to, "I got this and you ain't got it," you know, to his friends and stuff. So that's why I ain't, I ain't even thinkin' about him. He ain't gonna do nothin' for me. And he used to, when we was together, he used to, but now, see, he like, he believe in this thing. He always told me, "Love the one you with," you know. Me and him can't be together. And so, the only person I can probably could deal with, not deal, well, you know, be around is my father. But he's makin' me mad now. 'Cause I haven't seen him. OK, first he kept comin' back once my mother died. All of a sudden he just stopped. And, I guess just, I guess he came around for about, about six months after my mother had died. Then he left, and he ain't come back. And I seen him one time after that. And now, you know, I, I didn't know how to get in touch with him. And he know how, if he wanted to, he know how to get in touch with me. But I don't guess he, you know, feel like he want the responsibility. I guess he feel like he could do what he want to do. Even though if, if it ain't me, he's still got two younger boys that he could, you know, take them. Take them off my sister's hands. My sister say she want to give me everything, you know, just leave, you know. 'Cause all of them almost grown. She can't do it, though. 'Cause they not ready to be out on their own. My sister she sent, she sent my brother eighteen to the Job Corps. He came back, he came back, about the end of May. No, about the end of June he came back. And so he told us he was just, you know, he say he got into a fight and they sent him home for a couple of days. But I didn't really believe they kicked him out because he hasn't went back yet. So she mad about that, too, you know. 'Cause she tried to do something and she just couldn't deal with it. He, he, my mother spoiled her sons. She spoiled them. And even my older brother, he twenty, what? Seven or eight, and he, he's spoiled rotten. And he, he, he used, he used to my mother pattin' him so much that he just be up under his womens all the time, you know. He had came over here a couple of times for, he stopped by. He hadn't been up here a couple of times. ... What do I need? I need at least about, at least about five hundred more dollars, and, uh, I don't, I just need a chance. I, I, if I get the chance, I'm not gonna, if I, I don't, if anybody gets the chance, I believe they can if they want to, you know.

INT.: What kind of chance?

DENISE: Like at least, uh, a half a step. You know, if I can get a job, even though I couldn't get me a job, if I got one I couldn't work it because I have too many children. You know, I'm pregnant and I have a little baby. And I got another baby and then I have a toddler and then I couldn't work. I couldn't work.

INT.: What were you sayin' about the job?

DENISE: Uh, if, I couldn't work now. I couldn't. 'Cause, um, I got too many childrens. I mean when they get older I'd probably be able to 'cause, OK, when I make, uh, I'll be twenty-six and my daughters will be ten and eleven and my sons'll be six and seven. And I think, I think I could work then. But that'd be about as soon as I could.

INT.: But you still need somebody to take care of them even then?

DENISE: Right. Part time 'cause they'll be in school then. But, you know, like after school. I mean that'd be probably for a couple of hours. So they'd be in regular school. Goin' all day. But, after school, so I don't know if, you know, you get a job you probably work nine to five. Somethin' like that. They get out of school at two-thirty. So about two hours later, right? Um, you need a baby-sitter. If, you know, if I can get a job and I worked once. I used to work a summer job. And they, uh, cut my check for it. It just got right. They was takin' out forty dollars a month.

INT.: For what?

DENISE: A summer job.

INT.: You had a summer job, so they took it out of your ...

DENISE: Check.

INT.: What you were making they took out of your check, so you didn't get ahead by working?

DENISE: Right.

INT.: Was that the only job you've ever had, the summer job?

DENISE: I had a summer job before. I had summer jobs from since I was fourteen until I was twenty.

INT.: Summer jobs. Like what kind of jobs? What were you doing?

DENISE: I worked, OK, the first one I just, I didn't do nothin'. I used to clean up. ... And then the second one I worked in the Eighteenth District Police Station. Uh, the third one, I worked with the, uh, Methodist Youth Home with boys, like as livin' in shelters. I worked it in there. And then the fourth one I'm, I worked with handicapped peoples. And I guess that's that. Yeah.

INT.: Do you have a high school degree? You workin' on that now?

DENISE: I go for my GED.

INT.: You mean right now?

DENISE: We takin' our test Tuesday. If you pass that, then you ready for to go for your degree. But if you don't, then you have to stay there and study for some more and, you know, they know you ain't ready to take your GED yet.

INT.: So are you gonna pass it?

DENISE: I hope so. I am gonna study hard.

INT.: What's the most money you ever made per hour at those jobs you had?

DENISE: They all makin' the minimum wage. So I don't know. One sixty-seven every two weeks and then I was—I used to give, you know, give it to my mother and stuff. Like, I, I didn't, I didn't get on Aid with my first child. I got on Aid, OK, my mother was gettin' it for me. My mother was gettin' it for me. Then ...

INT.: How old were you when you had your first child?

DENISE: Sixteen.

INT.: So, your mother was gettin' Aid for you?

DENISE: And my child. But my mother would give me whatever I needed, you know. She, she was a nice, she was there. My mother would give me whatever I needed. And my mother still took care of us, so then, when I got pregnant with my second child, that's my daughter eight, I guess I was about seven months pregnant and so my mother, the most money I had was that first check. They gave me five hundred and forty-nine dollars. I gave my mother two hundred and fifty dollars of that and then after that I was gettin' three hundred and two.

INT.: Why'd you get five hundred and forty-nine at first?

DENISE: I don't know. They gave me that much money for gettin' on Aid.

INT.: How old were you when you had your second child?

DENISE: My second?

INT.: Two years later?

DENISE: Mm hmm. And this one [points to the child she is pregnant with]. Well, I'll be twenty-two in September, but it'll be here before I make twenty-two.

INT.: Is that what got in your way of finishing school, high school?

DENISE: Well, I coulda still went. I coulda still went. 'Cause my mother woulda took care of my child. But, I, I was, see, I wanted her. I planned my first child. Then when I got her, I was, I wanted to be around and stuff, but it was like a conflict between me and my mother. 'Cause my mother wanted her just as much. My mother used to always try to push me out the way. You know, my mother always like, she wanted to do everything. When it comes to pictures, she didn't want me around. When she take her picture, she wanted to get her dressed and all that kind of stuff, you know. So it used to be like me and my mother'd get into an argument and so my grandma's baby would run and my mother'd be ready to kill me, you know, "Don't touch my baby. You just get out. You don't have to take her."

INT.: You need money to get housing, is that right? You need money that will match housing prices?

DENISE: Right.

INT.: In this city?

DENISE: Uh huh.

INT.: For, uh what, three bedroom ...

DENISE: For a three-bedroom apartment.

INT.: You need to be free to work? When you're free to work, you need a job?

DENISE: They didn't let that bill pass. They, you ain't see it on the news? They, Sister Connie [the director of the shelter] did it. She put all the, um, she went out and had all these folks tryin' to get in that we should get more money, you know.

INT.: You mean the assistance check?

DENISE: Right. That we should get more money and they wouldn't pass the bill. They, they vetoed it and ...

INT.: The State of Illinois?

DENISE: People, people have to be um, eatin', what'd they say? Caviar or some stuff. You know, they, well, she said that he [the governor] bought he, he, he ... Libya or somewhere and sent back a plane full of caviar and, oooo, I can't say the names of all them old rich people. But he spent six million dollars on this stuff.

INT.: Governor Thompson?

DENISE: Yeah, him. He's spent all this money and bought all this food and, and it costed one point two million dollars for the gas to go in this plane and he couldn't give us six million, six million dollars for each one of us to have twenty dollars more on our check every month. He wouldn't pass it. And that still ain't enough. It still ain't enough for a, for a nice apartment.

A Final Note on the Simplicity of Homelessness

Although the concrete experience of homelessness reveals its complexity, there are political and policy dangers inherent in emphasizing this complex reality.

As more and more "sophisticated" social science analysis (often a more "accurate" analysis) of the problem of homelessness has occurred over the past decade, it often serves only to detract from the basic contradiction that produces the problem. As we have documented throughout, the basic socioeconomic contradiction generating homelessness in American cities arises from economic trends expanding and intensifying poverty and welfare state rollbacks on the one hand and the decreasing number of affordable housing units resulting from forces at work in the urban housing market and cuts in public housing on the other. But even in "good" social science research, the basic contradiction is increasingly de-emphasized. The promotional material for a recently published work on homelessness, a "sophisticated," "accurate," sound ethnography of homeless persons, illustrates our point:

> *Checkerboard Square* reveals the daily struggle of street people to organize their lives in the face of rejection by employers, government, landlords, and even their own families. Looking beyond the well-documented causes of homelessness such as lack of affordable housing or unemployment, Wagner shows how the poor often become homeless through resistance to

the discipline of the work place, authoritarian families, and the bureaucratic social welfare system. He explains why the crisis of homelessness is
not only about the lack of services, housing, and jobs but a result of the very
structure of the dominant institutions of work, family, and public social
welfare. (Wagner 1994)

In other words, what makes for good social science and good analysis
of homelessness, what is good for publishing and selling books about
homelessness, may be bad for social policy. "Complexity" actually di-
verts more attention away from the "simple" policy solutions that are required and need to be implemented immediately. The lower levels of extreme poverty and homelessness in Canadian cities, and in the cities of
many of the social democracies and welfare states of Europe, for example, essentially result from basic government programs promoting income security and the public provision and subsidy of affordable housing, programs absent in the United States.

The dangers of the "complexity" of homelessness are most apparent
in the United States when public officials and government justify "not
throwing money at" poverty and homelessness through income and
housing programs because "the problems are more complex than that."
Unfortunately, in the name of fiscal austerity, both major political
parties and the Clinton administration are quick to use this ideology as
the rationale for the federal government's lack of response to the whole
of industrial and urban decline. In this way, the "simplicity" of
homelessness is not addressed. The "simple" public policies that would
address the basic socioeconomic contradiction in American cities that is
the source of growing poverty and homelessness remain unfunded and,
indeed, not even a part of any major political actor's agenda.

13

Making Homelessness Go Away:
Politics and Policy

The structural approach informs our analysis and understanding of homelessness. We do *not* examine faulty people or faulty values but rather the changing nature of work, urban decay, the absence of welfare state protections, and the shortage of affordable housing. Homeless persons and families are not the only Americans suffering, but they are the hardest hit. They are experiencing the extreme consequences of the basic structural contradiction: that of increasing levels of poverty combined with decreasing availability of affordable housing. Since the homeless are *not* a special population, they do not demand special solutions. The solutions to homelessness are structural. Good theory leads to good policy; bad theory leads to bad policy.

Industrial Decline

De-industrialization and globalization have created a low-wage, high-risk economy for individuals and families. As corporations respond to declining profits by downsizing, hiring temporary workers, and moving to countries with cheaper labor, workers are increasingly insecure. The collective bargaining power of unions, once a source of worker opposition to corporate demands, declines. Blacks and other racial minorities are most susceptible to these negative trends and suffer intensifying economic marginalization.

The recent ratification of NAFTA (North American Free Trade Agreement) will only exacerbate unemployment and underemployment in the United States. By allowing (if not encouraging) companies to relocate in Mexico, with its lower wages, lax environmental laws, tax breaks, and other potential subsidies in exchange for jobs, NAFTA is good for business but bad for workers.

Policy Recommendations

A model "Workers' Bill of Rights" was recently introduced to the U.S. House by Representative Bernard Sanders (1993:17). Sanders's bill includes five major components: (1) raising the minimum wage to at least $5.50 per hour, (2) increasing paid vacation days, (3) cutting military spending in order to invest significant sums in infrastructure, (4) passing legislation to protect workers forming labor unions, and (5) instituting a single-payer Canadian-style national health care system.

Sanders's bill would result in higher wages for our lowest-paid workers. Even when an employee earning minimum wage (currently $4.25 per hour) can work forty hours a week and fifty-two weeks a year, which is more and more the exceptional case, the full-time wage is a poverty wage. A family of three remains a full 30 percent below the federal poverty line with such an income. Increasing the minimum wage to $5.50 would pull this family's income up to the official poverty line, which, though not generous, would at least separate official impoverishment from year-round, full-time employment. Additionally, as Sanders points out, such an increase in the minimum wage would stop the taxpayer subsidy currently given to low-wage employers, in the form of food stamps, Medicaid, and other federal programs, which supplement the meager wages paid their employees.

An increase in vacation days and shorter work hours would result in less stress in the workplace and at home. Workers are being stretched to the limit, expected to work longer and longer hours. Overtime has reached record levels, according to the Bureau of Labor Statistics. In April 1993, the average overtime for a factory worker rose to 4.3 hours a week, the highest level since the bureau began keeping records in 1948 (New York Times News Service 1993). The average worker has added one month per year to his or her working time since 1969 (Matas 1993), the consequence of employers' tactic of hiring fewer workers to save on the costs of recruiting, training, and per person benefit packages. The Labor Department reports that nearly $900 million a week is going to overtime pay—an amount that would, if redirected, provide for about 1.3 million new employees, each with an average wage of more than $11 per hour (New York Times News Service 1993).

Following the example of other major industrial nations, paid vacation days could be considerably more abundant in the United States. Whereas American workers average just under eleven paid vacation days a year, Spain offers an average of thirty-two paid vacation days, and multiple other nations, such as the Netherlands, Germany, the United Kingdom, Japan, and Australia, have an average that more than doubles our own (Shapiro 1992:103). Guaranteeing additional time off, shortening the workweek, and reducing work hours would allow more workers to enter the workplace, thus lowering unemployment.

Lowered unemployment and underemployment are directly related to an investment of significant sums in rebuilding America. Our roads, sewer systems, bridges, schools, mass transit, and other elements of the infrastructure have been left to deteriorate as billions have been poured into military spending. As the January 1993 meeting of the U.S. Conference of Mayors reported, the infrastructure needs of America's cities are at a crisis level. From the 7,000 infrastructure construction projects currently approved in 500 cities but lacking sufficient funding, 400,000 jobs would be created if federal funds were forthcoming (Holmstrom 1993). Particularly given the end of the Cold War, our domestic needs warrant a reorienting of budget priorities.

The reemergence of a strong trade union movement is critical to an increase in the standard of living for all working people. Unions have traditionally been organized to protect the interests of workers, from wages and working conditions at the job site to broader social and political concerns away from it. The twelve years of Reagan-Bush labor law have taken their toll; only 16 percent of all American workers (12 percent of those with private employers) are now members of labor unions, compared to 40 percent in Canada and even higher percentages in other industrialized nations, including the Netherlands, Denmark, France, and Germany. Sanders's bill calls for new federal legislation that would provide workers with the legal protections they need to establish new labor unions and negotiate contracts with their employers. The Industrial Union Department of the AFL-CIO (American Federation of Labor and Congress of Industrial Organizations) has demanded that such legislation include a striker replacement or "scab" bill preventing employers from permanently replacing workers on strike. In addition, they have called for a "card check recognition" allowing workers to unionize as soon as a majority in the workplace sign union cards. Under current law, union certification is delayed for months or even years while the National Labor Relations Board sets up an official election. Finally, the Industrial Union Department wants "first-contract arbitration." This legislation would require employers to bargain first contracts after union certification, preventing them from delaying negotiation implementation of a collectively bargained agreement (McClure 1993).

Sanders's Bill of Rights would also provide for comprehensive health insurance coverage for all Americans, using as its model the Canadian single-payer system. Thirty-seven million Americans lack any health insurance, and millions more are underinsured. By controlling fees and profits, a single-payer system would contain the exorbitant costs of medical treatment in the United States while offering all citizens preventative and emergency health care. As Sanders writes, "By eliminating the waste and inefficiency inherent in 1500 private insurance companies, each with their own program and paperwork, and by controlling doctors' fees and drug company profits, we could save over $80 billion dollars a year—more than enough money to provide comprehensive health insurance for all Americans" (Sanders 1993:17).

In addition to Sanders's detailed suggestions, we would add federal policies making it more difficult for corporations to move their businesses to other countries. At the very least, minimal standards on wages, health and safety, and other working conditions must be a part of any international free trade agreement. Unless and until these worker safeguards are in place, the corporate profit motive will cause increasing exploitation of workers, pitting laborers in developed countries against those in Third World nations.

Urban Decline

The social and economic problems discussed in this book are concentrated in America's cities. Job loss resulting from de-industrialization and corporate flight, a declining tax base as more affluent white residents retreat to the suburbs, and disinvestment by financial institutions result in spiraling urban decay. These trends are magnified for racial minorities, who constitute a larger and larger proportion of the urban poor. The decline and deterioration of cities continues at an unrelenting pace, unchecked by federal and state action. In fact, it can be argued that federal policies in particular have promoted the decline of U.S. cities—by encouraging suburbanization, metropolitan deconcentration, corporate and job flight, and disinvestment in urban areas.

Policy Recommendations[1]

The federal and state abandonment of urban centers must be stopped. We advocate a policy of massive intervention by both regional and federal governments, a government plan for rebuilding urban areas that rivals the Marshall Plan, which rebuilt Europe after World War II. Public investment in U.S. cities needs to proceed on a level never seen before.

Regional government should be encouraged. Here, more affluent suburbs and edge cities share tax revenues and services with less affluent cities, improving the quality of life throughout the metropolitan area.

This will, of course, be opposed by many suburbanites who do not see it as serving their interest. There is some precedent for it, however: Louisville, Kentucky, and its suburbs have come to such an agreement. In Minneapolis–Saint Paul, any county in the metropolitan area that exceeds the average growth rate by 40 percent or more shares the excess tax revenue with the rest of the area, including the central city (*Economist* 1992).

For its part, the federal government must stop underwriting the deconcentration of metropolitan areas with its policies and subsidies. It must enforce prohibitions against disinvestment in the city. On the positive side, it must fund a public works job creation program modeled after those of the Great Depression and the New Deal era. This public works program could be used to rebuild the decaying urban infrastructure. The federal government's urban policy ought to increase public assistance and welfare payments, build more affordable public housing, develop an adequate public mass transit system, and fund the cleanup of toxic and hazardous waste, particularly in poor and minority neighborhoods. The federal government must provide health insurance to all people, including inner-city residents, and increase financial assistance for urban public hospitals. It must also, along with state government, take on a greater share of the funding of public schools. This will help remove the educational inequalities between suburban and urban schools that result from the reliance on local property taxes.

These changes in the federal government's urban policy will not come easily. Presently, urban residents are not viewed as a constituency by either major political party. Compared to the past, fewer members of Congress represent cities. More congressional districts incorporate cities and suburbs. Members of Congress, even those from the cities, are now more loyal to national political action committees than they are to local urban political machines and organizations. And in the post–Cold War era with cutbacks in military spending, the Democratic-controlled U.S. Senate and House passed legislation preventing the transfer of funds from the military budget to the domestic budget. This ensured that no peace dividend would be available to rebuild urban areas. Democrats, long the party of the cities, could have stopped this, but they chose not to (Dreier 1992).

Meanwhile, city governments, city employees, and poor and working-class residents lose ground as cities cope with the myriad of problems by raising local taxes, cutting services, and, through the process of privatization, turning as many city functions as possible over to the profit-making sector.

Meager Welfare State

Even when the government's own conservative definition and calculation of the poverty line is used, the number of poor Americans reached a twenty-seven-year high in 1991 (Watson 1992:8). The welfare system in the United States is justly criticized for failing to deal with increasing and deepening poverty. It has been deficient in at least two ways: (1) It restricts assistance to certain limited categories of persons and (2) the assistance given does not lift the poor out of poverty.

The welfare state in the United States limits most aid to impoverished women and their children. Programs set up to provide assistance, such as AFDC, Medicaid, food stamps, and housing subsidies, are insufficient for a decent standard of living. Through the 1980s and into the 1990s, already paltry AFDC grants were reduced by the effects of inflation. During the Reagan era, eligible families were kept off the rolls or terminated for technical reasons.

Black mothers and their children face persistent discrimination in the welfare bureaucracy. Applying for and receiving assistance is often demoralizing and humiliating. And the disdain of society toward the poor is reflected in the disdain of welfare workers. Single men and women without children are assumed to be "able-bodied workers" or "employable" and as such receive very little if any aid. Some states, counties, and cities offer General Assistance (GA) funds, but these are even more meager than federal programs.

A recent examination of the United States and other Western democracies by the Joint Center for Political and Economic Studies singled out the United States for the "depth and breadth of its poverty and the ineffectiveness of its institutions in improving the lot of the poor" (Talbot 1991:6). The study noted that social programs in the United States do not lift recipients above the poverty line, in contrast to other industrialized nations. In the Netherlands, for example, two-thirds of that nation's poor residents are elevated above the poverty line by welfare programs.

Policy Recommendations

A "safety net" of welfare state protections must be instituted, providing basic security for those who are most at the mercy of structural economic transformation. Providing a job at decent wages to every American who wants and needs to work is surely the ultimate goal. Present historical conditions, however, make such a goal, given its massive scope, unattainable and therefore unrealistic. Given current fiscal constraints and the public outcry for reducing the federal deficit, government may not be willing or able to create decent-paying jobs in sufficient numbers. The private sector is not the answer either, given the competition inherent in an increasingly global economy. Whereas the creation of good jobs remains an essential aim, a concurrent requirement must be the improvement of all impoverished Americans' lives, whether currently employed or not, through the institution of welfare state protections. Such protections would include guarantees of affordable housing, comprehensive health care, legislated increases in the minimum wage, lengthened unemployment compensation, revisions in the funding and delivery of education, pay equity for women and minority groups, federally subsidized child care, and guaranteed income security. These programs would assist single adults as well as mothers and children. Ironically, instituting such protections would allow a different definition of what wage level constitutes a "decent" job. With welfare state protections, workers would not need to purchase such necessities as medical care out of their own earnings, for example, and could be adequately housed using a smaller percentage of their household incomes.

Urban Housing Crisis

Low-income and affordable housing is dwindling, particularly in U.S. cities. The urban housing market has been transformed by gentrification, investments in middle-class and luxury housing, the destruction of SROs (single-room occupancy hotels), slumlording, and rising rents. The shrinking supply of low-income and affordable housing has been exacerbated by failed federal housing policies, including urban renewal and rollbacks in public housing. Subsidizing the private sector to provide low-income housing has proven to be inefficient, ineffective, and costly. Blacks and other racial minorities in our cities have suffered disproportionately from these negative housing trends.

Policy Recommendations

What can be done to counter these trends in the urban housing market? How can government assist, rather than hinder, its citizens' search for affordable housing? If subsidies to private developers do not work, what will?

Rent control is not the answer. There is no consistent evidence that cities with or without rent control develop more affordable or low-income housing or that average rental costs decline. At least potentially, strong rent control does preserve the existent stock of affordable housing and should be supported. However, in many cities with weak ordinances, there are numerous schemes by which rent control is circumvented. As Gilderbloom and Appelbaum write in *Rethinking Rental Housing*, "Rent control has had a more political than economic impact" (1988:148).

Voucher programs are not the answer. Vouchers, intended to fill the gap between what a poor family can afford and the cost of housing in the private market, fall into the same trap as subsidy programs in general—they try to solve a problem caused by the market with a market-based solution. The Reagan administration allocated 1 million housing vouchers for 1988, substituting this program for the scandal-ridden HUD developer loan programs of the early and mid-1980s. The need for vouchers in that year is estimated at minimally six times the 1 million vouchers distributed (Dreier and Atlas 1989:29). Even if vouchers were given to all who need them, however, the program still would not work, as it fails to expand the supply of affordable housing. Vacancy rates for this housing are so low in many cities than one-half or more of all voucher holders would not be able to use their certificates. Using Dreier and Atlas's analogy, "It is similar to giving out food stamps when the supermarket shelves are empty" (1989:29). The only way voucher programs can work is if the grants are so generous that certificate holders compete for middle-class or upper-middle-class housing. This size voucher is certainly not what its advocates intend, and it is not politically feasible in the United States.

Selling off public housing to tenants is not the answer. Even if these properties were sold for $1, this response is unworkable. Given the extremely low household income of persons currently residing in public housing, without significant subsidies, the poor cannot afford the utility costs, maintenance, and taxes associated with home ownership. And once again, this response does nothing to increase the stock of affordable housing.

So what is the answer? The answer is a massive infusion of federal funds into low-income and affordable housing, part of a "Marshall Plan" to rebuild American cities (mentioned earlier). This initiative would include sums for the construction of new public housing, maintenance and rehabilitation of existing public housing, and encouragement of not-for-profit, community-based housing production, ownership, and management.

Nonprofit organizations build new or renovate existing housing, rent out the units, and manage the development. Without the necessity of making a profit, rents can be set at considerably lower levels than in the private sector. Publicly funded nonprofit housing banks could provide construction or rehabilitation loans to the nonprofit organizations at very low rates of interest, further reducing the costs of building and maintaining these developments (see Zarembka 1991). This solution to the housing crisis increases the supply of units and keeps them permanently affordable. Housing is removed from the private market, remaining in the control of local communities.

This is not a new idea. Nonprofit developers in the United States, including groups representing churches, unions, and community development corporations, have increased tenfold over the past decade, numbering about 2,000 today (Dreier and Atlas 1989:34). Their emergence coincides with the federal government's withdrawal of support and funding for affordable housing through the 1980s. Most of the affordable housing constructed or rehabilitated through that period and into the present results from the efforts of these nonprofit groups.

In addition to the nonprofits in our own country, we can look to Canada for examples of innovative, small-scale, low-income housing built, restored, or rehabilitated by nonprofit groups. In short, both from our own and from other societies' experience, we know how to build and run affordable housing. The issue now: Are we willing to fund it? Nonprofits have been able to scrape together necessary funds on a local level, but the housing needs of this country are far beyond their limited scope.

Only the federal government has the power and resources to forcefully confront the nation's massive housing needs, and it must be dedicated to that end. Sorely needed is a federal housing initiative, which would funnel significant sums of money into nonprofit organizations for the express purpose of providing low-income and affordable housing. This program must also address new construction and maintenance and rehabilitation of current public housing stock. Legislation outlining such a comprehensive housing program has been drafted by Congressman Ron Dellums of California. The passage of this or similar legislation, with an estimated price tag of more than $50 billion, would signal a genuine commitment to the housing needs of all American citizens.

The Shelterization Response[2]

The overriding societal response to the problem of homelessness has been the provision of emergency shelters and shelter services, including job training, health care, education, and substance abuse counseling. These programs have been funded primarily through the Stewart B. McKinney Homeless Assistance Act, passed by Congress in 1987. Once shelters and their services are assumed to be the answer to homelessness, social service professionals operating these institutions are defined as the experts who know best how to proceed. But do they? Are shelters and their services necessary stopgaps (if not perfect, at least benign) or debilitating, dependency-creating institutions? We often ask what shelters do *for* the homeless; perhaps we should ask, what do shelters do *to* the homeless?

Shelterization as a solution to homelessness is at best a temporary necessity—emergency food and a bed when there is no other alternative. At its worst, the shelter contributes to the further victimization of the homeless by labeling these persons as deviants. Shelters may in fact harm those they intend to serve.

The Negative Impacts of Shelterization

In his critique of human services and the social work bureaucracy, John McKnight (1989) offers one route to such a conclusion. McKnight's analysis rests on two basic premises: (1) Human service interventions have negative effects as well as positive benefits and (2) human service interventions are only one of many ways to address the condition of "disadvantaged" persons. This critique of negative effects concentrates on four characteristics of the human services approach to problem solving.

1. Emphasis on "deficiencies": Persons with *specific* needs are labeled as *generally* deficient and incapable.
2. Unacknowledged monetary impact: Dollars spent on service programs (including the salaries of professional providers) are not available as cash income to the poor.
3. Impact on the community: Social service professionals become the authority figures in the neighborhood. Local citizens become impotent as problem solvers.
4. Impact on "clients": Human service programs in the aggregate create an overwhelming environment of deficiency, resulting in dependency and deviance and negating the potential for positive effects that singular programs may offer. (McKnight 1989)

An emphasis on deficiencies, McKnight's first point, is evident in the shelterization response to homelessness. Homeless persons are regularly labeled as mentally ill, substance abusers, and otherwise generally incapable of, or unwilling to, live productive lives. This downplays and obscures homelessness as the simple lack of permanent housing. Social service providers then attempt to "fix" these deficient persons, rather than "fixing" the underlying causes of homelessness.

Timmer's (1988) study of shelter ideology supports this conclusion. As he observed,

> The programs tend to treat their residents' homelessness as a matter of values, more specifically as a matter of culture of poverty values. Homeless persons tend to be regarded as the classic culture of poverty in action. They are often perceived as fatalistic, irresponsible, unable to sacrifice the moment and delay gratification (drinking instead of job hunting or buying cigarettes instead of saving their money), valuing education or training very little if at all, and suffering from a low achievement drive or lack of initiative and aspiration which is at once thought to be the cause of their homeless predicament and their inability to overcome it. (Timmer 1988:164)

McKnight's second point, the unacknowledged monetary impact of social services, can also be seen in the shelterization response. Funds spent on shelter beds, food, and services are not available for federal and state cash assistance programs. Public investments for services would be more enabling as cash income. Putting this issue another way, McKnight's critique calls for a recognition of the trade-off between social services and housing. To give more to one set of activities—shelters and their programs—arguably means giving less to another—the construction and rehabilitation of low-income housing.

Shelterization also has a negative effect on the community and its willingness and ability to confront the problem of homelessness. Putting the homeless into shelters removes these persons from the streets and thus from public view. If the homeless are "hidden" in shelters, others do not have to see them or step around them. Homelessness thus disappears to an increasingly antagonistic public (Ferguson 1990), which can assume that other people—paid professionals—will deal with these issues. As McKnight writes,

> Human service professionals with special expertise, technique, and technology push out the problem-solving knowledge and action of friend, neighbor, citizen, and association. As the power of profession and service system ascends, the legitimacy, authority, and capacity of citizens and community descend. The citizen retreats. The client advances. The power of community action weakens. The authority of the service system strengthens. And as human service tools prevail, the tools of citizenship, association, and community rust. Their uses are even forgotten. Many local people come to believe that the service tool is the only tool, and that their task as good citizens is to support taxes and charities for more services. (McKnight 1989:9)

McKnight's fourth point, the negative impact on "clients" of an all-encompassing definition of deficiency, can be seen in the shelter as an institutional setting. People there live wholly surrounded by services and service providers. As McKnight argues, this enveloping of the person creates a distinct environment—one in which a circular process develops. The institutional environment causes persons in it to adapt, sometimes in deviant and dependent ways, but the adaptive behavior itself is taken as proof of the need for the services the institution provides.

An example of this circular process is found in Timmer's (1988) ethnographic account of a Chicago shelter for homeless mothers and their children. There was conflict in the shelter between women residents and the staff over the parenting of the women's children. Corporal punishment was not allowed under any circumstances, even though this mode of discipline was the most established and consistent method these mothers had in dealing with their children's misbehavior. The parenting assistance of an extended kin network, generally present prior to these women coming to the shelter, was also missing. Living in the shelter, under the shelter's rules, these mothers were denied the ability to parent in their accustomed way. They responded to their felt lack of authority by generally ignoring their children's actions, which resulted in the staff defining these mothers as incompetent. To complete the circular process, these "incompetent mothers" were required to attend parenting classes as part of their shelter stay.

The negative effect of shelters on their residents is not a new phenomenon. Hoch and Slayton's discussion in *New Homeless and Old* (1989) of the use of shelters during the Great Depression exemplifies the lengthy history of negative consequences for shelter residents:

> The effect on the men was predictable. They became despondent and often child-like, dominated by authority, going through the motions of life. One resident said that there should be no fear of communists' organizing the men in the shelters because "There's no life in these shelters. ... They wouldn't fight nothin' in here." (Hoch and Slayton 1989:82)

The shelter's effect on its residents helps justify the professional and public emphasis on pathology and deviance. The homeless are seen as degenerate or sick, unable to make their own decisions and care for themselves.

The Politics of Compassion

Hoch and Slayton (1989) offer another approach from which to view the harmful effects of the shelterization response. They point out how in the mid-1980s social service providers succeeded in formulating the language of the homeless debate so as to emphasize the physical and social vulnerabilities of homeless persons rather than the right of all citizens to housing. Homelessness was thus defined as a social problem requiring professional caregivers and their skills. A population of "clients" whose "needs" warranted professional intervention was created. This ideological position portrayed and treated the homeless as passive, needy victims.

The Rejection of Shelterization by the Homeless

The "politics of compassion" results in the provision of shelters and shelter services. But these "refuges" have been rejected by the homeless themselves, who resent the numerous rules and regulations common to the shelter experience. The overt control exerted over every aspect of life, including the scheduling of waking, sleeping, eating, and showering, restrictions on personal habits, and demands to be enrolled in required programs to continue to receive shelter, is compared by many shelter residents to that of correctional facilities. Perceiving shelters as places lacking in autonomy and privacy, most homeless persons avoid them. They use shelter facilities only when absolutely necessary, as when winter cold becomes life-threatening.

The rejection of the shelter must be placed in historical context. As Hoch and Slayton's (1989) work highlights, the economically marginal in America's cities have not always had such limited choices. Earlier in this century, a variety of housing options, from the SRO, to the lodging house, to the working-class cage hotel, to the "flop" hotel, gave the poorest of the poor housing alternatives. Even though this housing may have been physically deteriorated, it provided residents what they most cherished: personal freedom and a lock on the door.

Suspicion and resentment of the shelter and its services are evident in reports of a growing "shelter rebellion" among homeless people. In New York, for example, homeless persons set up a tent city in Tompkins Square rather than enter the city's shelter system (Ferguson 1990). Similar protests have occurred in Los Angeles, where a short-lived tent city was constructed in 1984, and Chicago, where homeless squatters broke into vacant Chicago Housing Authority units in 1988 (Hoch and Slayton 1989). This rejection of shelters is also evident in occupancy rates. In Chicago, for example, the average shelter occupancy rate in 1987 hovered around 84 percent, and the 4,250 available beds were filled to capacity less than half the time (U.S. Dept. of Housing and Urban Development 1989:40). These vacancies exist even as the City of Chicago Department of Human Services estimates the number of homeless at 40,000 to 49,000 over a year's time (1990:2).

Those homeless persons who do enter shelters recognize them as dismal places of last resort, not welcomed "treatment centers." In the words of Kitty, a shelter resident in Tampa, "It's like a correctional institution and I'm not a criminal. ... I haven't done anything wrong" (Timmer 1988:163). Other first-person accounts speak of the hope of "escaping the shelters" and existing "on the verge of madness, so hungry for a little privacy and peace that I was afraid I'd start screaming in my sleep." "No one should have to live like that" (Russell 1989:52). Interviewing homeless persons in Chicago, researchers from the National Opinion Research Center found that most who had used shelters agreed that they offered a clean and decent place to sleep, but almost half complained about a lack of security and privacy and resented the restrictions on their personal freedom (Rossi, Fisher, and Willis 1986:136). Shelters are perceived by the homeless not only as demoralizing but also as dangerous. Fear, both of losing one's meager possessions and suffering personal injury, is often cited by those who have experienced shelter life.

Increasing numbers of homeless people are organizing, speaking out for themselves and against shelterization. One group, the National Union for the Homeless, consists of fourteen local chapters representing 30,000 homeless individuals. This organization's underlying principle, and the basis for its collective protest, is that citizens have a right to housing. In the words of Alicia Christian, a union member, "Homeless people are saying they don't want any more stopgaps. They don't want shelters, they want houses. They don't want welfare, they want jobs. That's a profound threat to people who say they want to enable, but really want to control" (cited in Ferguson 1990:55). Christian's statement also indicates a class difference between the homeless and their "advocates." Many homeless advocacy groups are dominated by middle-class and upper-middle-class persons, including professional service providers and shelter operators. These professionals and the homeless they "serve" have quite distinct, if not opposing, agendas and ideologies. This supports McKnight's (1989) critique of social service caregivers as creating dependency rather than self-sufficiency and gives credence to the National Union for the Homeless in its claim that the homeless must speak for themselves.

Policy Recommendations

Shelters and shelter services are *not* the solution to homelessness. In addition, these responses detract both financially and politically from the *real* solution—the provision of sufficient low-income and affordable housing. Emergency food and shelter must continue to be available, but only as a *temporary* response in crisis situations. Shelterization must not persist as the primary institutional response to homelessness.

Clinton and the New Democrats

The Reagan-Bush era is over. A new administration has assumed power in Washington, D.C. President Clinton's winning slogan focused on change and returning government to the people. It would seem that the time is right for a sincere dedication to the Housing Act of 1949, which guaranteed all Americans "decent, safe, and sanitary" housing.

But the rhetoric has not been translated into reality. Given the Clinton administration's New Democrat politics and focus on reducing the deficit, it is unlikely that any significant housing initiative will occur. Actually, the Department of Housing and Urban Development will have difficulty meeting its current bills. In addition to deferred maintenance expenses and increased costs tied to new subsidies for landlords, federal accounting practices require that entire multiyear costs of a contract be charged against the department's budget in the year the contract is renewed. This is a looming problem for HUD, as subsidy programs begun in the mid-1970s and financed through fifteen-year contracts come due. Just under a third of HUD's current budget of $25 billion is allotted to these renewals, with the figure expected to grow to more than $15 billion by 1997 (DeParle 1993). Although some have argued that this issue has no real significance—it is only an accounting problem—HUD's budget will have to grow significantly just to cover these contract renewals and maintain current levels of housing assistance. This means that even if the HUD budget is increased by the Clinton administration, actual expenditures for housing low-income persons remain the same or even decrease.

HUD Secretary Henry G. Cisneros remarked in an April 1993 *New York Times* article (DeParle 1993) that he would like to increase the number of families given housing assistance by 100,000 per year. But even at that pace, which is unlikely to occur, it would take fifty-one years to house the 5.1 million families on the department's list of the most in need.

President Clinton's new federal budget, unveiled in February 1994, actually *cuts* funding for public housing by more than $2 billion. Section 8 rental assistance, a problematic market-based program (as discussed earlier), is increased from $1.1 billion to $2 billion. Spending for homeless persons is increased by nearly 50 percent, from $800 million in fiscal 1994 to $1.2 billion in fiscal 1995, but this increase is targeted primarily for shelters and temporary housing (Fram 1994). Secretary Cisneros has proposed to turn abandoned military bases into more homeless shelters.

Any increase in welfare state protections is unlikely to materialize under the present administration. Discussions currently under way propose that AFDC recipients be required to accept work after receiving benefits for two years and that welfare payments be linked to changes in personal behavior, such as forcing unmarried teenage mothers to live with their parents (Shogren and Brownstein 1993). Even the health care reforms currently under consideration retain the power of the five largest private insurers in the country through "managed" competition. And with the support of President Clinton, NAFTA has passed.

Policy, Not People

The structural contradiction between an increasing "at-risk" population and decreasing low-income and affordable housing supply will only worsen if not confronted immediately. The homeless on city streets and in shelters will multiply. As long as we focus on the particular characteristics and/or "deficiencies" of homeless persons rather than on expanding poverty and the urban housing crisis, the root causes of homelessness will not be addressed. As emphasis is placed on individuals, it is all too easy to accept a behavioral explanation of homelessness, blaming victims for their own plight. Even when this attention is couched in sympathetic terms, as in the "politics of compassion," with its provision of shelters and shelter services, the political agenda moves away from justice and empowerment and toward charity rather than real change.

Neither blaming the victim nor compassion will end homelessness. Structural transformation is required, and this will not occur without major modifications in public policy. As Dreier and Appelbaum write in "American Nightmare: Homelessness," "Public policy was responsible for creating this epidemic, and changes in public policy will be required to resolve this mounting problem" (1991:46). The issue now: Do we have the will to act?

Notes

1. This section is from Doug A. Timmer, "Urban Problems in the United States," pp. 118–159 in D. Stanley Eitzen and Maxine Baca Zinn, *Social Problems*, 6th ed. Boston: Allyn and Bacon, 1994.

2. This section is from Kathryn D. Talley and Doug A. Timmer, "Resisting Shelterization: The Politics of Housing and Homelessness," *Housing and Society* 19 (3) (1994).

References

Adams, Carolyn Teich. 1986. "Homelessness in the Postindustrial City: Views from London and Philadelphia." *Urban Affairs Quarterly* 21:527–549.

Apgar, William C. 1989. "The State of the Nation's Housing: An Update." MBA Homeless/Affordable Housing Task Force.

Appelbaum, Richard P. 1989. "The Affordability Gap." *Society* 26 (May/June):6–8.

Associated Press. 1991. "'80s Housing Didn't Shelter the Poor" (December 12).

———. 1993. "Poor Families Hit Harder by Health Costs" (April 14).

Baca Zinn, Maxine, and D. Stanley Eitzen. 1993. *Diversity in Families*, 3d ed. New York: HarperCollins.

Bahr, Howard. 1973. *Skid Row: An Introduction to Disaffiliation*. New York: Oxford University Press.

Banfield, Edward. 1974. *The Unheavenly City Revisited*. Boston: Little, Brown.

Barlett, Donald L., and James B. Steele. 1992. *America: What Went Wrong?* Kansas City: Andrews and McMeel.

Baumohl, Bernard, Marc Hequet, and Elaine Shannon. 1991. "Permanent Pink Slips." *Time* (September 9):54–56.

Baurac, Deborah Rissing. 1993. "Working Isn't Worth Cost to Some Moms." *Denver Post* (March 3):1E, 6E.

Bausch, Louise, and Mary Kimbrough. 1986. *Voices Set Free: Battered Women Speak from Prison*. St. Louis: Women's Self Help Center.

Black Scholar. 1990. "Report by U. S. House Select Committee on Hunger: Obtaining Food." *Black Scholar* 21 (January–February):6–16.

Bogue, Donald. 1963. *Skid Row in American Cities*. Chicago: University of Chicago Press.

Boyce, Joseph N. 1992. "L.A. Riots and the 'Black Tax.'" *Wall Street Journal* (May 12):A16.

Brenner, M. Harvey. 1973. *Mental Illness and the Economy*. Cambridge: Harvard University Press.

Burawoy, Michael, et al. 1991. *Ethnography Unbound: Power and Resistance in the Modern Metropolis*. Berkeley: University of California Press.

Burns, Greg. 1993. "Study Tracks What Blacks Spend on What." *Chicago Sun Times* (August 13):41, 45.

Burt, Martha R. 1992. *Over the Edge: The Growth of Homelessness in the 1980s*. New York: Russell Sage Foundation.

Carliner, M. 1987. "Homelessness: A Housing Problem?" In R. Bingham, R. Green, and S. White (eds.), *The Homeless in Contemporary Society*. Beverly Hills, Calif.: Sage.

Castro, Janice. 1993. "The Disposable Workers." *Time* (March 29):43–47.

Chavkin, Wendy. 1987. *Monthly Vital Statistics Report*. Washington, D.C.: National Center for Health Statistics.

Cherlin, Andrew J. 1981. *Marriage, Divorce, Remarriage*. Cambridge: Harvard University Press.

Chicago Coalition for the Homeless. 1993. *Alone After Dark: A Survey of Homeless Youth in Chicago*. Chicago: Chicago Coalition for the Homeless.

Chicago Sun-Times. 1993. "How Welfare System Could Be Improved" (August 11):33.

Children's Defense Fund. 1988. *Vanishing Dreams: The Growing Economic Plight of America's Young Families*. Washington, D.C.: Children's Defense Fund.

_____. 1989. *A Vision for America's Future*. Washington, D.C.: Children's Defense Fund.

_____. 1991. *The State of America's Children 1991*. Washington, D.C.: Children's Defense Fund.

City of Chicago Department of Human Services. 1990. *Stewart B.Mckinney Homeless Assistance Act: Title IV Comprehensive Homeless Assistance Plan*. Chicago.

Clay, Phillip. 1979. *Neighborhood Renewal*. Lexington, Mass.: Lexington Books.

Community Emergency Shelter Organization and Jewish Council on Urban Affairs. 1985. *SROs: An Endangered Species*. Chicago.

Coontz, Stephanie. 1992. *The Way We Never Were: American Families and the Nostalgia Trap*. New York: Basic Books.

Coughlin, Ellen K. 1993. "Author of Noted Study on Black Ghetto Life Returns with a Portrait of Homeless Women." *The Chronicle of Higher Education* (March 31):A7–A8.

Daley, Suzanne. 1987. "In New York, the Hidden Homeless Increase." *New York Times* (June 17):1, 14.

Demos, John, and Virginia Demos. 1973. "Adolescence in Historical Perspective." In *The American Family in Social Historical Perspective*, Michael Gordon (ed.). New York: St. Martin's Press, pp. 209–222.

Dentzer, Susan. 1992. "Why Workers Have Little to Cheer." *U.S. News & World Report* (August 17):26–27.

DeParle, Jason. 1991. "Poor Are Increasingly Facing a Tough Choice on Housing." *New York Times* (December 12):A1, A13.

_____. 1992. "Why Marginal Changes Don't Rescue the Welfare State." *New York Times* (March 1):E3.

_____. 1993. "Big Bills Come Due, and H.U.D. Is Forced to Scramble for Money." *New York Times* (April 8):A1.

Dibble, Ursula, and Murray Straus. 1980. "Some Social Structure Determinants of Inconsistency Between Attitudes and Behavior: The Case of Family Violence." *Journal of Marriage and Family* 42 (February):71–80.

di Leonardo, Micaela. 1992a. "Boyz on the Hood." *Nation* (August 16/24):178–186.

_____. 1992b. "White Lies Black Myths: Rape, Race, and the Black 'Underclass.'" *Village Voice* (September 22):28–36.

Dionne, E. J., Jr. 1989. "Poor Paying More for Their Shelter." *New York Times* (April 18):A20.

Downey, Kirsten, and Paul Taylor. 1991. "Poor Renters Attempt to Stave Off Homelessness." *Washington Post* (November 12):A12.

Dreier, Peter. 1992. "Bush to Cities: Drop Dead." *Progressive* 56 (July):20–23.

Dreier, Peter, and Richard Appelbaum. 1990. "Nobody Home: The Housing Crisis Meets the Nineties." *Tikkun* 5 (September–October):15–18.

_____. 1991. "American Nightmare: Homelessness." *Challenge* (March–April):46–52.

Dreier, Peter, and John Atlas. 1989. "Grassroots Strategies for the Housing Crisis: A National Housing Agenda." *Social Policy* (Winter):25–38.

Dubin, Murray. 1992. "Child-Care Costs Soar 35%: Number of Available Relatives Dips as Weekly Tab Averages $54." *Denver Post* (September 6):1A, 19A.

Dugger, Celia W. 1992. "Tiny Incomes, Little Help for Single Mothers." *New York Times* (March 31):A1, A8.

Duis, Perry. 1983. *The Saloon*. Urbana: University of Illinois Press.

Easterlin, Richard A. 1987. "The New Age Structure of Poverty in America." *Population and Development Review* 13 (2):195–208.

Economist. 1992. "America's Cities: Doomed to Burn?" (May 9):21–22, 24.

Edelman, Marian Wright. 1991. "Children at Risk." Pp. 295–306 in Jerome H. Skolnick and Elliott Currie (eds.), *Crisis in American Institutions,* 8th ed. New York: HarperCollins.

Eitzen, D. Stanley, and Maxine Baca Zinn. 1989a. "The Forces Reshaping America." Pp. 1–17 in D. Stanley Eitzen and Maxine Baca Zinn (eds.), *The Reshaping of America: Social Consequences of the Changing Economy.* Englewood Cliffs, N.J.: Prentice-Hall.

_____. 1989b. "The Reagan Domestic Legacy: Greater Inequality and Destabilization." Pp. 94–103 in D. Stanley Eitzen (ed.), *Society's Problems: Sources and Consequences.* Boston: Allyn and Bacon.

_____. 1993. *In Conflict and Order: Understanding Society,* 6th ed. Boston: Allyn and Bacon.

Eleff, Bob. 1990. "Proposed Housing Plan Commits Few Resources. *In These Times* (May 2–8):7.

Farley, W. Reynolds, and Albert I. Hermalin. 1971. "Family Stability: A Comparison of Trends Between Blacks and Whites." *American Sociological Review* 36:1–17.

Feagin, Joe R. 1982. *Social Problems.* Englewood Cliffs, N.J.: Prentice-Hall.

Feagin, Joe R., and Clairece Booher Feagin. 1990. *Social Problems: A Critical Power-Conflict Perspective,* 3d ed. Englewood Cliffs, N.J.: Prentice-Hall.

Feagin, Joe R., and Robert Parker. 1990. *Building American Cities: The Urban Real Estate Game.* Englewood Cliffs, N.J.: Prentice-Hall.

Ferguson, Sarah. 1990. "Us vs. Them: America's Growing Frustration with the Homeless." *Utne Reader* 41:50–55.

Flanery, James Allen. 1993. "Husbands Killing Wives: A Problem Resists Solution." *Omaha World-Herald* (October 24):1.

Fram, Alan. 1994. "Clinton Plans Public Housing Cuts." *Chicago Sun-Times* (January 8):14.

Freeman, Richard B., and Harry J. Holzer (eds.). 1986. *The Black Youth Employment Crisis.* Chicago: University of Chicago Press.

Fulwood, Sam, III. 1993. "Out-of-Wedlock Births Soar in U.S., Study Says." *Denver Post* (July 14):1A, 20A.

Gaines, Donna. 1992. *Teenage Wasteland: Suburbia's Dead End Kids.* New York: HarperPerennial.

Garb, Maggie. 1992. "City Marks Low-Cost Housing Needs." *Chicago Sun-Times* (April 19):pullout 1.

Geertz, Clifford. 1983. *Local Knowledge: Further Essays in Interpretative Anthropology.* New York: Basic Books.

Geronimus, Arline T. 1987. "On Teenage Childbearing and Neonatal Mortality in the United States." *Population and Development Review* 13 (June):245–279.

Gilderbloom, John I. 1991. "Housing in America: It's Time for a New Strategy." *USA Today* (magazine) 120 (November):30–32.

Gilderbloom, John I., and Richard P. Appelbaum. 1988. *Rethinking Rental Housing.* Philadelphia: Temple University Press.

Gillis, Michael. 1991. "City Warned of Loss of Residential Hotels." *Chicago Sun-Times* (January 30):14.

Gioglio, Gerald R. 1989. "Homelessness in New Jersey: The Social Service Network and the People Served." Pp. 113–129 in Jamshid Momeni (ed.), *Homelessness in the United States, Vol. 1: State Surveys.* Westport, Conn.: Greenwood Press.

Glasser, Irene. 1988. *More Than Bread: Ethnography of a Soup Kitchen.* Birmingham: University of Alabama Press.

Greenhouse, Steven. 1993. "Where Will Jobs Come From?" *Denver Post* (April 26):2A.

Gugliotta, Guy. 1992. "Nation's Poor Can't Afford Scarce Rental Housing Units." *Coloradoan* (Fort Collins) (November 27):A6.

Hacker, Andrew. 1992. *Two Nations: Black and White, Separate, Hostile, Unequal.* New York: Charles Scribner's Sons.

Harris, Sara. 1956. *Skid Row, U.S.A.* Garden City, N.Y.: Doubleday.

Harrison, Bennett. 1990. "The Wrong Signals." *Technology Review* (January):65.

Henderson, Harold. 1993. "The City File." *Reader* (August 20):Section 1, 40.

Hewlett, Sylvia Ann. 1991. *When the Bough Breaks: The Cost of Neglecting Our Children.* New York: Basic Books.

Hirsch, Arnold R. 1983. *Making the Second Ghetto: Race and Housing in Chicago, 1940–1960.* Cambridge: Cambridge University Press.

Hoch, Charles, and Robert A. Slayton. 1989. *New Homeless and Old: Community and the Skid Row Hotel.* Philadelphia: Temple University Press.

Holmstrom, David. 1993. "Activists Urge Clinton to Frame Urban Strategy." *Christian Science Monitor* (February 1):6.

Horwitz, Allan V. 1984. "The Economy and Social Pathology." *Annual Review of Sociology* 10. New York: Annual Reviews.

Hudson, Frances, and Bernard Ineichen. 1991. *Taking It Lying Down: Sexuality and Teenage Motherhood.* London: Macmillan Education Ltd.

Illinois Coalition Against Sexual Assault and the Illinois Coalition Against Domestic Violence. n.d. "Male Violence Against Women" (pamphlet).

Inniss, Leslie, and Joe R. Feagin. 1989. "The Black 'Underclass' Ideology in Race Relations Analysis." *Social Justice* 16 (4):13–34.

Jackson, T. H. 1993. "What Is Happening to U.S. Workers' Wages? *People* (March 20):2.

Jones, Tim. 1993. "Cast as Budget Villain, Emil Jones Rejects Role." *Chicago Tribune* (July 11):1, 3.

Joravsky, Ben. 1993. "Give Us Shelter: Activists Press City with a Billion-Dollar Housing Initiative." *Reader* (September 3):Section 1, 3.

Kasarda, John D. 1985. "Urban Change and Minority Opportunities." Pp. 33–67 in Paul E. Peterson (ed.), *The New Urban Reality.* Washington, D.C.: Brookings Institution.

Kasinitz, Philip. 1984. "Gentrification and Homelessness: The Single Room Occupant and the Inner City Revival." *Urban and Social Change Review* 17:9–14.

Kilborn, Peter T. 1993. "Temporary Help Now Half of New Hires." *Denver Post* (March 28):29A.

Kozol, Jonathan. 1988a. "Are the Homeless Crazy?" *Harper's Magazine* 277 (September):17–19.

_____. 1988b. "Distancing the Homeless." *Yale Review* 77:153–167.

_____. 1988c. *Rachel and Her Children: Homeless Families in America.* New York: Crown.

Kreck, Carol. 1992. "Child-Care Figures 'Too Low': Area Parents, Experts Scoff at Government's $54-a-Week Figure." *Denver Post* (September 17):4A.

Kritz, Fran. 1993. "Battered Women Go Unassisted, Report Says." *Chicago Sun-Times* (August 20):31.

LaGory, Mark, Ferris J. Ritchey, and Kevin Fitzpatrick. 1991. "Homelessness and Affiliation." *Sociological Quarterly* 32:201–218.

Lee, Barrett A. 1987. "Homelessness and Community." Paper presented at the Annual Meeting of the American Sociological Association.

Levitan, Sar, and Clifford M. Johnson. 1982. *Second Thoughts on Work.* Kalamazoo, Mich.: W. E. Upjohn Institute for Employment Research.

Levitas, Mitchell. 1990. "Homeless in America." *New York Times Magazine* (June 10):44–45, 82–91.

Lewis, Oscar. 1971. *Five Families: Mexican Case Studies in the Culture of Poverty.* New York: New American Library.

Liebow, Elliot. 1993. *Tell Them Who I Am: The Lives of Homeless Women.* New York: Free Press.

Lips, Hilary M. 1991. *Women, Men, and Power.* Mountain View, Calif.: Mayfield Publishing.

Lubeck, Sally, and Patricia Garrett. 1983. "Child Care 2000: Policy Options for the Future." *Social Policy* 18 (Spring):31–37.

McBean, Bill. 1992. "No Car Often Means No Job at New Airport." *Denver Post.* (October 4):1C, 5C.

McClure, Laura. 1993. "Rush to Compromise." *Progressive* 57 (June):22–25.

McGovern, Tim. 1983. "Tenants Lose Again in Legislature." *Denver Post* (April 6):18.

McKnight, John. 1989. "Do No Harm: Policy Options That Meet Human Needs." *Social Policy* 20 (1):5–15.

McWhirter, William. 1992. "The Temping of America." *Time* (March 29):40–41.

Matas, Alina. 1993. "Shrinking Workplace Takes Toll." *Denver Post* (April 26):5H.

Mercer, Marcia. 1990. "Homeless Are Worse Off Than a Decade Ago." *Rocky Mountain News* (January 3):31.

Mihaly, Lisa K. 1991. "Homeless Children: A National Tragedy." *USA Today* (July 30):9A.

Miller, Bryan. 1993. "Life Saver." *Reader* 22 (August 13): Section 1, 1.

Miller, Nancy. 1990. "Housing Study: No Doomsday or Utopia." *USA Today* (July 19):B1.

Mills, C. Wright. 1959. *The Sociological Imagination.* New York: Oxford University Press.

Moberg, David. 1992. "Decline and Inequality After the Great U-Turn." *In These Times* (May 27–June 9):7, 22.

Moore, Charles H., David W. Sink, and Patricia Hoban-Moore. 1988. "The Politics of Homelessness." *PS: Political Science and Politics* 21:57–63.

Morganthau, Tom. 1986. "Abandoned." *Newsweek* (January 6):14–19.

Moynihan, Daniel P. 1988. "Our Poorest Citizens—Children." *Focus* 11 (Spring):5–6.

National Center for Children in Poverty. 1990. *Five Million Children: A Statistical Profile of Our Poorest Young Citizens.* New York: National Center for Children in Poverty.

New York Times. 1988. "Despite a 5-Year Upturn, 9.7 Million Jobs Are Lost" (December 13):A12.

_____. 1991. "Study Finds Bias in House Hunting" (September 1):14.

New York Times News Service. 1993. "High Cost of Hiring Spurs More Overtime." *Denver Post* (May 16):1A.

Nicodemus, Charles. 1993a. "50,000 Wrongly Denied Aid, Study Says." *Chicago Sun-Times* (August 10):4.

_____. 1993b. "UIC Study Sounds Alarm on Affordable Housing." *Chicago Sun-Times* (September 1):50.

_____. 1993c. "Welfare Reform Group Gets Hostile Greeting." *Chicago Sun-Times* (August 11):20.

Noyelle, Thierry, and Thomas M. Stanback, Jr. 1984. *The Economic Transformation of American Cities.* Totowa, N.J.: Rowman and Allanheld.

O'Reilly, Brian. 1992a. "The Job Drought." *Fortune* (August 24):62–74.

_____. 1992b. "Your New Global Work Force." *Fortune* (December 14):52–66.

Pacelle, Mitchell. 1991. "Rental Squeeze Hurts Low-Income Tenants." *Wall Street Journal* (December 3):B1.

The People. 1992. "Decline of Family Has Economic Roots" (September 1):1.

_____. 1993a. "Growing Poverty Demands Working-Class Response" (January 3):3.

_____. 1993b. "More Workers Being Employed on a 'Contingency' Basis." (March 20):3.

Piliavin, Irving, Herb Westerfelt, and Elsa Elliot. 1989. "Estimating Mental Illness Among the Homeless: The Effects of Choice-Based Sampling." *Social Problems* 36:525–531.

Pollitt, Katha. 1990. "A New Assault on Feminism." *Nation* (March 26):409–418.
Population Today. 1986. "Counting the Uncountable Homeless." *Population Today* 14:3,8.
Quinn, Jane Bryant. 1992. "How to Improve Odds of Buying a Good Used Car." *Rocky Mountain News* (February 3):31.
Reed, Adolph, Jr. 1988. "The Liberal Technocrat." *Nation* (February 6).
_____. 1992. "The Underclass as Myth and Symbol." *Radical America* 24 (January):21–40.
Richman, Louis S. 1992. "Struggling to Save Our Kids." *Fortune* (August 10):34–40.
Rimer, Sara. 1989. "The Rent's Due, and for Many It's Homelessness Knocking." *New York Times* (March 24):1, 10.
Ringheim, Karin. 1993. "Investigating the Structural Determinants of Homelessness: The Case of Houston." *Urban Affairs Quarterly* 28 (June):617–640.
Rocky Mountain News. 1992a. "Black Teen Jobless Rate Tops 50%" (June 6):59.
_____. 1992b. "57% of Black Children Live with One Parent" (July 21):4.
Rom, Mark. 1992. "Reversing America's Welfare Magnets." *USA Today* (magazine) (March):16–18.
Ross, Sonya. 1992. "1 Million Women Attacked by Lovers in 1991." *Denver Post* (October 3):2A.
Rossi, Peter H. 1988. "First Out, Last In: Extreme Poverty and Homelessness." Paper presented at the American Sociological Association meetings, Atlanta, Georgia (August).
_____. 1989. *Down and Out in America: The Origins of Homelessness.* Chicago: University of Chicago Press.
Rossi, Peter H., G. Fisher, and G. Willis. 1986. *The Condition of the Homeless in Chicago.* Chicago: National Opinion Research Center.
Rothenberg, Paula S. 1992. *Race, Class, and Gender in the United States: An Integrated Study,* 2d ed. New York: St. Martin's Press.
Russell, Colette. 1989. "A Day in the Homeless Life." *Utne Reader* 41:52–53.
Sanders, Bernard. 1993. "A Workers' Bill of Rights." *Z Magazine* 6 (March):17.
Sapiro, Virginia. 1990. *Women in American Society,* 2d ed. New York: St. Martin's Press.
Scarpitti, Frank R., and Margaret L. Andersen. 1992. *Social Problems,* 2d ed. New York: HarperCollins.
Schwadel, Francine. 1992. "Poverty's Cost: Urban Consumers Pay More and Get Less, and Gap May Widen." *Wall Street Journal* (July 2):A1, A9.
Schwarz, John E., and Thomas J. Volgy. 1992a. *The Forgotten Americans.* New York: W. W. Norton.
_____. 1992b. "Out of Line." *New Republic* (November 23):16–17.
Sclar, Elliott D. 1990. "Homelessness and Housing Policy: A Game of Musical Chairs." *American Journal of Public Health* 80 (September):1039–1040.
Sexton, Patricia Cayo. 1983. "The Life of the Homeless." *Dissent* 30 (Winter):79–84.
Shapiro, Andrew L. 1992. *We're Number One!* New York: Vintage Books.
Shapiro, Joseph P. 1989. "A Conservative War on Poverty." *U.S. News & World Report* (February 27):20–23.

Sheak, Robert. 1988. "There's More to Poverty Than the 'Feminization of Poverty': The Trends, 1959–1983." *Humanity and Society* 12:125–141.

———. 1990. "Corporate and State Attacks on the Material Conditions of the Working Class." *Humanity and Society* 14:105–127.

Shogren, Elizabeth, and Ronald Brownstein. 1993. "Welfare Panel Backs Jobs Plan." *Chicago Sun-Times* (December 4):3.

Sidel, Ruth. 1992. *Women and Children Last: The Plight of Poor Women in Affluent America.* New York: Penguin Books.

Siegel, Norman, and Robert Levy. 1985. "The Real Problem Is Housing." *New York Times* (December 17):B17.

Simons, Janet M., Belva Finlay, and Alice Yang. 1991. *The Adolescent and Young Adult Fact Book.* Washington, D.C.: Children's Defense Fund.

Sklar, Holly. 1993a. "The Upperclass and Mothers N the Hood." *Z Magazine* 6 (March):22–31.

———. 1993b. "Young and Guilty by Stereotype." *Z Magazine* 6 (July/August):52–61.

Skocpol, Theda. 1992. *Protecting Soldiers and Mothers: The Political Origins of Social Policy in the United States.* Cambridge: Harvard University Press.

Snow, David A., and Leon Anderson. 1993. *Down on Their Luck: A Study of Homeless Street People.* Berkeley: University of California Press.

Snow, David A., Susan G. Baker, and Leon Anderson. 1989. "Criminality Among Homeless Men: An Empirical Assessment." *Social Problems* 36:532–549.

Snow, David A., Susan G. Baker, Leon Anderson, and Michael Martin. 1986. "The Myth of Pervasive Mental Illness Among the Homeless." *Social Problems* 33 (June):407–423.

Sosin, Michael R. 1992. "Homeless and Vulnerable Meal Program Users: A Comparison Study." *Social Problems* 39 (May):170–188.

Stein, Sharman. 1990. "Public Aid Doesn't Stretch as Far as It Used To." *Chicago Tribune* (August 5):1, 24.

Talbot, Basil. 1991. "U.S. Fails Its Poor, Study Says." *Chicago Sun-Times* (September 19):6.

Talley, Kathryn D., and Doug A. Timmer. 1994. "Resisting Shelterization: The Politics of Housing and Homelessness." *Housing and Society* 19 (3).

Timmer, Doug A. 1988. "Homelessness as Deviance: The Ideology of the Shelter." *Free Inquiry in Creative Sociology* 16 (2):163–170.

———. 1994. "Urban Problems in the United States." Pp. 118–159 in D. Stanley Eitzen and Maxine Baca Zinn (eds.), *Social Problems*, 6th ed. Boston: Allyn and Bacon.

Timmer, Doug A., and D. Stanley Eitzen. 1992. "The Root Causes of Urban Homelessness in the United States." *Humanity and Society* 16 (2) (May):159–175.

Trafford, Abigail. 1982. "New Health Hazard: Being Out of Work." *U.S. News & World Report* (June 14):81–82.

USA Today. 1993. "From Honolulu to Detroit, Homeowners Pay More" (May 6):10B.

U.S. Bureau of the Census. 1992. "Poverty in the United States: 1991." *Current Population Reports,* Series P-60, No. 181. Washington, D.C.: U.S. Government Printing Office.

U.S. Department of Housing and Urban Development. 1989. *A Report on Homeless Assistance Policy and Practice in the Nation's Five Largest Cities.* Washington, D.C.: Government Printing Office.

Usdansky, Margaret L. 1992. "Low-Pay Jobs Up; Rich-Poor Gap Widens." *USA Today* (May 12):1A.

Vander Kooi, Ronald. 1966. "Skid Rowers: Their Alienation and Involvement in Community and Society." Ph.D. dissertation. Michigan State University.

Vaughn, Roger. 1972. "Landlord-Tenant Relations in a Low-Income Area." Pp. 77–88 in Stephen Burghardt (ed.), *Tenants and the Urban Housing Crisis.* Dexter, Mich.: New Press.

Wagner, David. 1994. *Checkerboard Square: Culture and Resistance in a Homeless Community.* Boulder, Colo.: Westview Press.

Walker, Lenore E. 1979. *The Battered Woman.* New York: Harper and Row.

Watson, Jerome R. 1992. "U.S. Poverty Level Highest Since 1964." *Chicago Sun-Times* (September 4):8.

Wiegard, R. Bruce. 1985. "Counting the Homeless." *American Demographics* 7:34–37.

Wilson, William Julius. 1987. *The Truly Disadvantaged: The Inner City, the Underclass, and Public Policy.* Chicago: University of Chicago Press.

Windishar, Anne. 1992. "Disgust with Welfare May Change How Nation Deals with Its Poor." *Denver Post* (August 23):6C.

Wright, James D. 1988a. "The Mentally Ill Homeless: What Is Myth and What Is Fact?" *Social Problems* 35:182–191.

———. 1988b. "The Worthy and Unworthy Homeless." *Society* 25(5):64–69.

———. 1989. *Address Unknown: The Homeless in America.* New York: Aldine de Gruyter.

Wright, James D., and Julie A. Lam. 1987. "Homelessness and the Low-Income Housing Supply." *Social Policy* (Spring):48–53.

Zarembka, Arlene. 1991. "Housing Banks." *Nation* (June 24):837.

About the Book and Authors

This book is the first to combine a cogent explanation of the economic and historical causes of homelessness with accounts of individuals and families on the streets, in soup lines, and in shelters. The human side of the story, told from ethnographies conducted in three diverse cities—Chicago, Denver, and Tampa—shows that there is no "culture of poverty" that makes people poor, just as there is no "culture of homelessness" that leaves people without shelter. Instead, the authors show that large numbers of people became homeless through the processes of urban and industrial decline.

Homelessness is largely an urban phenomenon. It increased dramatically when cities witnessed the simultaneous loss of low-income housing and good-paying industrial jobs. However, the increase in the number of homeless people does not suggest a special social problem—arising from the character of individuals—but is the result of social and economic transformations in American cities since the late 1970s.

In this book the words of the homeless tell the stories of people who were "making it" before but eventually fell into circumstances of extreme poverty. The many paths taken to homelessness, revealed in their stories, speak to the changing conditions of inequality in the United States today and the need for new public policies.

Doug A. Timmer is associate professor of sociology at North Central College. **D. Stanley Eitzen** is professor of sociology at Colorado State University. **Kathryn D. Talley** is associate professor of sociology at North Central College.

Index

AARP. *See* American Association of Retired
Persons
Abuse
battered women, 140–151
drug, 118, 119, 132
from families, 112, 117, 118
fears of charges of child, 115
and foster care, 123
from social services bureaucracy, 99–
103, 115–116
See also Alcoholism
ADC. *See* Aid to Dependent Children
AFDC. *See* Aid to Families with Dependent
Children
AFL-CIO, 177
African Americans. *See* Blacks
Aid to Dependent Children (ADC), 43. *See
also* Aid to Families with Dependent
Children
Aid to Families with Dependent Children
(AFDC)
assistance received from, 94, 100, 149,
158–159, 171–172
need for additional funds, 19, 164, 172–
173
and paperwork, 63. *See also* Welfare
bureaucracy
and politics, 55–58, 133–134
reductions in, 29–30, 137, 171, 180
reluctance to use, 115, 116
and unemployed males, 43
See also Welfare
Alcoholism
as cause of homelessness, 50–52
and homeless people, 8, 13–15
and Skid Row stereotypes, 49–50
and teens, 119
Alcohol rehabilitation programs, 33
Alop, Alan, 95

American Affordable Housing Institute,
Rutgers University, 12
American Association of Retired Persons
(AARP), 56
Anderson, Leon, 7, 16, 36, 38–39, 121
Appelbaum, Richard, 182, 190
Archer, Michelle, 128–130, 134–135, 137–
139
Arizona, 44
Asia, 86–87
Asian Americans, 6, 57
Atlanta, 95
Atlas, John, 182
Audy Home, 118
Australia, 176

Bahr, Howard, 50
Bankruptcy, business, 88
Benefits. *See* Health care
Blacks
and "deviant behaviors," 131–134. *See
also* Deficiencies, personal
and divorce, 28
and domestic violence, 141
and education for children, 136
and employment, 26–27, 40–41, 95
and housing, 21–23, 94, 95, 181
poverty rate, 3, 6, 10, 175
and public assistance, 44, 57, 180
single mothers, 128–135, 137–139, 140,
141–151, 155, 156–173
"Black Tax," 95
Bogue, Donald, 37–38, 43, 50
Boston, 19, 53
Boyce, Joseph, 95
Burawoy, Michael, 9
Bureaucracy. *See* Welfare bureaucracy
Bureau of Labor Statistics, 176
Bush administration, 55, 177

Business, 87–88
  relocation, 86–87, 88, 178
  See also Economy; Employment
Buyouts, corporate, 88

California public assistance, 44
CAM. *See* Computer-aided manufacturing
Canada, 174, 177, 183
Caribbean nations, 86–87
CCC. *See* Civilian Conservation Corps
Center on Budget and Policy Priorities, 19
Centers for Disease Control and
      Prevention, 146
CHA. *See* Chicago, Housing Authority
Chicago, 7
  child welfare agencies, 123
  Coalition for the Homeless, 122
  cost of living in, 95
  homeless teens in, 117–118
  Housing Authority (CHA), 64–65, 148,
      157, 164–165
  housing discrimination in, 95
  housing, 52–53, 62–68, 70, 138, 160–161
  justice system, 96
  Main Stem/Skid Row, 36
  poverty in, 48
  public assistance, 43, 44, 156–159, 164
  shelters, 91, 105, 128, 155, 158, 159–160,
      162–164, 165–168, 187
  slumlording, 149–150
  social networks and taverns, 49
Child care, 137–138, 139, 170–171
  policy and subsidizing, 60–61, 134, 181
Children
  AFDC recipients and number of, 57, 134
  fears of losing, 35, 115
  health of, 135–136
  and life in shelters, 165, 166–168, 186
  in poverty, 130–131, 136–137
Children's Defense Fund, 61, 138
Christian, Alicia, 188
Cincinnati, Ohio, 53
Cisneros, Henry G., 189
Cities
  economic decline of, 6, 27, 178
  and homelessness, 4
  housing shortages in, 78, 92, 181
  increased cost of living in, 94–96
  policy recommendations for, 178–179,
      181–183

rebuilding infrastructure of, 177
  and urban renewal, 21–22
Civilian Conservation Corps (CCC), 47
Class
  differences between homeless and
      "advocates," 188
  discrimination, 14, 131–135
  divisions among homeless, 107–109
  and "old" versus "new" homeless, 35
Clay, Phillip, 21, 70, 93
Clinton administration, 55, 174, 189–190
Colorado landlord bill, 96
Computer-aided manufacturing (CAM), 86
Connecticut, 44
Consumer price index (CPI), 10, 26
Coontz, Stephanie, 41
Corporate flight, 86–87, 88, 178
Corruption
  and subsidizing private sector, 24
  See also Crime
Cost of living
  and child care, 60–61
  health care costs, 72–73, 177–178
  and housing, 18–19, 49, 69–70, 78–79, 82,
      93, 94, 149
  increases in general, 84
  in inner city, 94–96
CPI. *See* Consumer price index
Crime
  and apartment managers, 160–161
  housing subsidies and corruption, 24
  and stereotypes of poor/homeless, 47–
      48, 132
  theft in shelters, 165, 166
  violence against women, 140–151
"Culture of homelessness," 6, 104–109,
      115–116, 185, 186–187

DCFS. *See* Illinois, Department of Children
      and Family Services
Debt, corporate, 87–88
Deficiencies, personal
  as cause of homelessness, 6, 13–16, 34,
      49–52, 66–68, 112, 190
  social services bureaucracy on, 184–187.
      See also Welfare bureaucracy
  See also Alcoholism; "Culture of
      Homelessness"; Mental health
Deindustrialization, 26, 75, 85, 125, 175
Dellums, Ron, 183
Demographics, of homeless, 6, 16–17

Denmark, 177
Denver, 7, 53, 95
Denver International Airport, 27
Department of Housing and Urban
    Development (HUD)
  apartment regulations, 158
  current budget, 23, 189
  homeless estimates by, 12
  on housing discrimination, 94
  housing programs in 1980s, 22–23, 24
di Leonardo, Micaela, 22
Discrimination
  and black, single mothers, 137, 150, 151,
    180
  class, 14, 131–135. *See also* Class
  racial, 3–4, 6, 27, 59, 94, 95, 133. *See also*
    Blacks
  sex, 59
  and state distribution of social aid, 30,
    137
Divorce rate, 28
Dreier, Peter, 182, 190
Drug abuse
  and black youth, 132
  and teens, 118, 119

Economic Policy Institute, 84
Economy
  changing structure of, 24–28, 83–84
  factors in changing structure of, 85–89
  and increasing homelessness/
    marginalization, 75, 89–90, 173, 175
  See also Employment; Marginalization,
    economic
Edelman, Marian Wright, 131
Education
  connection between poverty and, 75–76
  and employment opportunities, 27, 150,
    171
  funding of public, 179, 181
  and homeless children, 136
  and teens, 119, 124, 172
Elderly, public assistance for, 47
Elliot, Elsa, 13
Ellwood, David, 138
Employment
  changing structure of, 25–27, 36–37, 74,
    82, 83–84, 85. *See also* Wages
  in cities, 27. *See also* Cities
  creating public, 177, 179, 180–181
  factors in declining, 85–89

and homeless, single men, 37–42
  increasing vacation days/decreasing
    work hours, 176–177
  racial discrimination in, 27, 59, 95, 137
  and welfare mothers, 58–60, 134, 137–
    138, 150–151, 170–171
  and young families, 70–72, 79–80
Ethnography, 6–7, 9
Europe, 174
Evans, Barbara, 140, 141–151
Eviction, 91–92, 93, 98, 156, 161

Families
  changing structure of, 28–29
  single-parent, 130–139. *See also* Women
  as solution for homeless people, 111–
    114, 161–162, 169–170
  and teen homelessness, 117, 118, 120–
    121
  and U.S. social policy, 113, 121–123, 126–
    127
  young, and economic marginality, 69–80
Family Leave Act, 60
Fathers, 169–170
Feagin, Joe R., 89, 97
Finance charges, 95
Florida, 81, 82. *See also* Tampa
Food stamps
  and bureaucracy errors, 45
  program reductions, 29–30, 180
  receiving, 63, 64, 94, 149, 169
Foster care, 123
France, 177

GA. *See* General Assistance
Gaines, Donna, 124
Geertz, Clifford, 7
General Assistance (GA), 43–44, 180
General Motors, 89
Gentrification, 20–21, 181
Germany, 176, 177
Geronimus, Arline, 135
Giancarlo, Jeffrey, 117, 118–120, 123, 125
Gilderbloom, John, 182
Glasser, Irene, 7
Globalization, 86, 175
Great Depression, 47, 73

Hacker, Andrew, 130, 135
Harvard University's Joint Center for
    Housing Studies, 93

HCH program. *See* Health Care for the Homeless program
Head Start, 139
Health care
  and children in poverty, 135–137
  Clinton plan, 190
  costs and uninsured, 72–73, 76–77, 177–178, 181
  as employee benefit, 84
  and poor health of homeless, 11, 33, 111, 116
  single-payer national plan for, 176, 177–178
  See also Medicaid; Mental health
Health Care for the Homeless (HCH) program, 13, 39, 47
Hispanics
  and "deviant behavior," 131–134
  and discrimination, 94, 95
  and education for children, 136
  poverty rate, 3, 6, 10
  and public assistance, 57
Hoch, Charles, 5, 16, 17, 38, 186–187
Homelessness
  and battered women, 147–151
  causes of, 3–6, 11, 17–30, 155–156, 175
  and children, 135–137
  "deserving" vs. "undeserving," 107–109. *See also* Ideologies
  and eviction, 91–92, 93, 98
  extent of, 12
  and families, 69, 79–80, 81–83
  and personal deficiencies, 13–16, 50–52, 66–68, 184–187
  policy recommendations for, 176–183, 188, 190
  and shelters, 104–107, 109–111, 183–188. *See also* Shelters
  and single men, 16–17, 34–54
  and single mothers, 55–68, 99, 156–173
  and teens, 117–127, 128–130
  and welfare bureaucracy, 100–102. *See also* Welfare bureaucracy
Household size, 29, 126
Housing
  costs, 18–19, 49, 69–70, 78–79, 82, 93, 94, 149
  doubling/tripling up, 69, 111–112
  home ownership rate, 78
  racial discrimination in, 94, 95
  recommendations on, 181–182, 182–183

shortage of low-income, 4, 11, 15, 17–24, 20(fig.), 30, 70, 92–94, 155, 173, 175
  and single men, 49, 52–54
  unmaintained, substandard, 93–94, 101–102, 149–150
  and young families, 78–79
  See also Housing, public
Housing, public
  bureaucracy in, 100–101, 156–158
  decreased funding for, 22–23, 92–93, 173, 180, 181
  decreasing availability of, 62–66, 70, 103–104, 138
  recommendations for creating, 182–183
  See also Shelters
Housing Act of 1949, 189
Houston, 19
Howard, Jeff, 136
HUD. *See* Department of Housing and Urban Development
Hudson, Frances, 129

IBM, 89
Ideologies
  behavioral stereotypes of poor, 37–38, 47–48, 49–50, 57–58, 131–135
  on dysfunctional families, 122–123
  in forming public policy, 174
  shelters and middle-class, 104–109
  and welfare bureaucracy, 99–100, 184–187
  See also Deficiencies, personal
Illinois
  Department of Children and Family Services (DCFS), 123–124
  Department of Public Aid, 102–103
  Juvenile Justice Commission, 119
  public assistance in, 44
  See also Chicago
Income
  decline in household, 74–75
  drop in U.S. per capita, 73
  and single-parent families, 130
  See also Employment; Poverty; Wages
Ineichen, Bernard, 129
Infant mortality rate, 135
Infrastructure, rebuilding, 177, 179
Institute of Real Estate Management (IREM), 97–98
Interest rates, 18

IREM. *See* Institute of Real Estate Management

Jackson, Sue, 55, 57–58, 60–61, 62–68
Japan, 176
Job Training Partnership Act (JTPA), 72
Johnson, Clifford M., 85
Joint Center for Political and Economic Studies, 180
Jones, Debbie, 91, 94, 96, 97
JTPA. *See* Job Training Partnership Act
Justice system
  and battered women, 146–147
  juvenile court, 118–119
  and landlord-tenant power relations, 96, 161

Kozol, Jonathan, 7, 12, 14

Labor pools, 41–42. *See also* Employment
Landlords/managers, 19, 96–98, 156, 160–161. *See also* Slumlording
Layoffs/downsizing, corporate, 89
Levitan, Sar, 85
Liebow, Elliot, 4, 7, 13–14, 99–100, 103–104, 115
Los Angeles, 53, 187
Louisville, Kentucky, 179

McKnight, John, 184, 185, 188
Main Stem, 36–37
Malnutrition, 11. *See also* Health care
Maquiladora program, 87
Marginalization, economic
  increasing rates of, 17–18, 30, 75, 173, 175
  and single men, 37–42, 48–49
  and single mothers, 59–61, 66. *See also* Women
  of teens, 124–125, 126–127
  and young, black men, 29
  and young families, 69–80, 83, 89–90
  See also Poverty
Medicaid, 77, 100, 134, 138, 180
Medicare, 47
Mental health
  and homeless people, 6, 8, 13–15, 66–68, 83
  and teens, 26
Mergers, corporate, 88

Metropolitan Ministries Shelter for Homeless Families, 82, 99
Mexico, 86–87
Michigan, 44
Migrant industrial labor, 36–37
Milano, Susan Murphy, 146
Military, 89
Mills, C. Wright, 8
Minneapolis–Saint Paul, 179
Moore, Diane, 99, 100–102, 104, 109–111, 113–114, 115–116
Moses, Denise, 155, 156–173
Moynihan, Daniel Patrick, 136–137

NAFTA. *See* North American Free Trade Agreement
Naples, Florida, 82
Nashville, Tennessee, 553
National Academy of Sciences, 59
National Association of Realtors, 97–98
National Coalition for the Homeless, 12
National Health Care for the Homeless Program, 117
National Opinion Research Center, 50, 188
National Union for the Homeless, 188
Native Americans, 6, 57
Near-homeless. *See* Marginalization, economic
Neon Street Center for Youth, 120
Netherlands, 176, 177, 180
New Deal, 52
New Homeless and Old (Hoch and Slayton), 5, 16, 17, 38, 186–187
New York City
  cost of living in, 95
  eviction in, 91–92
  homelessness rates in, 12
  housing in, 19, 53, 138
  rejection of shelters in, 187
  and reliance on family, 111–112
New York (state) public assistance, 44
Nonprofit organizations, 182–183
North American Free Trade Agreement (NAFTA), 87, 175, 190
Novella, Antonia, 140

Ohio, 44
Old Age and Disability Assistance, 43

Parker, Robert, 97
Patriarchy, 141

Pennsylvania, 44
Pensions, 84
Piliavin, Irving, 13
Politics
  of "compassion," 17, 186–187
  and "complexity" of homelessness issue,
    174
  and funding social programs, 55–58, 179
  See also Ideologies
Pornography, commercial, 120
Portland, Oregon, 53
Poverty
  children in, 122, 136–137
  and employed mothers, 59–60
  and homelessness, 3
  increasing rate of U.S., 6, 10–11, 24, 28,
    73–74, 93, 130–131, 175, 180
  official line of, 10, 57
  and single men, 48–49, 53
  See also Homelessness; Marginalization,
    economic; Wages
Power relations
  and patriarchy, 141
  and teens, 125–126
  tenant-landlord, 96–98, 160–161
  worker-management, 88–89, 175, 177
  See also Class
Pregnancy
  and battered women, 143
  and employment, 150–151
  prenatal care, 77, 135
  teen, 128–129, 131
Private sector
  and privatization, 179
  and subsidizing low-income housing,
    23–24
Project Chance, 102–103
Prostitution, 119–120
Public assistance. *See* Welfare
Public policy
  antifamily, 121–123, 126–127
  and children, 136–137
  and "complexity" of homelessness issue,
    174
  as exacerbating homelessness, 8, 21–24,
    29–30
  recommendations for, 175, 176–179,
    180–183, 188, 190
  See also Ideologies; Politics

Race
  and AFDC recipients, 57
  and employment discrimination, 27, 59,
    95, 137
  and homelessness rates, 3, 6
  and housing discrimination, 94, 95
  and public assistance cuts, 44, 137
  and unemployment, 40–41
  See also Blacks; Hispanics
Reagan administration
  defense spending during, 89
  homelessness estimates during, 12
  and housing programs, 22–23, 182
  and labor unions, 177
  and welfare programs, 29–30, 55, 56, 73,
    180
Reed, Adolph, Jr., 132
Reich, Robert, 26, 87–88
Rent
  control, 181–182
  inflation, 18–23, 78–79, 93
  See also Housing
Research methods, 6–7
Rethinking Rental Housing (Gilderbloom
    and Appelbaum), 182
Rhode Island, 44
Rossi, Peter, 43, 50–51, 112

Safety
  in shelters, 165–166, 188
  and subsidized housing, 65–66, 139
St. Martin De Porres Shelter, 91
"Sallies." *See* Salvation Army
Salvation Army, 33–34, 51, 82
San Antonio, Texas, 138
Sanders, Bernard, 176, 177–178
San Diego, 53
San Francisco, 53
Schwarz, John, 10
Seattle, 53
Section 8, 100–101, 103, 158, 189. *See also*
    Housing, public
Sexton, Patricia Cayo, 8
Shadow work, 47–48
Shagford, Bob and Nancy, 81–83, 89–90
Sheldon, Sam, 33–34, 39–40, 42, 44–48, 51–
    52, 53–54
Shelters
  battered women's, 145, 151
  building more, 189
  effectiveness of, 79–80, 183–188

health/safety in, 111, 135, 165–166, 188
life in, 64, 109–111, 128–130, 155, 158,
    159–160, 162–164, 165–168
middle-class ideology within, 104–109
SI. *See* Survivors Insurance
Sidel, Ruth, 141
Single males
    causes of homelessness for, 33–36
    and employment, 36–42
    and public assistance, 42–47
Single mothers. *See* Women
Single-room occupancy (SRO) hotels, 187
    loss of, 19, 52–53, 93, 181
    rental fees for, 49
Skid Row, 37–38, 41–42, 42–43, 47, 49–50
Skid Row in American Cities (Bogue), 37–
    38, 43, 50
Sklar, Holly, 134
Skocpol, Theda, 45
Slayton, Robert, 5, 16, 17, 38, 186–187
Slumlording, 21, 149, 181
Smith, Sara and Dave, 69, 70–73, 75–80
Snow, David, 7, 14, 16, 36, 38–39, 121
Social networks/relationships
    breakdown of black, 41
    homeless use of, 35
Social policy/programs. *See* Public policy;
    Welfare
Social Security
    and the elderly, 47
    Survivors Insurance (SI), 137
Sosin, Michael, 15
Spain, 176
SRO. *See* Single-room occupancy hotels
SSI. *See* Supplemental Security Income
Stereotypes
    of the poor, 131–133
    and Skid Row men, 37–38, 47–48, 49–50
    "welfare moms," 57–58, 131–135
    See also Ideologies
Stewart B. McKinney Homeless Assistance
    Act, 183
Sullivan, Louis, 132
Supplemental Security Income (SSI), 94
Survivors Insurance (SI), 137

Takeovers, corporate, 88
Tampa
    employment in, 82
    homeless in, 7, 33–34, 99

housing discrimination in, 95
public assistance in, 44
Taxes
    regional revenue sharing, 178–179
    regressive, 96
    shelters/deductions, 24, 60, 133
Technology, 86
Teenagers
    and homelessness, 117–124, 126–127
    marginalization of, 124–126
    as single mothers, 128–135, 137–139
Temperance Movement, 49
Temporary employment, 41–42
Tenants' groups, 96–98, 182
Timmer, Doug, 185, 186
Trade unions
    loss in strength of, 88, 175, 177
    protecting, 176, 177
Training programs
    and discrimination in job placement,
        150
    through Job Training Partnership Act, 72
    See also Education
Transiency, 37–38
Travelers and Immigrant Aid Society,
    Institute on Urban Poverty, 44

Underemployment, 85
Unemployment
    and blacks, 40–41
    compensation, 181
    and family violence, 141
    and management/worker power
        relations, 88–89
    permanent layoffs, 89
    U.S. rate of, 84–85, 175
    and young males, 74, 76
    See also Employment
Uniform Crime Reports, 140
United Kingdom, 176
Urban Institute, 95
Urban renewal, 21–22, 52. *See also* Cities
U.S. Conference of Mayors, 105, 138, 177

Vacation days, 176–177
Values. *See* "Culture of homelessness"
Vander Kooi, Ronald, 50
Veterans, 45–47
Volgy, Thomas, 10
Voucher programs, 182

Wages
  declining, for unskilled labor, 25, 26, 38–
    42, 74–75, 83–84, 85
  minimum, 176, 181
  and women, 28–29, 59, 171
  See also Employment
Wagner, David, 112–113
Walsh, Henry, 33–34, 40, 44–47, 51, 53–54
"Warehousing," 21
Washington, D.C., 138
Welfare
  alcoholics on, 50
  and bureaucratic abuse of poor, 99–104,
    115–116
  child, agencies, 123–124
  decreases/deficiencies in, 73, 74, 173,
    180, 189–190
  employment and decreases in, 171
  and low-income families, 70, 94
  to the nonpoor, 133
  recommendations on increasing, 179,
    180–181
  single men and, 42–47
  single mothers and, 55–58, 66, 115–116,
    133–134, 137–139
  See also Aid to Families with Dependant
    Children; Food stamps; Housing,

    public; Medicaid; Public policy;
    Welfare bureaucracy
Welfare bureaucracy, 44–45, 63, 100–104,
  115–116
  ideologies of, 99–100, 184–187, 188
Westerfelt, Herb, 13
Whites
  and AFDC recipients, 57
  poverty rate, 3, 6, 73
Wilson, William J., 29
Women
  battered, 140–151
  and child care, 60–61, 134, 137–138, 139,
    170–171, 181
  and employment, 26, 58–60, 134, 137–
    138, 150–151, 170–171
  and poverty/homelessness, 28–29, 59–
    60, 62–68, 91–92, 93, 98, 99, 100–102,
    109–111, 113–116, 130–131
  single mothers and welfare, 55–58, 66,
    115–116, 133–134, 137–139
  teen mothers, 128–135, 137–139, 155,
    156–173
Women and Children Last (Sidel), 141
Workfare, 56
Work hours, 176–177
Works Progress Administration (WPA), 47
WPA. See Works Progress Administration
Wright, James, 13, 15, 48